NATURE'S WILD

LOVE, SEX, *and* LAW *in the* CARIBBEAN

Nature's Wild

ANDIL GOSINE

Duke University Press   Durham and London   2021

Designed byAimee C. Harrison
Typeset in Minion Pro by Copperline Book Services

Library of Congress Cataloging-in-Publication Data
Names: Gosine, Andil, [date] author.
Title: Nature's wild : love, sex, and law in the Caribbean /
Andil Gosine.
Description: Durham : Duke University Press, 2021. |
Includes bibliographical references and index.
Identifiers: LCCN 2021002264 (print) | LCCN 2021002265 (ebook)
ISBN 9781478013655 (hardcover)
ISBN 9781478014584 (paperback)
ISBN 9781478021889 (ebook)
Subjects: LCSH: Homosexuality—Caribbean Area. | Human
beings—Animal nature. | Art, Caribbean—Social aspects. | Sex
and art. | Gays—Legal status, laws, etc.—Caribbean Area. | Queer
theory. | Caribbean Area—Colonial influence. | BISAC: ART /
Criticism & Theory | HISTORY / Caribbean & West Indies /
General Classification: LCC HQ75.16.C27 G67 2021 (print) |
LCC HQ75.16.C27 (ebook) | DDC 306.76/609729—dc23
LC record available at https://lccn.loc.gov/2021002264
LC ebook record available at https://lccn.loc.gov/2021002265

Cover art: Kelly Sinnapah Mary, *Nature's Wild*, 2020. Courtesy
of the artist.

Publication of this book is supported by Duke University
Press's Scholars of Color First Book Fund.

For A. and New York City, 2014

CONTENTS

ACKNOWLEDGMENTS, ix

INTRODUCTION, 1

1 *Puhngah!*, 13

2 Clothes Make the Man, 32

3 The Father, a Godfather, and the
Specter of Beasts Old and New, 62

4 *Désir Cannibale*, 103

NOTES, 153

WORKS CITED, 159   INDEX, 171

5 *Natures'* Wild, 130

ACKNOWLEDGMENTS

With sincere gratitude to and love for my families and friends; my teachers, students, and colleagues; readers of earlier drafts (Emily Anglin, Richard Fung, Latoya Lazarus, Tim McCaskell, and Duke's reviewers and editors) for their indispensable advice; everyone who sat for interviews, shared stories, or contributed images to this project, especially Colin Robinson; the artists whose works are its pulse, Lorraine O'Grady and Kelly Sinnapah Mary; and everyone engaged in "wrecking work," including my favorite public intellectuals, Crissle & West.

Introduction

I was late to learn of sex. I was thirteen years old and in my second year at Presentation College, a Catholic all-boys school atop San Fernando Hill in Trinidad. Twenty-something-year-old Mr. Ramkissoon (not his real name) was talking us through the brackets and multiplication and square roots that would lead us to a solution x, so much a favorite activity of mine that I often asked him for extra algebra homework. Mr. Ramkissoon was one of our few male teachers to don a stylish, contemporary wardrobe. Those teachers who were Brothers of the Order sported long white cotton robes, while a favorite of the older men was the "Shirt Jack," better known internationally as the Cuban-associated guayabera. Mr. Ramkissoon's daily wardrobe comprised a form-fitting shirt tucked into narrow-legged slacks, a sharp contrast to the shining navy blue polyester of the heavy-set, rosy-faced visitor who suddenly appeared and interrupted our lesson in algebra that afternoon. Father Larry (not his real name) would occasionally make these visits to provide moral instruction. Neither the students nor teacher were told in advance about when he might appear, thus ensuring that a sense of trepidation permanently hung in the air. The two exchanged a few words and after a quickly forgotten note indicating the transition, Mr. Ramkissoon abruptly left the classroom.

Father Larry pointed to the row of students in which I happened to be seated and ordered the five of us to stand up. "Prove to me," he instructed, "that you are not a homosexual." We stood silent in the nook between surface and seat of our creaky wooden desks. Father Larry paused, his slanted smile signaling sadistic delight about the humiliation that was certain to unfold. Another pause and I could see his hand ready to lift and point at one of us to prompt an answer. I was sure that his pointing finger was to land in my direction. Instead, a confident, cheerful voice broke the silence. "Show me the girls [at the adjoining Presbyterian school, Naparima] next door," snapped Ramsingh from the back row (where else would the appointed class jester sit?), "and I'll give you proof." Everyone, including Father Larry, erupted into laughter. This spontaneous burst of heterosexual teenage lust rescued the classroom's five potential homosexuals, including me, from the burden of proof. But I was so caught up in my shame that nothing he said registered after that, although I am sure he must have stayed for at least an hour. The minute Father Larry finally exited, I turned to a classmate for relief. "What," I asked, "is a homosexual?" His answer prompted another question: "But . . . what is sex?" He filled me in some more, much to my surprise and horror.

This provocation from Father Larry was my entry point for conscious thinking about sexual desire. Thirty years later, I am struck about how efficiently this encounter maps the complex terrain of historical antecedents for the production and regulation of sexualities in colonized territories like Trinidad and Tobago, identifies some of the main actors engaged, and signs important questions and tensions at the heart of contemporary debates about sexual rights. Our exchange with Father Larry, a microcosmic expression of a dynamic produced and reproduced in scales large and small, in contexts past and present, offers evidence of the key arguments presented about sexual rights struggles in the Anglophone Caribbean in scholarship and popular media, signing both the long, structured history of homophobia that actively delegitimizes nonheterosexual sex and the primary role played by the Christian Church and state institutions like schools in its production. As in the encounter with Father Larry, however, this history is complicated and layered with contradictions. Just as Father Larry's disciplining of homosexuality simultaneously introduced me and, I would guess, other boys to its very possibility, and may have even worked to sanction homoerotic imaginations, so too have related cultural and legal codes intended to control sexuality also produced ambivalent consequences, sometimes positing completely different effects consciously and subconsciously.

The exchange between Father Larry and us students is also an example of a five-centuries-long struggle put to Caribbean peoples: to prove ourselves human, and not wild, like animals. "Every culture feels that they've hard-won distances between themselves and the animals," West Indian American artist Lorraine O'Grady observed to me in a 2010 interview, "and anything that reminds you that you haven't come so far is problematic. [It] puts the culture in jeopardy." Negotiations of the distance between "human" and "animal" play out in all kinds of everyday acts and throughout the institutions governing our conditions of life, but what perhaps most threatens the ideological maintenance of this division is sex, and sex is therefore the target of intense regulation. The sex act, O'Grady says, reminds us of our animality and is "almost an affront to the ways in which culture has tried to circumscribe nature." In the artist's diptych *The Clearing* (plate 1), O'Grady draws a line between five hundred years of pairings between white men and Black women that imperil the human/animal divide propping up facades of civilization across the Americas in the subtitle of the work: *or Cortez and La Malinche, Thomas Jefferson and Sally Hemings, N. and Me.* Each subject holds a different position in the fields of power it occupies, but all, including the artist herself, are implicated in the messy execution of sexual desire; as Giorgio Agamben has also said of every culture that claims itself civilized, "man is the animal that must recognize itself as human to be human" (2004, 26).

In her related 1998 essay "Olympia's Maid," O'Grady theorizes that the relationship between the white male and the Black female was the start of the disruption of faith between the white male and the white female. On plantations in the American South, sex between white masters and enslaved Black people was evidenced by the abundance of light-skinned progeny. The masters' wives assumed a state of suspended disbelief, choosing, at least on the surface, to deny their own eyes rather than admitting the fractured trust embodied around them: "There were these children who obviously looked like their husbands, but they would have to believe the lies that their husbands were telling them, 'No, you're not seeing this,' right?," O'Grady observes. "The white male on the plantation was having to lie, a lot, and the white female was having to believe what she knew were lies." In her diptych, the white male is in chain mail to symbolize the French *roman* of courtly love, "and this was the end of [that] idea." O'Grady's work shows the lines drawn by sexual engagement as floating markers at a range of simultaneous levels, making and unmaking power and identity, an exposure of what is rendered invisible by normative culture, her couples reclining on multiple horizontal axes, in physical contests where the stakes are entitlement to acknowledgment, presence and representation, and humanity. The lines drawn between interracial sex and acceptability—and the ways in which the slippage across those lines reveals the fragile stability shored up by discursive and legislative strategies that put distance between more human and less human—are but one expression of how sex has been regulated to restrict access to self-constitution of identity in Euro-American and other cultures.

A major component of the expansion of European colonization in Africa, Asia, and the Americas was the introduction of legal statutes that set out "civil" parameters of sex, including laws forbidding interracial and homosexual sex. Father Larry's command that we prove our nonhomosexuality is, I argue, a manifestation of a five-centuries-long struggle in the Americas for each of its colonial and postcolonial-era cultures to place distance between ourselves and animals. In the same fashion, contemporary contests for power and meaning making between some religious organizations, the state, local and international sexuality rights activists, and others continue to unfold on the global stage with evolving significances for the contemporary Caribbean. Our realization of what M. Jacqui Alexander has theorized as "erotic autonomy" (1994, 6) therefore requires that we recognize and seriously attend to the production of and our response to anxieties about the threat of wild animality. The unfolding global climate emergency in which species extinction is a human life–threatening consequence further underlines the necessity of weighing and confronting the demarcation of humans from other animals in the most practical and urgent terms.

In the five chapters that comprise *Nature's Wild*, I take up the lens deployed in O'Grady's art practice, which helps us refocus the role of sexual desire in the human/animal divide that has long undergirded sociopolitical dynamics in the Americas, to examine the history of the regulation of homosexuality in Trinidad and Tobago and other Caribbean countries. I contend with the persistent identification of sodomy as a dividing line between human and animal, and think through how an acknowledgment of sodomy's role in the drawing of this line might alter how we understand, approach, and configure struggles over the regulation of sex. I begin with *puhngah*, a word that suggests anal sex. Long before I was familiar with sex in even the most basic terms, I heard this word used, including in the joke that anchors chapter 1. The broad currency of jokes that invoke the term suggests the cultural resonance of its subject: hinging on the fate of three doomed missionaries who have been captured by a native tribe, puhngah serves as the joke's punch line. As with O'Grady's art, which exposes submerged forms of knowing in the sexual and epistemological, the joke described in chapter 1 plumbs the depths of knowing for its uncomfortable humor. Any narrative joke works because it takes the listener across the line between not knowing and knowing, and this one conflates the experiential knowledge of what puhngah is with what the word means to unwittingly profound effect. In the joke, puhngah is shown to be something to fear if it is known but perhaps to be feared even more if it is not, for that is to relinquish control over it, and over the definition of those who practice it. In visceral terms, the joke shows that fears of puhngah transcend the bodily to take on ontological dimensions: the fears it reveals, significantly, are of puhngah as not just an erasure of the line between one body and another but also an erasure of the lines drawn between those who know it—in the linguistic, cultural, bodily, and biblical senses—and those who do not. This fragment of comic narrative, couched in both humor and in homophobia wielded as a tool for existential domination, creates a space for enacting the subversive ontological perils of crossing this line. In this first chapter, I parse the joke—in its disordering representation of some of the elements at play in Father Larry's intermittent capture of the classroom for moral training—to trace the operation of sodomy as a dividing line between human and animal since the moment of European encounter in the Americas.

Historical records from the sixteenth century show how Spanish invaders characterized Indigenous peoples, including Trinidad and Tobago's Kalinago (whom Columbus misnamed "Caribs"), as sodomites as an effective means of characterizing them as *less human* than their conquerors, and *more animal*. Such records build on a literature founded by early fifteenth-century colonizers, which from the earliest times used sodomy as a reductive key for dehumanization. In his much-cited and circulated letter of 1495, Michele da Cuneo, childhood friend and shipmate of Christopher Columbus, offers deliberately exaggerated claims that the Kalinago/Carib people he encountered widely practiced sodomy, although, significantly, he also notes that they were likely unaware of homosexuality as a sin (Lunenfeld 1991, 283). This complex denigration redoubles the sense of the Kalinago/Caribs as more animal by coupling the act of sodomy with an animal-like lack of ethical perspicacity about sexual behavior, and an unawareness of a European moral code that he presents as natural—an irony given that da Cuneo was a notoriously brutal rapist who preyed upon those same Kalinago/Carib people whose sexual morality he judged inferior to his own. Their dehumanization was necessary to justify their displacement, enslavement, and genocide, and the citation of sodomite practices was central to that justification.

Spanish colonizers' invocation of sodomy to advance colonization was consistent but not institutionally inscribed, except through church doctrine. This would change with the arrival of the Victorian era in Britain at the height of its imperial reach, when legislation against sodomy was imposed. In Trinidad and Tobago and other British colonies in the Caribbean, sodomy would become officially outlawed in 1861, through the adoption of the Offences against the Person Act. Notably, this law set out similar sanctions against and punishments for sodomy and bestiality, underlining the use of the former to prove the latter. In most scholarship, this pairing is conceived as a tool that has primarily functioned to further convey the immorality of homosexuality; by contrast, I propose that the pairing represents something more complex: the long-established role of sodomy as a defining line between human and animal, and a means of arbitrating who can claim access to the rights that come along with the much-desired "fully human" status. The criminalization of sodomy along with bestiality was maintained through the first fifty-six years of Trinidad and Tobago's political independence. In the discourses of both advocates and opponents of sodomy's decriminalization, as I will show, we find evidence of the parties' struggles over the definition of the distance and distinction between human and animal. The identification of heterosexual, Christian or Christian-mimicking marriage—along with its various ritualistic accoutrements—as the primary means by which nonwhite Trinidadians may be seen to graduate to the category of human further exemplifies how anxieties about animality shape the country's social organization and politics.

One of the reasons why sex is such an effective method for revealing our animality is that any sex act is typically performed in a state of being stripped bare, or at least bare of the usually most-covered parts, bereft of that ultimate material barrier between human and animal and basic signifier of the human condition: clothing. Nakedness exposes more than just skin; it reveals the subversive potential inherent in dressing, undressing, and changing clothes, and the undermining of clothing's use as a means of policing and determining identity and constituting prescribed versions of humanness. In chapter 2, "Clothes Make the Man," I describe and examine the nearly decade-long case of four Guyanese people who were arrested and subsequently fined for being bodies in the wrong clothes. Their arrest, harassment by the police and judiciary, and initial conviction rested plainly on nineteenth-century British colonial laws that prescribed gendered clothing as a fix for the base animality of Caribbean peoples. This chapter considers the large body of antivagrancy laws put in place by the British that both ascribe and propose recuperation from Caribbean peoples' animality. I argue that the eventual legal victory by the arrestees may be viewed as a decolonizing act that confidently refuses to respond to the demand to prove ourselves "not animal." While the persistent institutionalization of dress codes by Caribbean governments continues this colonial imperative, their authority is being challenged in creative ways.

Chapter 3, "The Father, a Godfather, and the Specter of Beasts Old and New," considers the discursive transposition between the Caribbean homosexual and homophobe over the past two decades, the latter now taking the place of the former as a demonized, bestial figure. This switch is echoed by a similar reversal of key generators of this fantasy. Once wrought by the European colonial officer, contemporary figurations have new authors: policy makers, politicians, businesses, and local and international activists together co-constitute the nonwhite homophobe as an animal. The world of gay international activists in particular has indulged this representation without acknowledging how the transference, with the Caribbean homosexual's position as a maligned and animalized figure assumed by the homophobe, is effectively a repositioning of this racialized, hierarchical perspective rather than an emptying out of this colonial dynamic. For this reason, the work of Trinbagonian LGBTQI+ activist Colin Robinson, the titular "godfather" in the chapter, is all the more significant. His leadership as cofounder and cochair of the country's most visible LGBTQI+ organization, CAISO, represents a significant departure from this contemporary trend. Refusing to engage the racist tropes that have been widely deployed to attack Caribbean governments, leaders, and people as homophobic, Robinson has instead pursued alternate strategies that challenge racialized and classist postcolonial reformulation of a politics of respectability. This chapter highlights alternative stories of Caribbean life that he and others from the region have tried to tell that depart from dominant representations, and traces the competing narratives told in Trinidad following the April 12, 2018, ruling by its High Court that effectively decriminalized sodomy for the first time in the country's history. I consider and contrast the varied and often-conflicting discursive arguments and strategies pursued in the advocacy of sexual rights. Tracing the nationalist impulse of Robinson's politics to those of the Father of the Nation, Eric Williams, I engage Sylvia Wynter's critiques to consider some of its limitations and possibilities. Similar to O'Grady's characterization of the dynamics of power in *The Clearing*, I seek out a subtler engagement that recognizes the difficult ambivalences of the distorted, varied afterlives of colonization.

Having spent the previous three chapters outlining how the animalization of Caribbean people has produced persistent racialized violence over the past five hundred years, I use the last two chapters to make a perhaps surprising proposition: that we who are so threatened with its slur embrace being marked "animal" or, at the very least, refuse to heed the call to prove ourselves not animal. Not all Caribbean people are similarly animalized, of course, but white, African, Indian, Chinese, Indigenous—all our humanities—are constituted in relationship to the demarcation of human from other animals, and with much varied ideological and material consequences. Rather than leaping to divert a charge like Father Larry's—to prove the civility of our bodies through a mimicking of Western, Christian, heteropatriarchal norms, as in the case of Ramsingh, the student who called out his willingness to dominate the girls of the nearby school to demonstrate his own acceptability—this book looks at these lines drawn for us, and those who refuse to cross them to prove something, who refuse to beg for recognition of "human, not animal."

Analysis of images, including of sixteenth-century renderings of colonial violence in woodcut, T-shirt designs by activist organizations, and contemporary Caribbean art, is also a central running thread in this project, reflecting the significant role visual cultural production has played in documenting—and disturbing—history, politics, and power. Each of the two final chapters shares a contemporary artistic response to the animalization of Caribbean peoples that confidently answers back: "We *are* animals; so what?" In chapter 4, I consider how Guadeloupean artist Kelly Sinnapah Mary's installation *Notebook of No Return* in the Martinican exhibition *Désir Cannibale* provides historical documentation and analysis of Indo-Caribbean people on the island that both weakens the violent intentions of colonial accusations of animality and also simultaneously complicates our subjectivities. And in chapter 5, I present and discuss my journey toward the production of artwork that shares and weighs my experience of growing up in rural Trinidad and the subsequent navigation of my Caribbeanness from outside my land of birth. I discuss how falling in love and heartbreak forced a contention with my own animality and the disciplining of it, which in turn became both catalyst and subject of my artwork. I argue against a divide between human and animal that is both cognizant of the history of racialized animalization that the previous chapters outline and an ecological commitment. Discussing the process of producing pieces of visual art I completed between 2011 and 2019, this final chapter is a reporting of the exploration that led me to a recognition and an aspiration shared with Sinnapah Mary: *We are animal*. This declaration, I argue, is layered with an awareness of the ongoing global ecological crisis and a statement of alliance with other animals and forms of life.

My interests in environmental justice, antiracism, and sexuality rights have been inseparable, and this final chapter explains in part how they are mutually constitutive. In so doing, my project attempts to carve out and begin to meditate on new questions in the contemporary theorization of sexuality in the Caribbean. In this now diverse and well-populated field that is seen to have "come of age" (McNeal and Quinn 2016, 1), conversations about Caribbean sexualities nevertheless consistently center questions, arguments, and policies around the notion of sexual citizenship, a consequence of broad and specific historical political and academic trajectories. M. Jacqui Alexander's "Not Just (Any) Body Can Be a Citizen" (1994) has (suitably) become the central framing text for scholarship and activism on sexual rights in the Anglophone Caribbean. Subsequent to the publication and circulation of this work in particular, scholars and activists have centered notions of "sexual citizenship" in relationship to analysis of sexual identity and the erotic. Lawyer and legal scholar Tracy Robinson, who has been a key figure in debates about and struggles for sexuality rights and protections over the last two decades, draws on Alexander's articulation of connections between property ownership, respectability, and erotic agency to formulate "sexual citizenship" as the basis of various sexual and gender rights claims (2007). Setting up her *Citizenship from Below*, for example, Mimi Sheller explains that in the Caribbean, "to act and make claims as a free citizen, political subjects must first position themselves as raced, gendered, national, and sexual subjects of particular kinds . . . , in discursive performances that always rest on the exclusion and repulsion of others" (2012, 21). Aaron Kamugisha further clarifies that citizenship in the region "has been constructed not merely on the denial of the experiences of black and Indian masses but also on the denial of the experiences of women and homosexuals—in short everyone who did not fit the template of 'white bourgeois heterosexual man' in its now brown/black male Caribbean configuration" (2007, 35). Echoing the vast body of scholarship on Caribbean sexualities, Rosamond King asserts that "both Caribbean cultures and laws stipulate that the ideal Caribbean citizen is a heterosexual, gender-conforming, biological man" (2014, 16). The task at hand, it follows, is affirmation of the rights of all citizens, and the extension of claims of citizenship and citizen rights to the whole community, beyond this figurative white man.

Because this focus on citizenship is an iteration of the confrontation with the ways in which "human" has been historically powerfully defined to render the nonwhite subject inhuman, theorization of "human" by Caribbean scholars provides a telling analysis. While "sexual citizenship" and claims to recognize the fullness of marginalized subjects' humanities can be effective and tangible means through which struggles over policy and politics can often be negotiated, particularly in reference to policy and law as experienced in the most availably coherent terms, Wynter warns us against this perpetual pursuit of recognition as a universal human subject that, she points out, is singularly formulated through Western European cosmogony. Is "citizenship," even if extended beyond European "Man," ever possible if its constitution is invested in the supremacy of the white man? Developing Frantz Fanon's concept of sociogeny, Wynter traces the specific historical development of the universal "Man, which overrepresents itself as if it were the human itself, and of securing the well-being, and therefore the full cognitive and behavioral autonomy of the human itself/ourselves" (2003, 260). "All our present struggles with respect to race, class, gender, sexual orientation, ethnicity, struggles over the environment, global warming, severe climate change, the sharply unequal distribution of the earth resources," Wynter adds, "are all different facets of the central ethnoclass Man vs. Human struggle" (260–61). "Man" as we know it only operates through its investments in these social discourses and hierarchies.

Zakiyyah Iman Jackson further develops Wynter's theorization of "Man" to challenge the "virtuousness of human recognition or humanization"—that which often feels like the endgame of much sexual rights advocacy work—to show that *we* are *human*, like *Man*. Reexamining the presumed stripping of Africans' humanity during the Atlantic slave trade, Jackson concludes that "humanization is not an antidote to slavery's violence; rather slavery is a technology for producing a *kind* of human" (2016, 96). She cites Toni Morrison's *Beloved*, where the author juxtaposes the degradation of enslaved people with that of animals, to demonstrate how "the slave's humanity (the heart, the mind, the soul and the body) is not denied or excluded but manipulated and prefigured as animal, whereby Black(ened) humanity is understood paradigmatically, as a state of *human* animality, or 'the animal within the human'" (97). *Beloved*, Jackson says, details "the violence of liberal humanism's attempts at humanization" (97–98). Taking a similar position, Saidiya V. Hartman writes,

> Suppose that the recognition of humanity held out the promise not of liberating the flesh or redeeming one's suffering but rather of intensifying it? Or what if this acknowledgment was little more than a pretext for punishment, dissimulation of the violence of chattel slavery and the sanction

given it by the law and the state, and an instantiation of racial hierarchy? What if the endowments of man—conscience, sentiment, and reason— rather than assuring liberty or negating slavery acted to yoke slavery and freedom? Or what if the heart, the soul, and the mind were simply the inroads of discipline rather than that which confirmed the crime of slavery? (1997, 5–6)

For Fanon, "the black soul is a white man's artifact" (1967, 14). He declares, "I am not a prisoner of history. . . . I should not seek there [history] for the meaning of my destiny. I should constantly remind myself that the real leap consists in introducing invention into existence. In the world which I travel, I am endlessly creating myself" (229). These provocations challenge the near-universal embrace by Caribbean rights advocates of notions of "sexual citizenship," whose claims are implicitly tied to the particular constitution of humanity of European "Man"; the plea is to become treated as He is treated. But as Wynter has argued, this task is an impossible one, as this "Man" is premised on the degradation of the nonwhite subject. Instead of continuing to center European Man, Wynter asks, "might there be a post-humanism that does not privilege European Man and its idiom?" She proposes that

> if we are to be able to reimagine the human in the terms of a new history whose narrative will enable us to co-identify ourselves each with the other, whatever our local ethnos/ethnoi, we would have to begin by taking our present history, as narrated by historians, as empirical data for the study of a specific cultural coding of a history whose narration has, together with other such disciplinary narrations, given rise to the existential reality of our present Western world system. (D. Scott 2000, 198)

Nature's Wild strives toward this reimagination of "human" through examination of some historical aspects of anxieties about homosexuality that have shaped the contemporary Caribbean. Neither a complete interrogation nor a fully developed manifesto, this project wrestles with the specific possibility of refusal of a demarcating line between human and nonhuman animal that "Man" impels. Whether colonialism's structured violence is read as either a consequence of the dehumanization of nonwhite bodies or as enabled, as Hartman argues, through its particular constitution of human, the separation of the human from nonhuman animal has remained a driving feature of postcolonial states in the Caribbean. Throughout *Nature's Wild*, I point to examples of how what Agamben calls "anthropogenesis," the separation of the human from the animal that results in the constitution of human (2004,

80), has already been challenged in various ways and also meditate on what possibilities both disregard to demands to prove ourselves human and our embrace of our animality might produce. These efforts trouble and sometimes struggle against the human/animal separation that Agamben argues is "the decisive political conflict [of the Western culture], which governs every other conflict" (80).

This book is as much a personal account as it is a social historical contention with the call for the colonized subjects to prove their own humanity. Throughout, therefore, I reference events and experiences from the first fourteen years of my life growing up in the rural space of George Village, Trinidad, as well as from the spaces in which I have worked and lived since. Readers will recognize that through this project, I am confronting my indoctrination into ideology of "Man" and striving to reclaim my own animality. This gesture toward unruliness is echoed in the interdisciplinarity of this project, moving across various fields but also offering both art criticism and the creation of visual art as part of the analysis and in support of my argument. Indeed, it is through artistic practice and cultural production that I have most grappled with O'Grady's observation that sexual desire entirely undermines humans' self-constitution as not animal—hardly a surprise given that my own foray into artistic production was formatively defined by my work with and study of O'Grady. The formative influence of O'Grady, as well as artists Richard Fung, Leor Grady, Wendy Nanan, Sur Rodney (Sur), and, through his work, Félix González-Torres, has shaped my art-making practice as primarily an expression of one's search for truth. Such an approach, as I have understood it, requires critical self-examination and an awareness that our instincts and intimacies are fully entwined with, but never fully captured by, social history. This engagement with these visual artists and with visual art practice has also influenced the style and form of my written expression, shaped by a desire to open up more explorative space than reach strongly decisive conclusions.

1   *Puhngah!*

FATHER LARRY'S FIXATION ON HOMOSEXUALITY was as likely an expression of his own internal struggles as an expression of his commitment to spreading (an interpretation of) the Gospel. But it also reflected the realities of homoerotic sexual socialization that happen at a place like Presentation College, its student population composed entirely of adolescent boys in the throes and aftermath of puberty. When explorations were not openly sanctioned and cast as acceptable homosocial behavior, boys found crevices and corners in this environment to indulge curiosities about their own and one another's changing bodies. I have since learned from other Presentation alumni, for example, that my inability to carry a single musical note meant that I missed out on an early initiation to oral sex, a not-infrequent ritual shared between boys behind auditorium curtains during choir practice.[1] Other graduates of the school have shared stories of Presentation being the site of their first experiences of same-sex kissing, mutual masturbation, and even—if somewhat on the nose for a Catholic school—an introduction to and perhaps socialization toward sadomasochism. One Presentation alumnus who went to the school in the 1970s shared with me stories of being cruised by other students in the classroom and even an attempted (but failed) "match" with another boy facilitated by a school administrator who himself seemed titillated by the prospect. The wily delight of Father Larry's facial expression when he directed us to prove ourselves "not homosexual" suggested that the pleasure he derived from the experience was not entirely due to his indoctrination in religious morality.

Inside and outside the classroom at Presentation, homoerotic socialization was often meted out under the guise of discipline and punishment, and boys often mimicked priests' condemnation of homosexuality in the creation of rituals that would ironically engage practices of it. During the entirety of my three years at the school, we junior boys most lived in fear of "poling" by the senior boys. Those of us who ventured near the senior block buildings risked being grabbed by some of the older boys and having our legs spread apart as we were pushed against and up and down a pole, all for a boisterous audience cheering on the intended degradation.[2] I lived in fear of this exercise because the space I most occupied at the school was its library, which was located adjacent to the Sixth Form block. Although I carefully mapped out a path that entirely avoided this area, its close proximity meant that I was always alert to the possibility of being grabbed for an attack. At least twice I exited the library and saw ongoing brutal attacks a few meters away.

I was terrified and horrified, understanding in some way, even if I didn't know the term, that poling constituted sexual assault. The institutional accommodation of this kind of violence has mostly gone unrecognized, perhaps because rituals like it have been normalized in exclusively male spaces.[3] Getting poled was the most visible homoshaming/homoeroticizing ritual during my time at Presentation, but former alumni also told me about "rose," a common bullying game at the school in the 1970s, in which the target boy would be surprised by the insertion of the bully's finger through his green polyester uniform pants to tickle his anus. What was "rose" in 1970s Presentation College was called "the Elephant's Walk" at the Southern California fraternity of one of Jane Ward's informants. In this hazing ritual, participants would be required to strip naked and assemble in a circle. Each young man would place one thumb in his mouth and the other in the anus of another boy: "Like circus elephants connected by tail and trunk, and ogled by human spectators, they walked in a circle, linked thumb to anus, while older members of the fraternity watched and cheered" (Ward 2015, 1–2). Elephant's Walk explicitly links sodomy and animalization; the transformation into elephants is what grants permission for the boys to enact anal penetration. While Ward's text emphasizes examples of homoerotic hazing in Euro-American institutions (a group in which I would include Presentation College, since for most of the school's existence, it was administered from its order's headquarters in Ireland), contemporary reports of similar practices in Asian countries, especially in the context of military and college environments, have been documented in mass media (cf. Chong 2020). In these rituals, like Father Larry's discursive provocation about the homosexual, sexual heterodisciplining and homoerotic titillation were executed at once, in the same moment.

My own adolescent explorations were crutched by my delayed maturation and by my cautious aversion to experimentation resulting from anxieties about the kinds of sexual assault that rituals like poling presented. Nevertheless, Presentation was still where I would first see other boys' naked bodies and where I would witness savvier boys' sexual experimentation, however undereducated I was about sex itself. I joined the Photography Club in my second term at the school. Besides learning how to develop and print film, the big reward of membership was access to the air-conditioned private space of the photography lab, tucked behind the three first-year classrooms on the ground floor. This location meant that sounds from the room were out of earshot when classes were out of session. The lab's privacy afforded particular kinds of play. By the end of that first year at Presentation, I was introduced to a "game" called puhngah. There wasn't much to the game besides boys fighting in pairs. Each battle began with the boys facing each other in warrior pose. This combat was not fought with fists, however, but with the hips, pelvis up against pelvis, until one boy had subdued the other on the floor. Sometimes boys remained entirely clothed during the exercise. Often, their blue-and-gold-crested uniform shirts came off, freeing torsos to meet. Bragging rights were claimed by whichever boy ended up on top. I was so oblivious to sex in those days—making mixtapes and building Lego sets held more of my attention—that I cannot even remember if boys were turned on by this or what other homoerotic affection might have transpired during or after a battle. During puhngah, I usually fled to the secondary lab space in the darkroom, put off by and probably a little fearful of the aggressive, masculine physicality and never quite understanding what the boys were doing.

I had heard the word *puhngah* long before the Photography Club shenanigans, however. It became familiar to me in its many channels of covert circulation, including jokes like the one translated here from its more charming Trinbagonian vernacular and bereft of its usually animated delivery.

> Three Christian missionaries leave Europe for Africa to spread their Gospel. But soon after they reach land, the three men get captured by members of a native tribe and are taken to their chief. The three plead their case and good intentions. Instead of just killing them, the chief gives them a choice: puhngah or death. The missionaries are relieved. None of them knows what puhngah is, but they think that it must be better than death. The first missionary steps forward and says he chooses puhngah. The chief takes him aside and buggers him. The second missionary makes the same choice, and the same thing happens. Seeing what has happened to the other two, the third missionary decides he would rather face death than be sodomized and announces, "I choose death." "OK," the chief replies, "death by puhngah!"

Something about it—perhaps simply the thrill of taboo crossing or the frisson of colonial power structures upended—caused schoolboys and some grown men to become very animated in telling and responding to the joke. Despite my improved vocabulary and memories of other boys' and men's passionate cackling response to the joke, the joke falls as flat with me now as it did when I was a child. But I have a new appreciation for the oddly concise way it packages and presents the history of sodomy in the Americas, from colonial encounter to the present form of the postcolonial state. Further, its positioning as a kind of anticolonial vengeance against invading missionaries is also curious, echoing the kind of ambivalence and contradiction inherently present in the life of the postcolonial state and of the postcolonial subject within that state, especially as formulated around the demarcation between human and animal.

MAN AND BEAST

Since at least the beginning of the colonial period, people in Africa, Asia, and the Americas have been characterized as more animal, less human. This view of colonized people justified the occupation of their lands, genocide, and their enslavement. Recalling the appraisal of enslaved people following the death of a plantation master, Frederick Douglass (1845) noted, "We were all ranked together at the valuation. Men and women, old and young, married and single, were ranked with horses, sheep, and swine. There were horses and men, cattle and women, pigs and children, all holding the same rank in the scale of being." "Slavery's archival footprint," as Zakiyyah Iman Jackson observes, "is a ledger system that placed black humans, horses, cattle, and household items all on the same bill of purchase" (2016, 95). "The black body," she adds, "is an essential index for the calculation of degree of humanity and the measure of human progress" (96). Not just enslaved African peoples' different physiognomies made them less than "Man." Nonwhite peoples' sexualities were very often held up as evidence of the kind of behavior that made them more like animals. In *The History of Jamaica*, published in 1774 and for a long time afterward considered an authoritative source on the subject, slavery advocate Edward Long describes African and Indigenous Jamaicans as "libidinous and shameless monkeys, or baboons," thus making them uncivil (quoted in Joffe 1999, 20). Familial and sexual attachments and structures in places that lay outside the borders of normative and in many ways mythological European heterosexual aspirations were also frequently named as a justification for the colonization of less civilized peoples of the Global South. In puhngah, sodomy is the fitting focus of a joke about colonial encounter and a thought experiment playing out the postcolonial subject's possible revenge, because right from the start, the act of sodomy has been viewed as a persistent threat to the constitution of human as not animal. The knowledge of sodomy's normative Western moral significance was currency that purchased ascription of human status, and it is this tension in the joke—the linguistic barrier preventing the missionaries from anticipating their own unknowing acceptance of puhngah and their shaming by their own code—that charges the joke with its ironic sting. Throughout the European colonization of the Global South, invasion of occupied lands was premised on the demarcation of Indigenous peoples as less than human. Evidence of participation in sodomy was presented as evidence of their animality and identified as a rationale for their extermination.

One of the most circulated examples of how evidence of sodomy was viewed as justification for the use of brutal force and of how scenes of brutal visual spectacle were staged to enforce association between colonized peoples and animals took place at the beginning of the sixteenth century in the territory of Quarequa (now Panama). The reproduction of this scene into a visual narrative of natural domination and illustration of the divide between human and animal was captured by a 1594 engraving based on a woodcut by Theodore de Bry, *Balboa Setting His Dogs upon Indian Practitioners of Male Love Whom He Ordered Eaten Alive by the War Dogs* (figure 1.1). De Bry's image adapts an account of a 1513 massacre by Spanish explorer Vasco Núñez de Balboa, who used dogs to brutalize men allied with the chief Torecha in

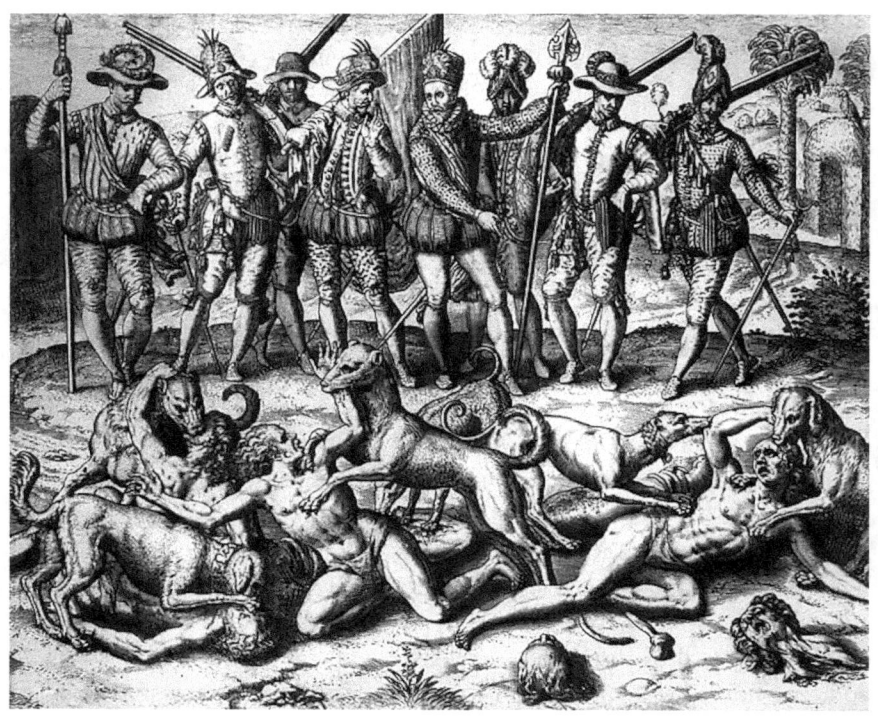

FIGURE 1.1 Theodore de Bry, *Balboa Setting His Dogs upon Indian Practitioners of Male Love Whom He Ordered Eaten Alive by the War Dogs*, 1594. Engraving, 160 mm × 169 mm, New York Public Library, Rare Book Room, de Bry Collection, New York.

the domain of Quarequa, producing one of the most famous and horrifying depictions of the use of dogs in colonial violence. The scene of this massacre was described three years later by Italian historian Peter Martyr d'Anghiera in his text *De Orbe Novo*: Balboa "founde the house of this kynge infected with most abhominable and unnaturall lechery. For he founde the kynges brother and many other younge men in womens apparel, smoth & effimiately decked, which by the report abowte hym, he abused with preposterous venus. Of these abowte the number of fortie, he commanded to bee given for a pray to his dogges" (quoted in Goldberg 1992, 180).

Martyr's narration of this event consistently underlines how participation in sodomy marked one as animal. He calls Balboa's victims "contagious beastes" and likens the attack on the men to the slaughtering of animals. They were "hewed," he wrote, "in pieses as the butchers doo fleshe . . . , from one an arme, from an other a legge, from hym a buttock, from an other a shuldre, and from sume the necke from the bodye at one stroke" (quoted in Goldberg 1992, 182). The dogs threw themselves on the men "as though they were wild boars or timid deer" (quoted in Boorstin 1983, 257). The visual implication that the men massacred are somehow akin to the animals used to destroy them is conveyed in stark, dichotomizing terms by de Bry's woodcut, in which a horizontal line in the center—a long, shadowed hillock in the landscape—divides the image in half, with the Europeans positioned standing, elaborately dressed and posed against a backdrop of sky in the top half of the woodcut and their near-naked Indigenous victims relegated to the bottom half, blended with violent fluidity into the roiling dogs. Both European colonists and Indigenous victims are located on the same bare earth, although most of the soldiers' standing bodies overlap with a lush space that includes signs of civilization represented by built structures. The implied sexual violence of the scene is present in the contrast between standing and lying, clothing and nakedness, human and less than human. The sodomy used by the colonizers to justify the violence is transformed into a sexually tinged spectacle of domination, one that is subtly undermined by the hypocritical contrast between the fine dress and seeming cultivation of the Europeans, whose agents of violence, the animals, are in fact extensions of their own bodies rather than those of the purportedly "more animal" men under attack. Curiously, the nimble, playful, fey poses and feather-decorated attire of the invading colonizers might, in the contemporary context, be read as "queer."

Throughout the late fifteenth- and early sixteenth-century Spanish invasion of the Americas, evidence of sodomy was cited as proof of Indigenous peoples' animality and used as justification for genocide. In Lorraine O'Grady's *The Clearing* (plate 1), Spanish conquistador Hernán Cortés's interracial relationship with the Nahua woman he was "gifted" as his slave, La Malinche, is identified as an enabling factor for his conquest of Yucatán/Mexico, but Cortés more explicitly invoked the sexual vice of sodomy to advance colonization. Bernal Díaz del Castillo's 1576 account shows us that Cortés attacked priests of the Indigenous peoples of Cempaloa as men with women's hair who "indulged in the foul practice of sodomy" (quoted in Goldberg 1992, 202). In sermons and instructions to Indigenous peoples, Cortés insisted over and over again that they give up sodomy. Columbus similarly accused Trinidad's Kalinago (Carib) men of "having long hair like women" and the women of being manly (quoted in Goldberg 1992, 198). In 1525, Spanish colonist Tomás Ortiz claimed that they "were sodomites more than any other race," and

Spanish colonial historian Gonzalo Fernández de Oviedo agreed that "the Indian eat flesh and are sodomites" (quoted in Goldberg 1992, 193).

In most accounts, general accusations offer no further elaboration, and invaders often reached the conclusion that Caribbean Indigenous peoples were sodomites because their societies' genders and gender norms did not match those of the Europeans or because they simply found it expeditious to do so. There is also evidence that some of the circulating tales about sodomy were actually drawn from the Indigenous peoples' reading of the Spanish colonists' society, arriving as they did as an exclusively male group, without female companions (Goldberg 1992, 185). Was colonizers' fixation on sodomy a result of what they witnessed among Indigenous peoples or a projection of their own anxieties and possible desires? Since the invaders came to the Americas in the midst of the Spanish Inquisition, in which sodomy was brutally punished, it is not surprising that fears about their own desires would be projected toward the Indigenous population, offering a familiar and efficient means of achieving dehumanization. The widespread shame, fear, and stigma surrounding sodomy in Spanish society provided a ready shorthand by which the domination of colonized peoples could be easily codified, naturalized, and communicated among colonizers and to the populace at home.

The puhngah joke is suggestive of this reading of sodomy's complex new meanings for colonizers, a tool for both colonial disciplining and self-normalizing and a contradictory territory of behavior and morality marked by violence, anxiety, desire, and fear. In the joke, homosexual sex is the main iterant, and the colonial missionaries' subjection to real or symbolic penetration is meant to humiliate them, both in the joke itself and in the telling of the joke. The joke establishes that while natives have some ease with homosexuality, at least in the role of aggressor, Europeans are terrified by it—or at least terrified by a public baring of their homosexual desires. In the joke, both the first and second missionaries choose puhngah over death; the second missionary still chooses puhngah even after it is revealed to mean sodomy. But for the third, so terrifying is sodomy—or perhaps the revelation of his homosexual desire—that death seems like the better option, a kind of escape hatch from the potential dehumanization enabled by sodomy. He escapes neither. The joke thus operates as a kind of return gaze to the colonizer. The joke also draws a line of continuity between colonizer and the resisting colonized; similar to the double effects of poling and Father Larry's classroom exercise, the intended use of sodomy as humiliation demonizes anal sex but in so doing also offers recognition and thus validation of the act and likely a kind of titillation.

Chapter One

This strategy of returning the gaze onto the colonizer specifically through the imagined act of sodomy takes center stage in the work of Toronto-based Cree artist Kent Monkman, whose painting *Daniel Boone's First View of the Kentucky Valley* (figure 1.2) depicts an Indigenous character sodomizing a British colonial settler. Monkman's painting signs its reference in the title, adapted from William Tylee Ranney's canonical 1849 reification of colonial manifest destiny, *Daniel Boone's First View of Kentucky* (figure 1.3). Monkman's painting pursues a number of reversals of Ranney's work. First, as in all his works from this series, Monkman represents the absented Indigenous population with the inclusion of a single man. The five male companions and two dogs in Ranney's painting have been removed. Left to his own devices, Boone—as signaled by his erect penis—is taking pleasure in being not the sodomizer but the sodomized in the colonial encounter. Like the puhngah joke, Monkman's painting reverses the structure of power established through sodomy. Lying on the ground atop a phallic land mass, Boone is not a guiding conqueror. He has instead become the willing conquest. Consistent with O'Grady's framework of pleasure and violence as simultaneous, the act of sodomy is imbued with ambivalence: Is it a "revenge" act, as in the puhngah joke? Or is the scene about the yearning by the sexually repressed European colonizer for the sexual liberty—or, one might say, the free animal desire—of the Indigenous American? While Boone's erect penis shores up the latter interpretation, it's unclear what's in it for the other man in the painting: Is his penetration of Boone an act of violence, revenge, redemption, or pleasure? The persistent idealization of white male bodies throughout Monkman's oeuvre adds another layer of complexity as well; it's difficult to also not interpret the work as a longing for sexual attention from gay white men.

Monkman's reimagination of colonial power struggles puts sodomy at the center of the colonial encounter in the Americas. Indeed, it was through British colonization of the Caribbean that anxieties about homosexuality were institutionalized through the adoption of harsh disciplinary legal regulations. The British captured Trinidad from the Spanish in 1797, when the island's population was 17,643—2,086 whites, 4,466 free people of color, 1,082 Amerindians, and 10,009 African enslaved people (Williams 1942, 1–4). Infrastructurally undeveloped during the period of its Spanish colonization, Trinidad would undergo an institutional transformation with the arrival of British settlers in greater numbers over the next century, a period that overlapped with the multiplied generation of discourses on and regulation of homosexual desire in Europe. As Michel Foucault (1978) has shown, starting in the eighteenth century, the generation of discourses about sexuality entered a new

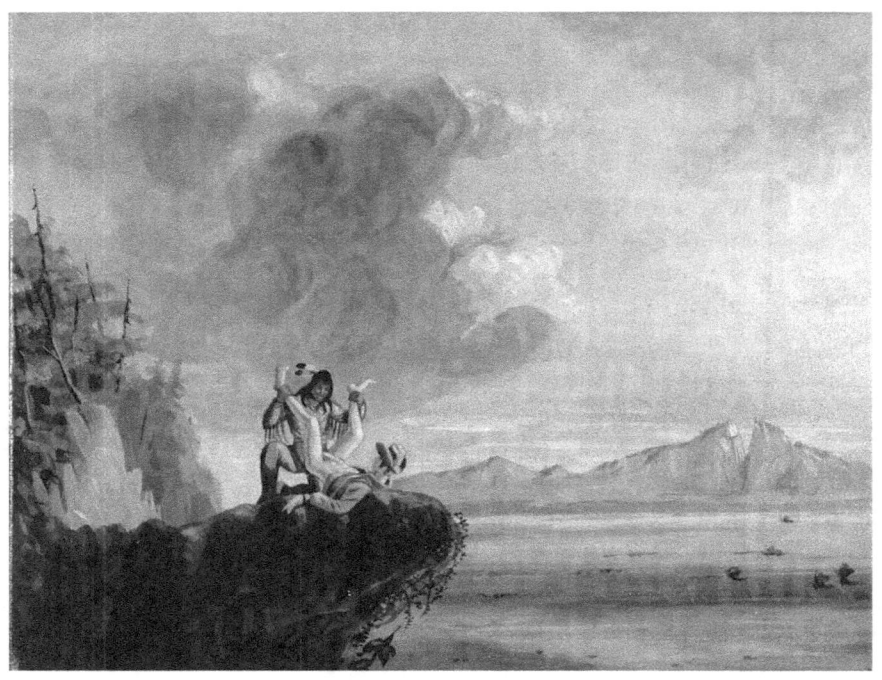

FIGURE 1.2 Kent Monkman, *Daniel Boone's First View of the Kentucky Valley*, 2001. Acrylic on canvas, 8 in. × 10 in. Courtesy of the artist.

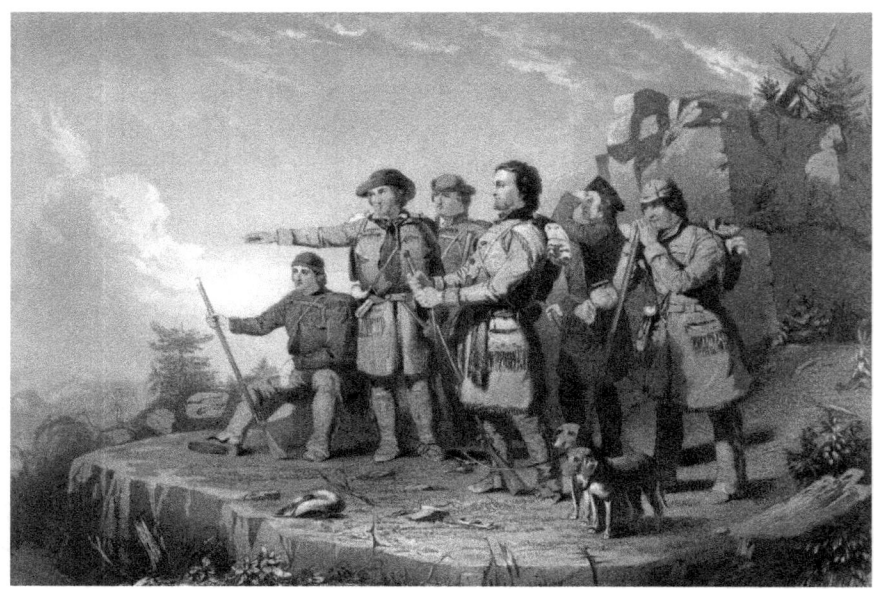

FIGURE 1.3 William Tylee Ranney, *Daniel Boone's First View of Kentucky*, 1849. Painting, framed 41⅝ in × 59 in × 3⅝ in.

period, and it became subject to aggressive regulation by the state, especially during the Victorian era (1837–1901). Foucault argues that the development of the capitalist system produced a new focus on human sexuality concerned with the production of the workforce to serve its needs. Over the nineteenth century especially, medical professionals and researchers became fixated on sex and particularly concerned with aberrations from the procreative norms, like masturbation and homosexuality. These developments in Europe coincided with the abolition of slavery in 1834 and 1838 in most of the British Caribbean colonies and the subsequent arrival of Indian indentures and with them Hindu and Islamic forms of marriage and familial structures. Sexual regulation laws introduced by the British in the Caribbean were shaped by these developments. Legal scholar Tracy Robinson observes, "Enduring post slavery sexed raced and gendered criminal laws which were all made during the flurry of lawmaking after slavery" were ushered in by colonial elites anxious about managing a population of free Black persons and large numbers of Indian indentured workers (Bulkan and Robinson 2018). Consequently, regulations introduced in the postemancipation period were perpetually concerned with defining the human to create shadowlands beyond the boundaries of "civilized" behavior to which those who did not conform to the moral code could be relegated—a kind of cultural prison that was newly able to lead its inmates to literal prison, a path paved by the legally inscribed category of "more animal."

Criminal codes introduced in British colonies were themselves developed in the context of anxieties about any kind of sex for pleasure. British legislation about sodomy dates back to as early as 1290, when such law was first mentioned in the medieval treatise *Fleta*, which stated that those "taken in the act" of sodomy should be "buried alive" (L. Moran 1996, 213). State regulation of same-sex acts would be introduced during the reign of Henry VIII. The advent of these laws in British society in the midst of colonization suggests a general anxiety about the Pandora's box of competing norms and behaviors potentially opened by the Europeans' metaphorical and literal penetration of "new worlds," which held threatening examples of alternative versions of how humans might live outside the patriarchal, hierarchical Christian model. The need to suppress any possibility for these alternative social models to be read as legitimate was echoed by a compounded need to codify and enforce patriarchal norms within British society and to draw clear lines between acceptable and unacceptable sexual behavior and thus between human and animal. A 1533 law prohibited the "abominable act of buggery" with "woman, man or"—notably—"beast," thus characterizing the act as animalistic (quoted in Waites 2013, 148). *All* kinds of bestiality would only become illegal in England a full two decades later, in 1558. The timing of these developments coinciding with Britain's first colonial efforts in the Americas is significant, as both practices of sodomy and bestiality became marked as measures for constituting types and degrees of humanness in a colonial context. This new attention to disciplining British people at home at the same time that new, threatening alternative cultural norms were being learned through colonizers' travels was perhaps an indication of an anxiety about British people's own humanness that was made invisible by highlighting the so-called barbaric practices of others in other lands. The legal equivalence between bestiality and homosexuality would endure for centuries. In 1892, when the British Home Office set out to review former cases to determine which prosecutions had been brought against men who had sex with men and men who had sex with animals, officials noted that "the calendars do not always give particulars enabling a distinction to be made whether the crime was committed with mankind or beast" (quoted in Brady 2005, 100). The offenses of sodomy and bestiality remain twinned in law in many countries, including in the Caribbean. In Saint Kitts and Nevis, for example, Article 56 of the Offences against the Person Act (1873) establishes that "any person who is convicted of the abominable crime of buggery, committed either with mankind or with any animal," shall be punished with imprisonment of up to ten years, with or without hard labor.[4]

Fears about homosexuality and the increased likelihood of laws against sodomy being enforced as a means of shoring up heteronormativity and patriarchal power were fueled by fears of declining bourgeois values and perceived threats to the British Empire (see Upchurch 2009). These anxieties would be projected and reframed in the colonies and expressed in the imbricated discursive articulation of "race" and gender with sexuality (see McClintock 1995; Stoler 1992, 1995; Young 2005). Rules about sexual activity were not only seen as necessary to civilize colonized peoples out of their animalistic desires but also—as expressed in Monkman's paintings—about keeping the sexualities of repressed and perhaps yearning colonial officers in check, at least in service of the idealized colonizing state if not in actual lived practice. (Colonial officers generally enjoyed immunity for sexual transgressions, especially those involving the abuse or assault of colonized peoples.)

Chapter One

The end of slavery in the Caribbean created a new conundrum in the colonies: how to make the previously animalized, enslaved person *human*? For British colonial administrators, including abolitionists, the answer was to school them in respectability. Although slavery ended in 1834, full enfranchisement was permitted in the British West Indies only following apprenticeships of four to six years, during which plantation laborers were to be taught respectability. In this period, "a new body of Europeans appeared in the colonies . . . missionaries, stipendiary magistrates, doctors and Colonial Office officials . . . whose task it was to 'civilize' the ex-slaves" (R. T. Smith 1967, 234). Absent this direction, administrators believed, "slaves would succumb to the most base desires, regressing to the heathens they were before the 'disciplinary-effects' of slavery. Indolence, laziness, lust, licentiousness, vice, and vagrancy would inundate the island as liberated slaves fled the plantation, taking to the bush or heading to the city to join the ranks of the growing urban underclass" (S. Scott 2002, 278). Worries about the wanton sexualities of Africans preoccupied British administrators, who came up with responses that proposed civilizing tasks through four basic tenets: religious education, knowledge of the English language, knowledge of economy, and education in the basis of colonialism (S. Scott 2002, 279). English emissaries were deployed to advance this mission through schools, churches, and other institutions.

Father Larry's classroom visit was thus part of this long-established tradition of both marking non-Europeans as animals and making them into humans (or closer to human). Across the postemancipation Caribbean, a commitment to disciplined heterosexuality was foundational to becoming characterized as human, not animal, and thus established in law. Beginning in 1860 with the introduction of Section 377 of the Penal Code in India, the British Offences against the Person Act, which explicitly outlawed sodomy with man or animal, was introduced across the British colonies. This extension of a law used to police behavior within Britain was mapped onto the making of personhood in the colonies in the postemancipation period. The genealogy of the act and its significance in Europe and then in the colonies reveals complex anxieties about sodomy, sexual desire, animality, and the racialized determination of personhood. Underlining the symbiotic relationship between Britain and its colonies, each remaking the other, the British Parliament revised its own legislation concerning the sex acts at the heart of the Indian Penal Code in 1861 and passed the Offences against the Person

Act. Section 61 of the act substituted sentences of ten years to life in prison for Britain's three-centuries-old death penalty.

This act was then introduced in Jamaica on January 1, 1864, and remains in place today; it also spread across the British Caribbean. In British Guiana, for example, three sections of the Criminal Law (Offences) Act targeted sodomy: Section 351 punishes acts of "gross indecency" with a male person with a two-year prison sentence; Section 352 criminalizes any "attempt to commit unnatural offences," including a ten-year prison sentence for any "male [who] indecently assaults any other male person"; and Section 353 states that "everyone who commits buggery, either with a human being or with any other living creature, shall be guilty of felony and be liable to imprisonment for life." Other sections of the Guyanese criminal code reveal how this prohibition was part of a broad view of the population as animals in need of a civilizing human hand. Section 153(1)(xlvii) of the Summary Jurisdiction (Offences) Act, Chapter 8:02, prescribes sanctions against anyone "being a man, in any public way or public place, for any improper purpose, [who] appears in female attire; or being a woman, in any public way or public place, for any improper purpose, [who] appears in male attire." The same section of the law covers laws about animals as well, outlining punishments for "exposing for sale cattle in improper part of town (iv); beating [a] mat in [a] public way in town (vii); cleansing cask, etc. in public way (xl); driving cattle without proper assistance (xv), etc." The section, which treats various offenses mainly in relation to towns, also includes sanctions against discharging a cannon within three hundred yards of a dwelling house, roller-skating on public roads, and flying kites in Georgetown and New Amsterdam.[5]

While indictments for sodomy were often handed down in Britain, the laws against sodomy were generally not broadly implemented in the colonies, where attitudes toward sex were much more relaxed, at least for settlers (see Hyam 1991).[6] Between 1868 and 1872, for example, Britain had 359 indictments for attempted sodomy, with 201 convictions (Brady 2005, 99). Meanwhile, the colonies offered European settlers freedom and power to exercise their sexual fantasies.[7] Joseph Gaskins Jr. notes that during the first half of the colonial project, British colonizers lived in an almost all-male society with few outlets for heterosexual sex and few legal restrictions and that "sexual license was among the most distinctive characteristics of British colonial society" (2013, 432). Thus, the imposition of the Offences against the Person Act in the colonies had more symbolic than practical significance. Its primary purpose appeared to be definition of the human, whether through narratives of class or race or in relationship to the demands of familial reproduction by emergent capitalist economies.

In their most basic essence, the antisodomy laws constituted animals so that humans could be made. The colonial production of images of Indigenous peoples, enslaved Africans, and indentured Indians as animalistic in order to justify their abuse, exploitation, and genocide in turn defined the colonizing settler as human. Many would-be settlers in the Caribbean were themselves burdened with the task of proving themselves human in their home countries and had fled to the New World as an escape from various conditions of marginality in relationship to dominant doctrines, whether Victorianism or Catholicism, that defined their behaviors and moralities as lacking. The animalization of some to define others as human continued in the postcolonial period. This program, created and enforced through cultural constructions of civilized behavior that model and police dress, manners, speech, self-fashioning, and self-conception, has been called the politics of respectability.[8] This effort by dehumanized people to secure the status of "human" through the reproduction of themselves as "respectable" subjects not only reproduces and maintains the very forms of hatred developed throughout the colonial period but is similarly deployed through externally imposed and internalized anxieties about sexuality and gender. The effort was effective in helping constitute a new petite bourgeoisie of Black and colored educators, health care professionals, writers, journalists, and civil servants within a generation after emancipation. This group, Bridget Brereton notes, "attached great weight to cultural and intellectual life." These new elites "boasted of their command of British culture, their ability to speak and write 'good English,' their interests in things of the mind. It was literacy, familiarity with books, the possession of 'culture' which mattered, as well as an occupation which involved no manual labour" (1979, 94).

Stuart Hall describes his experience of this project while attending high school in 1940s Jamaica. Schools like the one he attended "were designed to cultivate and conscript a British-oriented, subordinate, 'native' elite," he says.

> Those schooled in such an environment would become "subjectified" from the inside by having their heads stuffed with a curriculum devoted to an idea of civilization to which, it was hoped, they would be motivated to aspire. This was a sort of "education of the feelings" as much as of the mind, the aim of which was evident both in the subjects we were taught and in the manner in which we were taught them. These valorized the British imagination, ways of life and habits of authority which the colonial

authorities believed to be embedded in the national literature, political institutions, social conventions, manners, values and ideals of "the mother country." (Hall with Schwarz 2017, 117)

In his memoir, Hall recalls a variety of small, ridiculous rituals pursued toward realization of civility. "Our English headmaster introduced tuck shops. On dress days, we sweated in blazers. On buses and trams, prefects struggled to keep the caps lodged somehow on the crown of their woolly heads, and laboured to keep their own caps white and free of swirling dust" (118). Although there were always ways in which acts of subversion emerged from this context, there was no doubt about the configuration of education as a practice of colonial mimicry.

This effort did not end with the security of political independence, as artist Christopher Cozier observes through his art installation *Attack of the Sandwich Men* (figure 1.4). The installation consists of one hundred white bread sandwiches wrapped in waxed paper. To each sandwich is affixed a miniature flag of Trinidad and Tobago, and all are spread across the floor like a fleet of ships. Along one side of the lines of sandwiches is an old radio playing a broadcast from the earliest days of Trinidad and Tobago's experience as an early independent nation. Cozier was born in 1959, three years before the country achieved political independence from Britain. In a 2003 interview with Annie Paul that appeared in *Bomb* magazine, Cozier explains, "The title music was from the *Nutcracker Suite* and the broadcasters all had fake BBC accents! They were attempting to correct all the wrong ways that people would have proceeded to sing the new anthem. The correct way turns out to be a kind of Victorian parlor style of singing. High-pitched with rolling *Rs*. So the contrast between Wonder Bread in neat rows and these instructions defined, for me, the relationship between those who had an American consumer template for 'progress' and those with a British template for civility and order" (Paul 2003). A mixed-ethnicity son of middle-class civil servants from Barbados, Cozier was viewed as a future leader in the new nation whose schooling demanded attention to the civilization of every detail of life, including what food he could eat. He recalls, "The other children with whom I went to school had admired my 'modern' sandwiches. The others had homemade lunches related to their cultural/ethnic backgrounds, like 'bakes,' something associated with African roots, or 'rotis,' which were associated with Indians. . . . My lunch was 'practical' and 'modern' and also easier to package and fit into my *Star Trek* or *Bonanza* lunch box (I had both), the little ones made of tin with the figures in relief, probably made in Taiwan or Hong Kong" (Paul

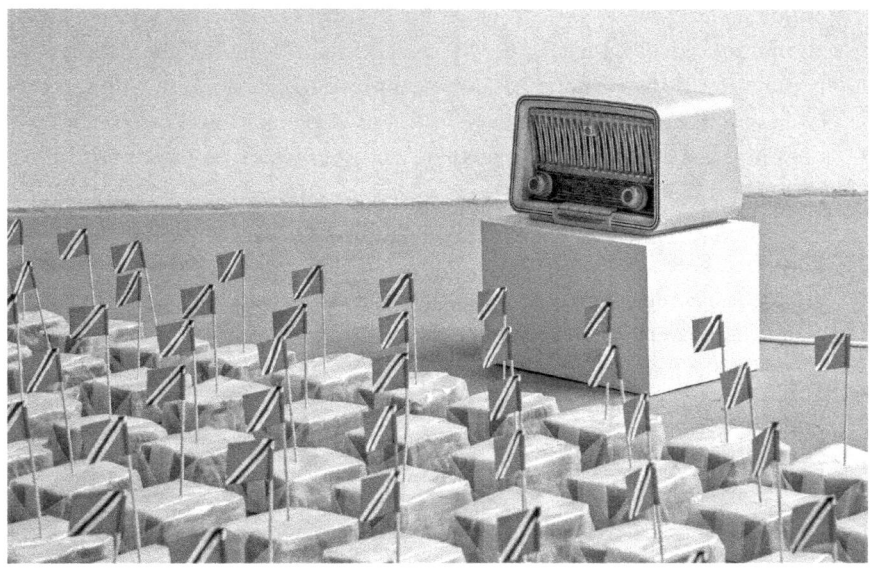

FIGURE 1.4 Christopher Cozier, *Attack of the Sandwich Men*, 2002. Installation, BKP-DAAD, Berlin.

2003). Four decades later, the sandwiches take on a different meaning. "I was quite haunted by the image of sliced bread wrapped in grease-proof paper," Cozier says. "To me it represented that time in my childhood just after independence, the promise of modernity and progress. . . . A sense of the march of progress and the aspirations came to me" (Paul 2003). Cozier and other middle- and upper-class aspirational families in the capital city would thus become invested in the politics of respectability because they would also be rewarded by it, a process that simultaneously made them more human and not animal—unlike the heathen roti-eating descendants of indentures in the countryside and economically marginalized Afro-Trinidadians.

Through their assumption of the respectability that colonial programs intended, the petite bourgeoisie could be defined as human, which most others in the society could not. For example, M. Jacqui Alexander (2005) and Kate Bedford (2009) show how the Bahamian state engaged in a program of heteropatriarchal recolonization in which the state's peoples were subsequently "sexualized and ranked into a class of good, loyal, reproducing, heterosexual citizens, and a subordinated, marginalized class of noncitizens who, by virtue of choice and perversion, choose not to do so" (Alexander 2005, 46). Taking charge after winning independence required proof of fitness to lead. Disciplined sexuality was a key component of civility. As Alexander argues, "Erotic autonomy signals danger to the heterosexual family and to the nation. And because loyalty to the nation as citizen is perennially colonized within reproduction and heterosexuality, erotic autonomy brings with it the potential of undoing the nation entirely, a possible charge of irresponsible citizenship, or no responsibility at all" (1994, 22–23). This ambition of creating "loyal, reproducing, heterosexual citizens" was folded into the development projects that promoted heteronormativity through education, health, and economic programs. Alexander concludes by noting that "respectability might well function as debt payment for rescue from incivility and from savagery" (1994, 14).

Following the achievement of political independence, colonial antisodomy laws were therefore preserved in most countries, and in some cases, punishments were made even more severe. In 1986, Trinidad and Tobago's Parliament raised the fines for sodomy and introduced a new sanction disallowing the entry of homosexuals into the country. This legislation also for the first time explicitly criminalized consensual sex between women. In Antigua and Barbuda, prior to 1995, there was one category for the crime of buggery, and it carried a maximum imprisonment of ten years. The 1995 Sexual Offences Act distinguished buggery and bestiality; the penalty for the latter remained ten years' imprisonment, while that for consensual and nonconsensual buggery between adults rose to fifteen years.[9] In 2011, Jamaica enacted a Charter of Fundamental Rights and Freedoms that added a limitation on the guaranteed rights with regard to laws relating to sexual offenses, obscene publications, and offenses regarding the lives of the unborn, thus reinstalling sanctions against sodomy.[10] A new clause also prohibited discrimination on the grounds of "being male or female," a determined resistance of transgender rights (see chapter 2), and a means to ensure that sex-based discrimination does not extend to prohibiting discrimination on the basis of sexual orientation. Guyana's colonial antisodomy laws were similarly kept in place by the country's constitutional review in 1980.

As Tracy Robinson points out, "The corpus of laws regulating sex in the Anglophone Caribbean today includes colonial criminal legislation dealing with rape, unnatural crimes, abortion, prostitution and vagrancy and can be traced to late nineteenth century omnibus criminal statutes, some codes, that were the products of a rash of lawmaking that ensued after slavery to control the freed population and those who came after as indentured workers" (2017, 8). These laws, Robinson argues, "have a dialogical quality." They are, she explains, "embodied and fluid processes that include the contradictory spaces in which official and unofficial actors make sense of sex laws and their lives, and work through the possibilities of legal change within what are often intimate arrangements of power. These processes are about national progress and vulnerability and who counts as a legal subject entitled to rights. New-old sex laws have an inherent indeterminacy as they are made sense of in different contexts, yet 'constrained by history, habit, social organization, and power'" (14). The purpose of these laws was twofold: to mark as savage the colonized peoples of the Caribbean, a group that had come to include the descendants of enslaved African people and Indian indentures brought by the British as well as the region's Indigenous population; and to justify the imposition of controls to curb that savagery, as evidenced by sexual and gender expression. "There are no other laws in the Caribbean which have the resilience of these laws," Robinson has observed (Bulkan and Robinson 2018).

Through the retributive acts of the chief in the joke, puhngah illustrates how colonial attempts to discipline homosexuality were taken up by post-colonial states following the retreat of European powers and the claim of independence. Emerging states' responses were not unlike the chief's, as they too refused formal symbolic and institutional expressions of colonial power as embodied by Europeans from the metropole, but maintained their forms of representation of and discipline through sexuality. Finally, the fact that both the game and the joke survive and resonate more than five hundred years after colonial encounters underlines the continuing resilience of these tensions. Puhngah invokes the facts of history that have formed contemporary sexual desires—themselves too unwieldy to fit easy categories and characterization—and exposes truths about the perseverance and effects of anxieties about sexual acts. Puhngah, imbued with its meanings by law, by word of mouth, by moral instructors like Father Larry, and by anxious jokes that refract tensions about centuries-old power dynamics built uneasily on moral prescription, shows the context and logic through which laws governing sexuality emerge and operate. As the ambivalence of Monkman's paintings suggests, while this context is clearly framed by the power asserted by the colonizing state over colonized peoples, it is also fraught with complications and ambiguities. Thus, rather than being seen as exclusively concerned with the control of colonized peoples, colonial laws might better be viewed as a manifestation of anxieties about desires of all subjects, including colonial officers, and as a response to fears about what might unfurl from the free, unregulated expression and exercise of sexual desire, including civilization itself. In other words, the fear is that without the laws, we might all be revealed to be the animals that we are. This view of the laws better explains their continuity and often their unchallenged reaffirmation in postcolonial governance in the Caribbean.

Clothes Make the Man   2

AT PRESENTATION COLLEGE, my considerable lack of savvy was evidenced in areas besides my ignorance about sex. I was also underschooled in gender, lacking clear instructions and investment in the performance of masculinity. For this, primary responsibility likely lies with the various Indo-Trinidadian women who raised me: my mother, my aunts, my grandmothers, the Sunday school teacher at the temple, and my teachers, all of whom were engaged in different ways in what I have termed "wrecking work" (2016a). "Everything slackens in a wreck" (Carter and Torabully 2002, 40), Khal Torabully wrote in *Cale d'étoiles*, his epic 1992 poem about the migration of Indians to the Caribbean via the British slavery-replacement system, indentureship. In this and subsequent work, Torabully's interest is in the sea voyage as "a place of destruction and creation of identity" (15). As theorized by other scholars of creolization, the cutting of ties and destruction of culture resulting from the ship journeys to the Caribbean provided openings for acts of resistance to oppressive forms of social organization, and for justice. Caribbean feminists have also pointed out that the imbalanced ratio of men to women and the organization of plantation life effectively interrupted gender norms during and after the indentureship period (cf. Mohammed 1999; Reddock 1986). This "wrecking work" continued to similarly ambivalent effect in the aftermath of political independence from Britain. The indenture-descended women who shared in the labor of my upbringing did not instill in me a loyalty to gender, whether through the examples they set or through more explicit instruction. To be fair, nor did the men, though fewer of them participated in my upbringing. My father's long work hours in a town that was far away (by Trinidad standards) were the main impediment to spending time together, while uncles were few and my grandfathers were not warm men by any measure and appeared to take no interest in me. Almost all of my schoolteachers were women, and many of them were single women appearing to be independently in control of their own lives. A medical student with progressive, liberal ideas would travel down from the city to run our Sunday school, and we mostly practiced meditation and breathing exercises. My mother married at a young age, but she was the only one of her sisters to do so. I was often shuffled between aunts on the weekend, and we would often end up at bookshops, hair salons, and sometimes bars.

Contemporary texts by Gaiutra Bahadur (*Coolie Woman*, 2013), Krystal Sital (*Secrets We Kept: Three Women of Trinidad*, 2018), and others underline the persistence of domestic violence in Indo-Caribbean families, but across the entire extended family, I have witnessed only one case of domestic violence, by a drunken uncle against his father, and my grandmother came to the rescue. That is not to say that my experience is "correct," fair, or complete and that other versions are not—on the contrary, data consistently report domestic violence as a major problem, especially in Guyana (Bahadur 2013, 236)—but to say that my experience existed too, and to suggest that the feminist "wrecking work" that surrounded my childhood strongly shaped my worldview and real, lived environment. Thus, I would have never felt the kinds of pressures to "act manly" that many gay Caribbean men report in other contexts (cf., for example, Crichlow 2004; Gill 2018; Wahab 2012). I cannot recall a single moment in which gender was used as a restrictive disciplining tool, and I was allowed a great deal of space to be whatever kind of child I wanted to be, and the people I wanted to be most like were my aunts.

One of the earliest ways in which I began to emulate these women was through fashion. I was comfortably obsessed with color-coordinating cute

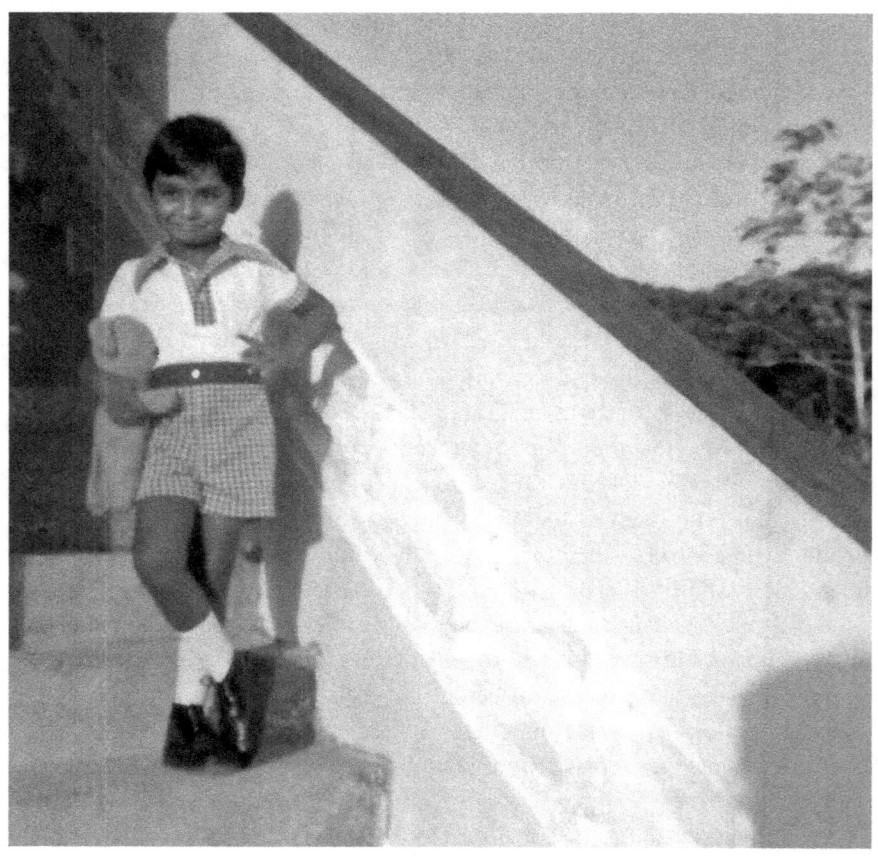

FIGURE 2.1 The author as a child in a favorite ensemble (ca. 1980).

wardrobes from as early as I had become aware that I wore clothes. At Robert Village Hindu School, beige uniforms were the daily rule, but whenever I could exercise the choice to construct my wardrobe, I did. That meant on no-uniform Fridays, I could put together cute outfits like the one shown in figure 2.1. Among my quirkier choices was a preference for Dutch clogs. From ages eight to nine, you couldn't get me into any other shoes—I even played cricket in them—and to be fair, no one ever tried, just as no one had a problem with my quick adoption of a Miss Piggy Muppet as my constant companion. Piggy and I shared a lot of picnics together and a lot of chats, and we often danced together to the only pop record I listened to repeatedly: the soundtrack for the first movie that my parents took me to see, at the Kay Donna drive-in in Valsayn, the campy cult classic *Xanadu*.

Chapter Two

As far as I can remember, no one pushed back against any of my alleged departures from what might have been imagined as more "proper," masculine boyhood behavior most of the time. It is quite possible that I was made to feel so confident about myself by George Village—and I do mean the whole village—that I might not have noticed challenges or criticism that was present. For example, because of the strong resemblance I bore to my mother and her sisters, I was often easily recognized as belonging to their tribe, but nothing bothered me about looking like these women I adored. Often I was told something along the lines of "you're pretty enough to be a girl" or "you're pretty like your mother/aunt." Looking back, one might read this as a double-edged gender-policing gesture, but I absolutely recall receiving the remark as a compliment, even a mark of pride. "Thanks!" I replied, firmly confident of *Xanadu*'s claim: "A million lights are dancing, and there you are, a shooting star." I saw my aunts as stars and was delighted to be thought about like them. What was shameful about being read as a girl?

In San Fernando, I would begin to experience a few more moments where I would come to understand that I deviated from something. In my first year at Presentation College, I arrived at a school bazaar positively gleaming about how my gift for color coordination had resulted in, I thought, quite the triumph of a wardrobe. I would learn that day and be reminded in the weeks that followed that perhaps an outfit of a silky pink shirt, bright-yellow baggy trousers, and yellow-and-pink moccasins that brought them together—the shoes accented with bright-green laces tied in a bow at the top—was not going to be the most well-received choice for a fourteen-year-old boy. The colors were read as both femme and unsophisticated, their gaudy brightness associated with undercultured rural Indians. I could easily endure the daily teasing that followed this colorful coming-out of sorts at the bazaar. But truthfully, it was like water off a duck's back; my aunts had raised a confident stylist who pitied the poor taste of these fashion-challenged boys who, I believed, clearly lacked my sophisticated palette.

That does not mean that my formative socialization by these feminist women—more my characterization of them that rings true as a retrospective observation than an identity or ideology explicitly or necessarily claimed by them in the moment—bore only the goodness of freedom from the confines of gender.[1] The flip side of indoctrination into fashion was that I also early on picked up on the uneasy relationships my aunts had with their bodies. Clothes were adornment, but they were also cover from shame and a means to negotiate more value for their bodies. Fashion is almost always consumer-capitalist endeavor and has always been dependent on the insecurities of women, and more recently also men, for profit: we need clothes to communicate identity and, often especially for marginalized subjects, add value. The poses I took in the photographs like figure 2.1 restaged my aunts' own poses in their outfits, their efforts to represent themselves as attractive. The structure and form of fabric, I would implicitly understand, hid natural deficiencies. The fact that my mother and aunts were "famously beautiful" (further elaboration about this quote appears in chapter 5) did not mean they were not preoccupied with naming and obsessing with "deficiencies" in their bodies. Despite having a different body from theirs, I nevertheless was similarly socialized to view my own as similarly lacking. From about age six or seven, I started to look at my stomach in the mirror—mimicking exactly the exercise I had seen my aunts do, perhaps focused in on those body parts we did share, like the ever-protruding belly. Boys tend to be indoctrinated into a male-focused regime of gaining muscle weight as a response to insecurity about their bodies—and indeed, both of my brothers, whose childhoods were mostly experienced in Canada, are evidence of that trajectory. But I implicitly understood from my aunts that my goal was to be thin. Of course, like them, I *was* thin but could never become thin enough. And not becoming thin enough, socialized to always see my body as only an itinerary of flaws, meant that I was deeply ashamed to be naked.

The first time I would even begin to understand that in that time, boys generally did not feel ashamed of their nude bodies was during my first physical education class at Presentation College. I was panicked about the change into and out of gym clothes, a feeling no one else seemed to share. I recall being surprised that while I was quietly and quickly shuffling from gym clothes to uniforms on the first day of class, there was one fully naked boy just strolling up and down the room's exterior, in full view of the rest of the campus. He was entirely unbothered about his own nakedness while I was so distraught about revealing just my upper body that I left behind and lost my new school shoes in the change room. Much to my long-term detriment, I also made every excuse to escape gym class from that day on. It is also not lost on me that the beauty ideals I adopted were ones that would really not serve me well as I grew into a man engaged in intimate relationships with other men. While I was being indoctrinated into my aunts' gospel of thinness in the 1980s, the AIDS epidemic was simultaneously making thin gay male bodies synonymous with the disease, and gay men consequently began to become much more invested in muscle building. If dominant representations of gay masculinity in pornography are our guide, the appeal of thinness generally expires with youth (cf. Kitzinger 1995).

Both outcomes of childhood socialization by the women around me—the confidence-building gender bending *and* the paralyzing insecurities I developed about public displays of the body—operated (still operate) in relationship to the dominant logic of colonization that clothes make the man. Regardless of how gender-coded dress has changed throughout time, there has been since at least medieval time a committed investment to the matching of wardrobe to gender. In his influential sermons, for example, Bernardino of Siena (1380–1444) accused boys of "inviting sodomy by wearing effeminate and elaborate clothing" and condemned mothers for "letting their sons dress up in order to gain the attentions of a wealthy lover" (quoted in Karras 2005, 138). From the moment of colonial encounter, people who have crossed Euro-centering gender norms of clothing have met serious violence in the Caribbean, from the Indigenous "men in skirts" slaughtered by Balboa in Quarequa, as depicted in the woodcut discussed in the previous chapter, to the present-day harassment and abuse of people who depart from these norms across the region.

Evidence of the endurance of these anxieties across time and politics, Fanon's much-cited note about homosexuality in *Black Skin, White Masks* foregrounds attire. Noting his inability to "establish the overt presence of homosexuality in Martinique," Fanon observes, "we should not overlook . . . the existence of what are called . . . 'men dressed like women' or 'godmothers.' Generally they wear shirts and skirts" (1967, 180). Rosamond King further takes issue with the simplified translation of "shirts and skirts" from Fanon's original French text, "une veste et une jupe": "While strictly speaking the 1967 translation of 'shirts and skirts' is not incorrect," she points out, "it is helpful to know that the French *veste* refers specifically to a *man's* shirt or jacket. This difference implies greater gender ambiguity than that of a man dressed completely in women's clothing" (2014, 54). This broader identification of ensembles thus places the subjects of Fanon's note on a continuum. King argues that "an outfit that is comprised entirely of clothing usually worn by women implies a desire to embody traditional femininity, whereas a man's jacket with a women's skirt implies a desire to simultaneously embrace *both* masculinity and femininity. In the latter case, 'men dressed as women' becomes shorthand for men dressed in any way that does not overwhelmingly endorse conventional masculinity. Though it is not clear which sense Fanon intended, both possibilities expand traditional notions of Caribbean gender" (54). In *Island Bodies*, King identifies a range of gender-nonconforming characters in Caribbean festivals as evidence of the long-standing visibility. In 2019, Akola Thompson added to King's archive with an example she found in the September 5, 1971, issue of Guyana's *Sunday Chronicle*. Titled "Men in Dresses—and a Village Is Divided," the original *Chronicle* article, Thompson reports, described men who were "decked out in Saris, miniskirts and high-heeled shoes, the trail-blazing Miss Anita the Iceberg, Miss Diamond, Shakira, Penny and Miss Viking Queen were said to simply ignore the men who had a problem with the way they lived" (2019).

The surveillance of dress and self-representation is conveyed in myriad forms, carrying a colonial legacy into contemporary lived experience in a tangible and continually policed fashion. In a 2018 fact-finding mission conducted by the Georgetown Law Human Rights Institute about the experiences of LGBTQI+ people in Guyana, respondents described many examples of harassment they experience at work and in public spaces. "Many transgender women talked about having to dress differently, always travel with others, and avoid areas that were known to be more homophobic," the report's authors noted (2018, 60). Processing their anxieties about the shamefulness of the naked body—developed from centuries-long Christian theology—European colonial officers in their encounter with Indigenous peoples in would-be colonies attached clothing to civility. Clothed men like them were men; those less clothed or not clothed like them were animals.

In this chapter, I draw attention to two cases tried in Caribbean courts over the past decade that demonstrate how "clothes make the man" in the colonial and postcolonial Caribbean, in both the gender-specific turn of this phrase and in terms of clothing's function as an arbiter of humanness/animality in the region: the arrest of Kennty Dave Mitchell in Trinidad in 2000; and of seven Guyanese persons accused of transgressing gendered regulations of clothing, which became known as the McEwan case in Guyana, in 2009. Analysis of these cases makes evident the ways in which the material of clothing is an interface through which colonial-era anxieties about "race," gender, class, and sexuality continue to powerfully underpin and structure negotiations about Caribbean peoples' animality. This function of clothing is observable in actions taken by police officers to violently remove or regulate wardrobes, in judicial commentaries and rulings that animalize some to humanize others, and in the systemic validation of these measures in law. Both the public responses and, in the instance of the McEwan case, the judgment of the Caribbean Court of Justice challenge convention.

The visual and material markers now used to signify or constrain who we are and what we can and should be, and to conceal and ornament our bodies, can in turn mean and be many things: clothing can variously and simultaneously be, among other things, protection, art, commodity, identity, sign of community membership, or legal requirement. Arbitration over what clothing is and what it means is itself therefore a highly contested and policed zone of thought, a fact evidenced perhaps nowhere more clearly than in the history of LGBTQI+ legal and social struggles, or in visual art engaging with gender and sexual identity.

Clothing is a defining feature of being human quite simply because humans are the only animals who cover their bodies as a lived daily practice. "Human bodies are dressed bodies," notes Joanne Entwistle (2000, 323). The seeming simplicity of this distinction, however, belies the complexity of its implications. The practice of wearing clothing plays a fundamental role in our continual process of constituting humanness, the self, and the other. Christian theology of course established a strong link between clothing, morality, and civility right from the start. In Genesis 2:25, we are told that Adam and Eve "were both naked, the man and his wife, and were not ashamed"; in Genesis 3:7, they are sewing fig leaves into aprons to cover their genitals; by verse 8, their nakedness has made them feel so ashamed that they are hiding from God.

Ruth Barcan observes that nudity "has divided the nonhuman from the human and divided humanness into types of gradations," such as male/female, civilized/savage, sane/insane, and normal/deviant (2004, 15). "Humans may be naturally naked," she points out, "but we have used clothing to define our kind (especially to differentiate ourselves from animals), and to differentiate ourselves from each other" (15). This symbolic use of clothing was especially activated during the European colonization of Africa, Asia, and the Americas. Philippa Levine points out that "while the sculptures and statuaries of ancient Greece that celebrated the heroic, naked male body were, and often continue to be, read as the pinnacle of a civilized aesthetic," the unclothed Indigenous subject across the Global South signified "an absence of civilization" (2008, 189–90). The use of nakedness to characterize nonwhite people as animals goes back to the very conception of natural history. The presence or absence of clothing was tied to civility in Carl Linnaeus's deeply influential classification of Homo sapiens in *Systema Naturae* into distinct racial types. The "wild man" was "four-footed, mute and hairy," the American "paints himself with fine red lines," and the African "anoints himself with grease," while the European was "covered with close vestments" and the Asiatic "covered with loose garments." Evidence of this connection between race and clothing included lawsuits. For example, in 1686, Blas de Horta called a witness to affirm that he wore "Spanish dress" in his attempt to prove that he was not in fact Indigenous (Earle 2001, 187). Following Linnaeus, in their epic 1817 four-volume set on the history of animals, French naturalists Frédéric Cuvier and Étienne Geoffroy Saint-Hilaire include a single image of a human body, that of African Khoe Khoe woman Sara Baartman (1824). Cuvier's ordering of animals was mirrored by his racist theories in other works that ranked different races, based on his assessment of the level of civilization achieved by each, and which implied the closeness of certain humans to animals because of their lack of "civilization," thus enabling the inclusion of Baartman's image in the history of animals. This literal stripping of colonized people's humanity was par for the course by the late nineteenth century. In 1869 leading British scientist Thomas Huxley received from the Colonial Office cooperation in providing nude photographs of natives from Asia, Africa, and the Americas. From her study of this period, Levine concludes:

> The trope of the "naked native" exercised a great deal of power throughout the era of British imperialism, and its power derived as much from the debates about the dispassionate representation of naked bodies as from the unequal power relations inherent in colonial rule. Together, these offered a potent means by which nakedness, as distinct from nudity inherited from the classical tradition, increasingly became emblematic of colonial primitiveness, savagery, and inferiority. Scientists excited about the prospect of uncovering truths quite literally elided undress and discovery, and nakedness as a means of documenting human "types" simultaneously became a lucrative avenue for photographers. (2013, 8–9)

"Unclothed," and "acutely aware of the camera," Levine says, "these photographic subjects were . . . not individuals but representatives, their exposed bodies revealing and demonstrating racial characteristics" (10). "Here was primitivism displayed quite literally in the raw, in the flesh, in the moment" (15).

Given the long-standing condemnation of nudity in Christian doctrine, it is no wonder then that European missionaries drew upon Christian theology to condemn nakedness among the people encountered. The association between nakedness and spiritual decay that was established in Genesis is also drawn in the New Testament. Revelation 16:15 reads, "Behold, I come

Chapter Two

as a thief. Blessed is he that watcheth, and keepeth his garments, lest he walk naked, and they see his shame." Consequently, "people who displayed no shame at being naked, then, were people whose souls were in danger" (Levine 2008, 191). Levine concludes that "to be naked was to be both ashamed and shamed" (191). Biblical texts' condemnation of nakedness propped up the characterization of colonized peoples as primitive. In *A Village in Pukapuka* (figure 2.2) from the 1870s, European colonization is seen to turn half-naked savages into more civilized humans. Among other examples cited by Levine in her research are Charles Darwin's encounter in the 1830s with the people of Tierra del Fuego, whom he described as "the most abject and miserable creatures I have any where beheld" and "quite naked," and British travelers' emphasis on the "nakedness of most Indians whom they encountered on their arrival" (Cohn 1996, 129). In Sergeant Wallace's photograph *Two Chamars*, as Levine notes, two Indians wearing rags appear mystified by the purpose of the shoes one holds up questioningly, and of the Western-style jacket lying on the ground. These objects, and their nakedness, comprise props used to construct a portrait of subjects whose relationship to humanity is artfully made to appear distanced.

As evidenced by Wallace's image, and by examples such as Baartman's inclusion in the natural history, nakedness, far from a natural state candidly observed by colonizers, was instead a state of being to be staged, curated, and deliberately styled to convey the distinction between human and animal. Such stagings rendered "natural" the colonizing relationship. In *Two Chamars*, the subjects are dressed in stylized nakedness for the photo.[2] Nakedness thus becomes a kind of dress, used to signify that dress is unfamiliar and unnatural to them, to show the imperfectness of the efforts to present them as fully human in a Western sense. Levine explains, "To be primitive was to be in a state of nature, unschooled, unselfconscious, lacking in shame and propriety—and nothing better signified the primitive than nakedness. Whether in the pages of the American magazine *National Geographic*, the textbooks from which generations of schoolchildren learned of the world beyond Britain, or the colonial fiction of the period of British imperial expansion, the native is frequently no more than semi-clothed" (2008, 191). "Placed thus low on the scale of progress and rendered pitiful rather than threatening, naked savages could find salvation only through clothing and Christianity, chastity and containment" (213). Christian missionaries thus sought to cover the bodies of "under-dressed" Indigenous people across the colonies of the Global South, from Mexico to Australia (Brock 2007, 4; see also figure 2.3 for a contrast to figure 2.2).

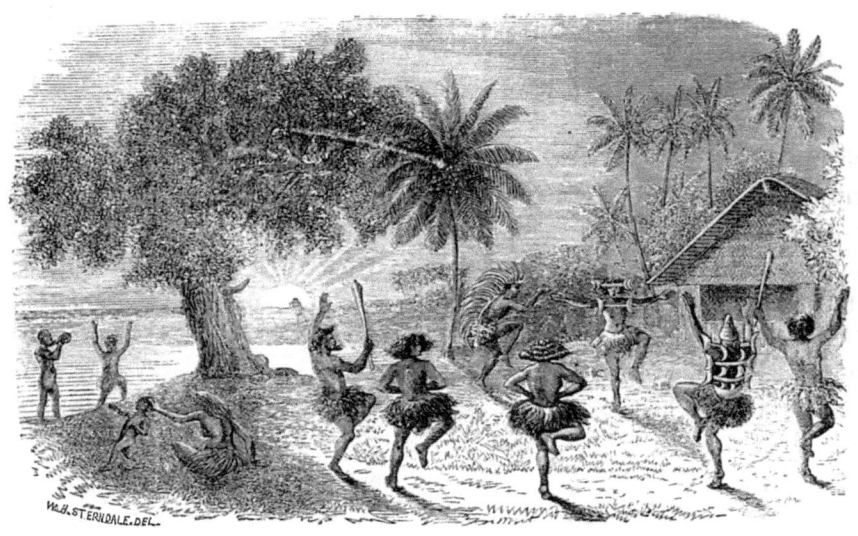

FIGURE 2.2 W. H. Sterndale, *A Village in Pukapuka, under Heathenism*, 1876. Drawing from William Wyatt Gill, *Life in the Southern Isles, or, Scenes and Incidents in the South Pacific and New Guinea* (London: Religious Tract Society, 1876).

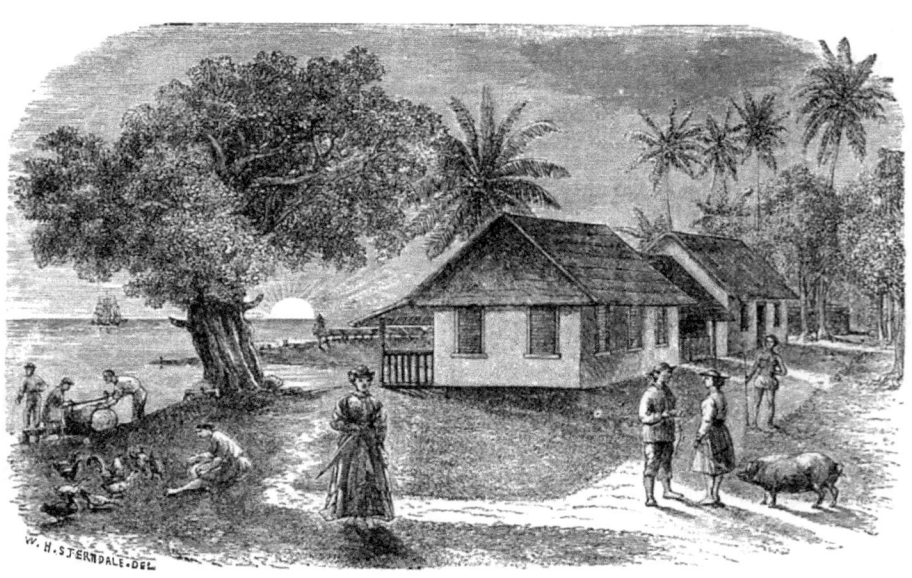

FIGURE 2.3 W. H. Sterndale, *The Same Village, under Christianity*, 1876. Drawing from William Wyatt Gill, *Life in the Southern Isles, or, Scenes and Incidents in the South Pacific and New Guinea* (London: Religious Tract Society, 1876).

This logic, harnessed throughout the colonization of the Caribbean, is still applied in the region in broad and specific ways. In the same way that clothing, or the lack of it, was deliberately used in photographs as a signifier of one's humanness, so too has the act of stripping been used to both identify and render a subject as animal / not human during the colonial era. This formulation of human/animal, morality/immorality, and nakedness has carried through to the present, as highlighted in the cases of Mitchell and McEwan et al. In July 2000, twenty-two-year-old Kenny Dave Mitchell and partner Kinno Jarvis were walking near a police station in Princes Town, Trinidad, when a uniformed officer called out to Mitchell. "Fat boy, come!" he instructed, as one might to a dog. No reports of the incident make clear what justified the callout to Mitchell. Perhaps the officer read the two men as a couple, or perhaps Mitchell's demeanor rendered a reading of him as queer.

Following his apprehension by police, Mitchell was subsequently taken to a cell and ordered to strip. While police officers routinely order suspects to strip, the primary intention of the act in Mitchell's case was clearly to enact his dehumanization, and the order was clearly gendered and inflected by his sexual identity. Mitchell subsequently filed a lawsuit against the police; his testimony recorded in court proceedings in 2007 recalled the experience.

I held my jersey in front of me to hide my body. He then told me to "take off the jockey shorts too." I obeyed. I held my jersey in front of my pelvic area in an attempt to hide my nakedness. At this point in time I was wearing no clothes. There was a table located next to us. P. C. Teasdale then told me to rest all my clothing on the said table. I was now completely naked and facing the officers. I attempted to hide my nudity with my hands. I was then told by P. C. Teasdale to move my hands from in front of me. I removed my hands. They both looked at me and started to laugh very loud. They ridiculed me. P. C. Teasdale then said to me "that you playing man and that small cuckoo you have" referring to the size of my penis. P. C. Teasdale then told me to squat on the floor facing them in full view of them. During this incident we were in full view of anyone who desired to pass along the corridor. Throughout this entire incident I was kept standing in the outer area of the cells. I was scared and totally embarrassed.[3]

By stripping Mitchell of the cover of clothing, the intent of police was to undo his manhood, in terms of both gender and humanity. Reenacted in the encounter between the police officers and Mitchell was the colonial rendering of the naked body of the colonized subject as shameless, as discussed by Levine, and as suggested by the staging of the photograph *Two Chamars* with the subjects' defamiliarized positioning vis-à-vis items of clothing, as though to suggest their ignorance of the moral reasons for wearing clothes and hiding the body. The exchange mirrors that between European audiences who came to see a naked Sara Baartman on display, right down to the specific emphasis on genitals. Although Mitchell's lawsuit against the state for wrongful imprisonment, assault, and loss of daily earnings succeeded, High Court justice Shaffeyei Shah was overtly hostile to Mitchell upon delivery of his verdict on July 4, 2007. Shah accused him of an opportunistic agenda to "demand his pound of flesh" and "get as much money from the State." The logic of Shah's verdict in support of Mitchell while criticizing him is easy to distill: Shah has to rule in favor of the law as it would be applied to a human, but Mitchell's class status and homosexuality endow him with a certain animality that makes it unlikely, or impossible, to feel shame from being naked. The judge's turn of the Shakespearean phrase *pound of flesh* reveals his dehumanizing intent. In *The Merchant of Venice*, Jewish moneylender Shylock uses the phrase in reply to the merchant Antonio about a loan he has given to Antonio's friend, thereby conjuring an image of cannibalistic decapitation as a teasing threat:

Go with me to a notary, seal me there
Your single bond; and, in a merry sport,
If you repay me not on such a day,
In such a place, such sum or sums as are
Express'd in the condition, let the forfeit
Be nominated for an *equal pound*
Of your fair flesh, to be cut off and taken
In what part of your body pleaseth me

It is telling that Shah uses a phrase that incites visualization of Mitchell as his flesh, to pointedly undermine his right to his legally due payment. Shah's response mirrors colonial officers' simultaneous rendering of their own nudity as shameless and that of colonized peoples as shameful. Levine points out that "as visually-based evidence became one of the dominant scientific modes of the nineteenth century, the uncovering of the native body for the purposes of knowledge trumped claims about what was appropriate in the public sphere" (Levine 2008, 209). The non-European body, with its absence of shame and its apparent normalizing or incomprehension of nudity, re-mapped that violation, creating a safe space for observing naked bodies belonging to nameless, oversexualized people to whom shame could not, allegedly, attach (Levine 2008, 218). Shah's comments to Mitchell thus activate a politics of respectability that simultaneously responds to and is complicit with the dehumanizing intent of colonial power.

This same logic of shame operated in the arrests of the seven Guyanese people nearly a decade after Mitchell. At around 8:30 p.m. on February 6, 2009, Gulliver McEwan (Quincy), Seon Clarke (Falatama), and one other person were waiting for a taxi at the corner of North Road and King Street in Georgetown. They were on their way to *Laugh It Off*, a local play at Guyana's National Cultural Centre in Georgetown that featured "transvestite" characters. In sworn affidavits submitted to the courts, McEwan described himself as wearing "a pink shirt and a pair of tights" as well as a black hairpiece (weave).[4] Clarke's wardrobe comprised slippers, a jersey, and a skirt. Clarke, McEwan, and the third person in their party were noticed by police officers passing by in a vehicle and arrested for appearing to be in women's attire. They were taken to the Brickdam Police Station in Georgetown. Six hours later, they would be joined by four others: Joseph Fraser (Peaches), Seyon Persaud (Isabella), Anthony Bess, and one other person. According to their filed affidavits, both Fraser and Persaud were dressed in red shirts and brown skirts and were wearing wigs. The four were having a meal at Stabroek market when hecklers started to taunt them. A physical fight ensued, and Fraser and Persaud ran off, only to be arrested by police near Georgetown's Parliament buildings. All four were placed in the same cell as Clarke and McEwan. As was the case with Mitchell's experience, in custody several of the Guyanese seven were ordered to strip, reducing them, too, to the "natural" and preculture state of the naked body. "We were made to strip off all of our clothing and were then searched thoroughly," stated Persaud in her affidavit. Police officers photographed them and then demanded that they take off all of their "female clothes." After the detainees stripped, the police told them to bend down to "search" them, as a way to mock their apparent homosexuality. They were then ordered to put on "men's clothing." Clarke noted, "It was one of the most humiliating experiences of my life. I felt like I was less than human." It is worth pausing to consider here that among all animals, only humans use clothing as the primary means through which to show their gender. We might therefore think of the removal of the gender-transgressive clothing of McEwan et al. as doubly violent: against both their chosen gender identities and their definition as human, not animal.

Adding to this rendering of Mitchell and McEwan et al. as animals is their jailing itself. Putting people in prison is to treat them like animals. Placing

Sara Baartman's body in Cuvier's natural history of animals as the sole example of a human considered as animal is to dehumanize her, to cordon her off like animals are in zoos, as an object for exhibition. Baartman is placed within Cuvier's book in a visual cage, on display. Similarly, as Fraser noted in her affidavit, "We were placed on an identification parade." In the same way that the violent, naturalized distinction between human and animal undergirds the almost entirely normalized caging, mistreatment, and domination of animals by humans, cages for humans are also normalized when the inmates of those cages are represented as more animal than human, through the stripping of clothing, the stripping of a "natural" sense of shame, and the stripping of a right to self-determined constitution of identity. Explaining a nationwide prison strike in the United States in August 2018, former inmate Kelvin Gadson noted, "You can't just treat people like animals," a quote that was repeated in the *USA Today* story about it (D. Brown 2018). After he was ordered to strip naked and mocked, Mitchell was put in a jail cell without ever being charged. The arrest of McEwan et al. on a Friday, Tracy Robinson and Arif Bulkan note, was par for the course. A Friday evening arrest ensures that the arrestees will remain in jail for the weekend without access to a lawyer or judge, and without being informed of what charges are being laid against them. A Friday arrest also gives the police and prosecutors the opportunity to find and craft a case for a crime, as they did in unearthing the 1893 statute. On Monday, they were finally read the charge justifying their detention over the previous seventy-two hours: that under the 1893 Summary Jurisdiction (Offences) Act, Section 153(1)(xlvii), for being a "'man,' and in 'any public way or public place' and for 'any improper purpose,' appearing in 'female attire.'" They were convicted and ordered to pay a fine of G$7,500 each. "The process is the punishment," Bulkan and Robinson observed (2018). The threat of jail is frequently made by police without necessary justification. In *Trapped: Cycles of Violence and Discrimination against Lesbian, Gay, Bisexual, and Transgender Persons in Guyana*, the 2018 Georgetown Law Human Rights Institute report on violence against sexual minorities, Guyanese lesbian "Denise" describes being under the seawall with her girlfriend when they caught the attention of the police.

> A few officers passed and apparently one of them saw and he came back with a few of his buddies. They [asked], "Can you kiss in front of us?" I looked at him and I said, "Dude if you know what's good for yourself I think you should leave us alone because that right there is harassment. I don't expect that from a police officer of all people." . . . And he said, "I

could arrest you." I said, "Arrest me for what? For refusing to kiss in front of you?" And he looked at me and said, "I will throw you in the lock up." I said, "By all means go ahead, because I am not smoking pot, I do not have any illegal drugs, I did not harass you, so please arrest me if you're going to do so." He walked up to me, and his buddies were looking at him, and [he] just looked at them and said, "Let us go." So they walked away. My girlfriend was so scared. (2018, 62)

In another incident named in the Human Rights Institute's report, a transgender woman recalled being sexually harassed by a police officer, who knew she was a sex worker: "[The police officer was] disrespecting me now because [he] know[s] I do this on the road, and [thinks] I should do it to [him]. . . . They were even telling me that if I don't do it, I'll go to jail. . . . I'm frightened of the police and I don't want to go to jail. . . . They will be very, very aggressive toward me" (2018, 64).

The actions of the police demonstrate the legal system's canny, institutionalized negotiation of a colonial line long-since drawn between human and animal; while technically human, the subjects oppressed by the system are entitled to legal rights, but because of the implicit lines drawn and voices repressed by colonial history, and by the contemporary reality of their dehumanization, the line is blurred. Thus, for instance, the judge can rule in favor of Mitchell while also stating that Mitchell is presumptuous, grasping, and shameless in his request for justice. Likewise, the police can systematically exploit a loop in the system (the Friday night arrest) that allows them to appear to follow protocol while instead simply caging their arrestees, without process and equally without recourse, while dodging the potential charge of violation of rights by being able to claim that it was a simple matter of timing. This context works to assure claims that it was simply the weekend's disruption of the working week that led, without any malicious agent performing the oppression, to the days of detention, punishment without process, and shaming of the arrestees for their expressions of gender and sexuality that are read to be outside the law and within a cage. Within this outside-the-system, inside-a-cage space, the removal of clothing is used almost ritually to further strip detainees of humanity and of rights. The act of caging is the controlled space where dressing and undressing is an act ordered and performed through the agency of the state rather than of the individual; it allows a space where the line between human and animal can be crossed and recrossed through the forced act of dressing and undressing, as a performance of control and domination that is the reverse of the kind of performance activated by theatrical works such as *Laugh It Off*, the play the arrestees were attending, which allow space for expressions of gender-nonconforming identities through dress. The court's description of the photographing of McEwan et al. as "an identification parade" is also noteworthy because it underlines the objectification of them, similar to the ways in which colonized subjects like Baartman were paraded to satisfy the colonizer's fetishizing gaze. This production of the seven as peculiar objects was reiterated in the first main story published about the case in the *Stabroek News* the day after the arrest, "He Wore Blue Velvet...? Seven Arrested for Crossdressing" (*Stabroek News* 2009). "Blue Velvet" is a reference to the popular 1963 Bobby Vinton recording whose opening lines were likely viewed as an efficient summary: "She wore blue velvet / Bluer than velvet was the night / Softer than satin was the light."

A DRESS CODE FOR HUMANS

Not just trans people are subject to the punitive disciplining force of dress codes. In many Caribbean states, dress codes are being used to define who can be properly presented as human. When Guyanese trans woman Petronella Trotman attempted in January 2017 to seek recourse through the courts for violence inflicted against her, she was barred entry by the presiding judge and told she would only be heard if she dressed like a man, effectively justifying the violence against her (Sharples 2017). He directed her to follow the dress code for men posted outside the courtroom that applied to everyone.[5] The text of the code posted in that courtroom outlined eight categories of forbidden wear each for men and women:

DRESS CODE TO ALL MEMBERS OF THE PUBLIC ENTERING THE COMPOUND

Please be advised that the following dress code is in effect:

MEN:

(a) sober colours such as black, blue, brown, cream, grey, etc.
(b) long pants,
(c) no vests, armless shirts, see-through shirts etc.
(d) no short pants, three-quarter pants, etc.
(e) no slippers,
(f) shirt jacks are allowed,
(g) shirts must be neatly tucked in pants

WOMEN:

(a) sober colours such as black, blue, brown, cream, grey, etc.

(b) no strap dresses or blouses

(c) no halters

(d) no mini skirts, short dresses, tights, etc.

(e) no curlers in hair

(f) no close fitted jeans

(g) no sweaters

These rules applied to all Guyanese people, and while gender is certainly a dominant focus of the code, like most others I have seen from the Caribbean, the code lists gender-determinant rules.

Dress codes in Jamaica generally do not appear to separate the rules by gender, but some clearly emphasize more rules related to women's bodies than to those of men.[6] A sign posted at a health clinic in Kingston named no gender but under the all-caps heading "DRESS CODE ENFORCED" listed clothing exclusively related to women under a large bold "NO": "Camisoles," "Tube tops," "Merinos," "Short shorts," "Mini Skirts," "Low Cut Garments Exposing the Bosom," "Tights," "Sheer (see through) garments" and "pants below the waist" (Chappell 2018). On a visit to the Southern coastal parish of Clarendon in 2019, Jamaican scholar-artist Honor Ford-Smith was struck by the visibility and very detailed character of dress code signage in the rural setting, an area commonly referred to as "Jamaica's breadbasket" because of its high concentration of small farms. Alongside a long list of no-nos that ban "rowdy behaviour," "loud talking," "illegal weapons," "gambling," "smoking," "alcoholic beverages," "loud music," "fast driving," and hair "setters" (rollers), these signs mandate wardrobe criteria that are clearly more directed to women than men: "NO MERINOS/VEST," "NO TIGHTS," "NO SHORT SHORTS SKIRTS," "NO BELLY SKIN BLOUSES," "NO TUBE TOPS," "NO HALTER TOPS," "NO SPAGHETTI STRAPS," "NO VISIBLE UNDERWEAR," and "NO TIGHT LOW-ENDING PANTS."

Ford-Smith's snapshots of signs at the two schools she walked past in the James Hill area of Clarendon—the only significant government institutions in that area, she noted—similarly focus on women's bodies (figure 2.4), as reflected in the drawings that appear in those of the primary school (figure 2.5), a likely consequence of conservative reaction to the growth of dancehall culture (see Cooper 2004). Notably, the high school in the area is named after the region's most known literary figure, Claude McKay. *If We Must Die*, one of his best known poems, makes a plea against dehumanization that employs animal-based metaphors. "If we must die, let it not be like hogs," it begins, "Hunted and penned in an inglorious spot." The 1919 poem's subsequent couplet, however, also returns the injury of animalization. "While round us bark the mad and hungry dogs," he writes, "Making their mock at our acursèd lot." McKay, who also authored the novels *Banjo* and *Banana Bottom* and autobiographies *A Long Way from Home* and *My Green Hills of Jamaica*, which are about his upbringing in James Hill, had his own respectability called into question by some of his peers, most notably W. E. B. Du Bois. In 1928 Du Bois described McKay's *Home to Harlem* as "a shameful novel." While he appreciated many aspects of the work and held high regard for McKay's skills as a poet, the Pan-Africanist philosopher argued that *Home to Harlem* catered to white people's fantasies in

> that utter licentiousness which conventional civilization holds certain white folk from enjoying—if enjoyment it can be called. That which a certain decadent section of the white American world, centered particularly in New York, longs for with fierce and unrestrained passions, it wants to see written out in black and white and saddled on black Harlem. [McKay] has used every art and emphasis to paint drunkenness, fighting, lascivious sexual promiscuity and utter absence of restraint in as bold and as bright colors as he can. . . . Whole chapters . . . are inserted with no connection to the main plot, except that they are on the same dirty subject. As a picture of harlem life or Negro life anywhere, it is, of course, nonsense. Untrue, not so much on account of its fact but on account of its emphasis and glaring colors. (*The Crisis*, June 1928, 202, quoted in Turner 1974, 16)

In Du Bois's biting critique, which most contemporary Black literary critics reject, we witness the furious anxiety caused by the onus placed on Black people to demonstrate their humanness through severe self-disciplining that would contain or deny any "animal" behavior.

I was most alarmed by the dress code signs I encountered in Trinidad. Where the wear and tear of the ones in Guyana and Jamaica clearly mark them as old, in Trinidad and Tobago, brand-new, gigantic, gender-defining dress codes are posted at most government offices (figure 2.6). These signs were installed shortly after the beginning of the current People's National Movement (PNM) government's tenure, in 2015. Taking a photograph of this sign is forbidden. In February 2019, I was in Port of Spain waiting to meet with my would-be brilliant cinematographer, Shari Petti. When she arrived a little late and a lot flustered, Petti explained that she was coming from visits to

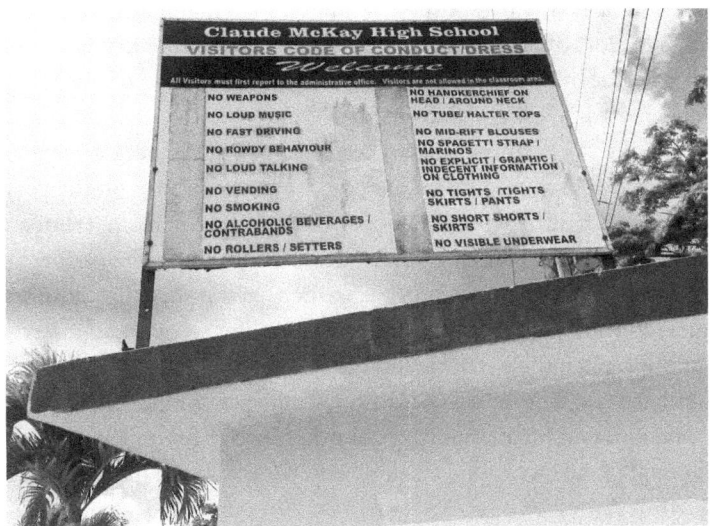

FIGURE 2.4 Dress code signage at Claude McKay High School in Jamaica, 2019. Photograph by Honor Ford-Smith.

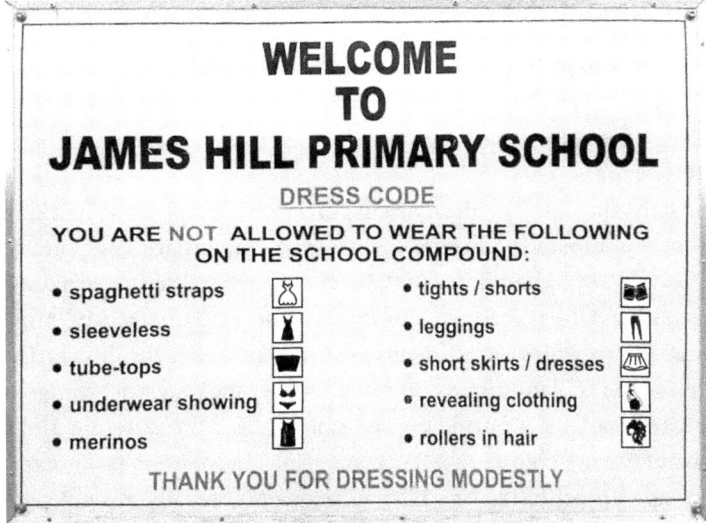

FIGURE 2.5 Dress code signage at James Hill Primary School in Clarendon, Jamaica, 2019. Photograph by Honor Ford-Smith.

two government offices (the passport office in Point Fortin and the Ministry of Legal Affairs in Port of Spain) but was at first barred from entry to them. Her wardrobe was deemed inappropriate because the hemline of her long-sleeve, turtleneck dress fell slightly above her knees.

Underscoring the state's investment in the dress code as a mark of civility is the prioritization of proper wear in the long list of regulations on the very large sign that greets visitors to the national botanical gardens in Trinidad (figure 2.7). Right at the top of the list at number 3, after a statement about the fact of regulation and the open hours of the gardens, is a notice that "visitors must be sufficiently and properly clad, and conduct themselves in an orderly manner," making explicit the perceived link between attire and civility (figure 2.8). Rule number 13 further states, "No visitor shall hunt or *molest* [emphasis added] any wild animals, birds, butterflies or other insects (except venomous reptiles or insects)," evidence of the entrenched imagination of the colonized subject as potentially bestial.

The application of gendered dress codes is not exclusively applied by public institutions. In Trinidad, nightclubs frequently detail appropriate clothing for men and women. In 2015 Shannon Jacob-Gomes was denied free entry into a nightclub in Port of Spain because she was determined by the club's bouncer to be "projecting the image of a man" (Ali 2015). There is an easy and not at all untrue explanation for this persistent investment in dress codes as a means to produce civility—to literally make the animal into human, that is, the enduring violence of colonization, reiterated in nationalist, neoliberal projects in the region.

From the start and into the present day, dress codes are about marking some people more human than others. Scholars of sumptuary law point to the Locrian code in seventh-century BC Greece as the first example of a dress code. It stipulated: "A free-born woman may not be accompanied by more than one female slave, unless she is drunk; she may not leave the city during the night, unless she is planning to commit adultery; she may not wear gold jewelry or a garment with a purple border, unless she is a courtesan; and a husband may not wear a gold-studded ring or a cloak of Milesian fashion unless he is bent upon prostitution or adultery."[7] However, it really was not until the thirteenth century that such laws took off in Europe, as a tool through which to maintain differences based on class. From this time until the seventeenth century, monarchs passed laws dictating permissible colors and styles of clothing, fabrics and textiles, all of it aimed at enforcing class divisions. Increasing trade with India and China, and more availability of "fancy" materials and metals, created fears about peasants dressing "above their station,"

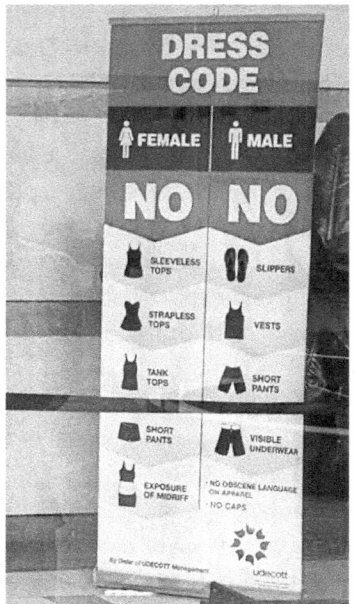

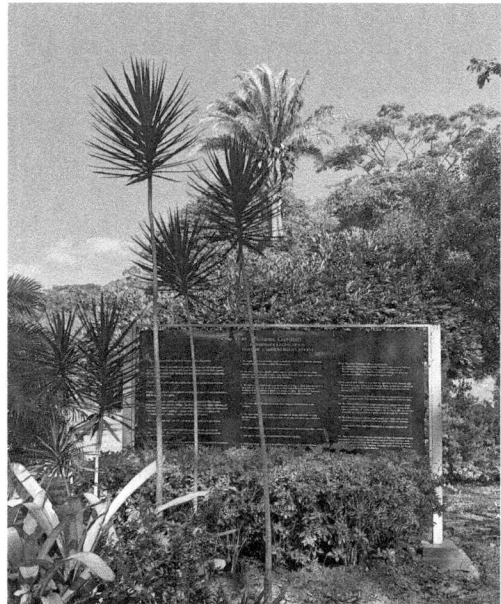

FIGURE 2.6 Dress code signage in Port of Spain, Trinidad and Tobago, 2019. Photograph by author.

FIGURE 2.7 Dress code signage in Port of Spain, Trinidad and Tobago, 2019. Photograph by author.

1. These Regulations may be cited as the Botanic Gardens Regulations.

2. The Gardens shall be open daily to the public from 6 a.m. until half an hour after sunset and on moonlight evenings until 8 p.m. On evenings when the Police Band is playing in the Bandstand in the Gardens, they shall be open until fifteen minutes after the end of the performance.

3. Visitors must be sufficiently and properly clad and must conduct themselves in an orderly manner.

FIGURE 2.8 Dress code signage in Port of Spain, Trinidad and Tobago, 2019. Photograph by author.

and thus undermining the visible identification of class. Importantly, it was just as those laws were being repealed in Europe that they were introduced in European colonies in the Global South. King James I had repealed most sumptuary laws in England before his reign came to an end in 1625. It was at this very moment, as Rebecca Earle notes, that they were being introduced in the Americas, reaching their "heyday" only in the seventeenth and eighteenth centuries. Earle points out that while legislation in the Americas similarly sought to control the clothing worn by different classes of person, these new codes were also explicitly invested in maintaining distinctions between different races. In "'Two Pairs of Pink Satin Shoes!!': Race, Clothing and Identity in the Americas (17th–19th Centuries)," Earle draws attention to several examples of racist sumptuary laws operating in the colonial Caribbean, including in Saint-Domingue (Haiti), where free people of color were forbidden from imitating clothing, jewelry, and hairstyles worn by whites; "free people of colour were instead required to dress in accordance with 'the simplicity of their condition'" (2001, 188). The eighteenth-century Spanish slave code for neighboring Santo Domingo similarly prohibited both enslaved people and free people of color from wearing "pearls, emeralds, and other precious stones" and, equally significantly, prohibited them from wearing the Spanish mantilla in place of the African headcloth, and comparable legislation was issued for the Dutch Caribbean islands in 1786 (188).[8]

By the nineteenth century, racialization of the body had been forcefully achieved and no longer required the support of fashion. Visible racial differences in the colonies tended to eclipse the class concerns of European laws, as the encounter with these "new" nonwhite bodies secured another abject, a less-than-human that would reassure the constitution of the white European as "Man." However, within postcolonial societies, the dress codes would find new purpose: "civilizing" the formerly colonized subject into humans and also invoking the divisions of class, effectively defining the poor as more animal, less human. Trinbagonian scholar Yvonne Bobb-Smith recalls a common saying of adopted mother Mrs. Mable Carr that demonstrated the normalization of this dictum. Carr was a former nurse at the Port of Spain General Hospital and a practicing nurse in 1950s Trinidad. She was also known as someone who could be counted on to help members of her local Belmont community take on the authorities. "Whenever she was upset about something the government was or wasn't doing, she'd threaten, 'Dey done want meh to put my clothes on now,'" meaning that if she was going to the effort to put on an outfit that specifically met the dress code, it was because she was readying herself to take on a government official. This was not mere rhetorical flourish. Mrs.

Carr understood explicitly that a compliant wardrobe was a necessary, minimal requirement to access treatment as a human constituent, and she had put together a specific wardrobe up to the task. "I recall a long-sleeve printed silk dress with a high V-neck. It was white with splashes of brown, gray, and black," Bobb-Smith recalls. "She had collars, perhaps three of them, that she would interchange. It was her only dress-up dress, which she washed with a special soap and kept in a pillowcase. She wore black patent leather shoes to match." Seventy years later, Bobb-Smith herself acknowledges that even as she approaches her ninetieth birthday in February 2021, she takes time to consider what to wear to suit the context of the space to which she is headed. Like Carr before her, the choice is a similarly strategic one that weighs the demands of normative codes and the exercise of her own agency to get what she needs. "My dressing serves as an empowerment tool," she says (Bobb-Smith 2020).

It is no secret in Trinidad and Tobago, like most other places, that class privilege can buy one out of the rules. Trinidadian labor activist Rawle Ramjag argues that the country's dress code is "for the rich, by the rich" (2016). Ramjag asks, "How can short pants be illegal? What, essentially, is the difference between a short pants and a skirt?" He goes on to charge: "Imagine our taxes are being used to pay an officer to prevent us from entering a building for which our taxes have paid." Ramjag argues, "In a plural society such as ours, we cannot afford to legalize, institutionalize nor regularize the way our people dress. Who will be the moral police? . . . Who are these purists who conceal themselves behind the veil of 'management' and draft up these archaic rules?" An editorial appearing in *Stabroek News* that criticized the arrests of McEwan et al. similarly emphasized this point. "The sentiment against men who express 'feminine' behaviour is very widespread in Guyanese society," the editors acknowledged, "even though traditional Indian and Eastern religions do not share the hard-line disavowal of such expressions as Christianity and Islam do." The editorial cited the example of the Hindu epic Mahabharata, in which "a famous warrior is an open cross-dresser who does not elicit any opprobrium."

Ramjag reports that when he tried to intervene in support of the women, a security guard told him that he "should go dong tuh de market an' buy a bra an ah panty an' put it on an try tuh see if yuh could come back in hyere." Eventually, his challenge to that officer resulted in his being surrounded by four more officers. Underlining the classist intentions of the rule, Ramjag admonishes the president's and prime minister's wives for wearing the same outfits forbidden to the social welfare clients. "Maybe if Mrs Rowley and Mrs

Carmona were poor and destitute, like many of the women who have to face (off) with Social Welfare Offices and other similar oppressive places," he says, "they would seek to retract this advantageous regulation. But a poor person cannot enter a Social Welfare Office in sleeveless." Notably, Ramjag closes his blog entry with a reference to animals, a turn of a phrase used in George Orwell's *Animal Farm*: "*Some pigs cannot be more equal than others*" (emphasis added).

"In trying too hard to be 'developed' and 'civilized,'" Peter Minshall (2013) writes in relation to dress codes, "we end up as an obscene caricature of ourselves." To be sure, the existence of these codes in the Anglo-Caribbean are a direct consequence of a legal mechanism that was put in place upon the retreat of colonial powers. When Jamaica, Trinidad and Tobago, Barbados, and Guyana achieved political independence from Britain, each new state integrated "savings clauses" into its legal codes. Savings clauses are statutes that limit the repeal of prior statutes. Thus, new laws introduced in each state were subject to preexisting legal codes. For example, the savings clause in the Constitution of Trinidad and Tobago is a general savings clause that saves all existing law from challenge, while the savings clause in Barbados is also a general savings clause, but it only protects written laws from such a challenge. When Guyana's chief justice Ian Chang ruled on the McEwan case in Guyana's High Court in 2013, he concluded that "it is not criminally offensive for a person to wear the attire of the opposite sex as a matter of preference or to give expression to or to reflect his or her sexual orientation [*sic*]" (quoted in Georgetown Law Human Rights Institute 2018, 40). Yet he also insisted that the 1893 colonial law that imposed fines for transgressing gender-regulating wardrobes was protected by the saving law clause, which limited human rights–related constitutional challenges to laws that were in force before the date the 1980 Constitution came into effect. Only in the final ruling on the case, issued by the Caribbean Court of Justice in 2018, nearly ten years after the charges against McEwan et al. were first made, did the judicial bench privilege the dignity and welfare of the litigants as Caribbean people over and above an old colonial law that would mark them as less than human.

AS NATURAL AS BREATHING AIR

Both Mitchell and McEwan et al. eventually found vindication in Caribbean courts. "Difference is as natural as breathing air" were the remarkable first words of the judgment issued by the Caribbean Court of Justice (ccj) on November 12, 2018, in the McEwan case.[9] In surprisingly poetic terms that deeply moved many sexual rights advocates in the Caribbean, many of whom reported becoming tearful in response, the judgment further elaborated: "Infinite varieties exist of everything under the sun." The introduction, read out loud by Chief Justice Saunders, continued: "Civilised society has a duty to accommodate suitably differences among human beings. Only in this manner can we give due respect to everyone's humanity. No one should have his or her dignity trampled upon, or human rights denied, merely on account of a difference, especially one that poses no threat to public safety or public order. It is these simple verities on which this case is premised." The appellants, the judgment's introduction further explained,

> are transgendered persons. Their sense of personal identity and gender does not correspond with their birth sex. As a result, their appearance, mannerisms and other outward characteristics are not consistent with society's expectations of gender-normative behaviour. That is their reality. It is a reality that is different from the one experienced by most persons. Unfortunately, it is a reality that, for whatever reason, confuses many and frightens, even disgusts, some in Caribbean societies often leading to derision of, and sometimes violence against, those who are different. It is for courts to afford the protection of the law to those who experience the brunt of such behaviour.

There are many paradoxes and contradictions inherent in the judgment. For example, there are "infinite varieties" of persons, yet at the same time, "most persons" agree on gender-normative behaviors. As seen with the mixed messages of the ruling in the Mitchell case, and the popular response to these cases, the tension between the "wrecking work" Khal Torabully speaks of is a powerful, entrenched force in Caribbean societies, a tension against the powerful force of respectability politics and a colonial surveillance apparatus not yet dismantled. As the next chapter demonstrates, international LGBTQI+ rights activists situated in the Global North have tended to broadly characterize the Caribbean as a homophobic space, and usually point to the existence of antisodomy laws as evidence of its incivility. However, these rulings in favor of human rights, despite shackling the progress and expression by legal residue from colonial rule, may instead be read as a decolonial assertion of this "wrecking work." The McEwan judgment was direct and clear: both the actions of the police against the plaintiffs and the law that was cited as justification were unconstitutional. In the official press release by the CCJ, the court conveyed that the panel, comprising Justices Adrian Saunders, Jacob Wit, Winston Anderson, Maureen Rajnauth-Lee, and Denys Barrow, "agreed that this law was from a different time and no longer served any legitimate purpose in Guyana." The justices accepted all three arguments from the legal team: that the law was also unconstitutionally vague, violated the appellants' right to protection of the law, and was contrary to the rule of law; that the law wrongly sought to criminalize a person's state of mind as there is no test to determine what is an "improper purpose"; and that the comments of the magistrate who first imposed fines against them, Melissa Robertson-Ogle, were inappropriate. In handing down sentences totaling GUY$45,000 (US$225) in 2009, Robertson-Ogle condemned McEwan et al. as gender "confused" men who were not fulfilling their "proper" role. They were, she said, "a curse on the family." "Go to Church," she implored them, "and give your lives to Christ." But the CCJ rebuffed her, pointing out that "judicial officers may not use the bench to proselytize, whether before, during or after the conclusion of court proceedings. Secularism is one of the cornerstones upon which the Republic of Guyana rests." The court ordered that Section 153(1)(xlvii), under which the litigants were first charged, be struck from the laws of Guyana and that costs be awarded to the plaintiffs.

As evidenced by the charges laid in both the Mitchell and McEwan cases, as well as by the dress codes outside government offices, the use of clothing as a means through which to mark human from animal persists in the postcolonial Caribbean. Indeed, part of Father Larry's mission in my Presentation College classroom was to mold us to become the politicians, judges, and state officials who would uphold this production of the poor and other marginalized subjects so that we ourselves could be made human, not animal. But I think the expressed public support for Mitchell and McEwan et al. beyond the courtrooms reveals Caribbean peoples' deep resonance and sympathy with their experience of dehumanization. In Guyana, the CCJ decision barely registered. "It was a non-issue," reports Society against Sexual Orientation Discrimination (SASOD) director Joel Simpson about the public response (2018). The government gave its assurance that it would follow the court's verdict in full, and only one significant statement of opposition registered in the press. Media coverage of Mitchell's case was overwhelmingly sympathetic to him because, I think, people from across various backgrounds could identify with his struggle to be treated as a human. Three weeks after his legal victory, in 2007, Trinidad and Tobago's main broadsheet, the *Trinidad and Tobago Guardian*, ran a picture of Mitchell on its Saturday edition front page, advertising a feature-length story inside and captioned "Give Gays Equal Rights," stating: "At 29 years, Kennty Mitchell seems to have everything going for him. He is a striving entrepreneur, a community activist and is involved in a nine-year 'common-law' relationship. Yet, he is put down by society and verbally and physically abused by many, including the police. Why? He is homosexual" (Wilson 2007). "Virtually all the people who wrote comments on the [newspaper's] website sympathized with him," recalls LGBTQI+ activist Colin Robinson in a interview I conducted. "[They] said, 'Whatever your sexuality is, you shouldn't be treated that way.'" Mitchell's win and the subsequent coverage, Robinson says, "transformed the face of GLBT organizing in Trinidad and Tobago. It said powerfully: I can stand up for myself, no matter who I am. I can stand up to the government. I can stand up to the police. And I can win. And people will support me."[10] Mitchell's court victory "had this really riveting effect," Robinson recalls. "He decided he was mistreated and was going to go to court and he won! He wasn't a posh middle-class person with lawyer friends. He hadn't completed a lot of school. But he was a really determined person: he ran a small business out of his home, he drove a maxi [taxi], and he'd done a lot of other things to earn a living." Shortly thereafter, Robinson and other same-sex-loving friends started to have more conversations and eventually reached out to Mitchell, and on August 1, 2007—Emancipation Day in the Caribbean, to mark the end of slavery—Mitchell and his partner met with a grateful and excited group. "That was the beginning of an incredible conversation," Robinson remembers. "We convened people across gender and across class that people commented they had not experienced before. It was very exciting, and people decided it was a moment to galvanize around, and mobilize. . . . There was just this moment to do this in Trinidad and Tobago." Mitchell's assertion of his human dignity would inspire others to demand respect for theirs too. As explained in the next chapter, Mitchell's victory would become a major catalyst and provide an enduring framework for LGBTQI+ organizing in Trinidad and Tobago.

Outside the courts, many Caribbean people continue to resist the application and tenets of sumptuary law, often nullifying its civilizing intent, and its demarcation of human from animal. When Shari Petti recalled her experience at the Ministry offices, my first thoughts went to the wardrobes of my aunts in the late 1970s and the 1980s, both images of them I could recall in memories and that are well documented in family albums. My mother is one of nine sisters and they have something of a reputation for fashion. To give you a sense of this: one evening in June 2012, one of my aunts had just dropped me off at the home of the painter Shastri Maharaj for a studio visit and interview. Recognizing her from forty-five years earlier, Maharaj tells me that my mum and her sisters were famous in 1970s South Trinidad for being among the only Indian country girls who would sport "Western clothes"—tube tops, short shorts, tight jeans. "We used to go to temple just to get a glimpse of them," he told me. They were also Indian country girls who loved mas, and many an Ash Wednesday of my childhood was spent rounding up the Trinidad dailies and weeklies before my grandfather could get to them, in case one of them was caught on camera.

While recognizing the ways in which their wardrobes and anxieties about their bodies were also reflective of and perhaps showed complicity with dominant sexist tropes of worth and beauty, I view my aunts' wardrobes as a sign of their confidence, and of their savvy usurpation of patriarchal authority, both in their homes and in public spaces. These women were caught between competing disciplining forces that recruit clothing as a tool—not just from the state but also from the patriarchal forces of religion, and those specifically contoured around notions of Indo-Caribbean morality, and executed in the rural space they occupied. Makeda Silvera's beautiful invocation of Jonesy in her landmark essay "Man Royals and Sodomites" similarly recalls how the Indo-Caribbeanness of her neighbor usurped the patriarchal pressures she faced. Silvera's grandmother describes Jonesy as "very loud. Very show-off. Always dressed in pants and man-shirt that she borrowed from her husband" (1992, 526). Silvera's response is like mine, in that we understood these deviations as *normal*. "I vaguely remember her pants and shirts," she writes, "although I never thought anything of them until my grandmother pointed them out" (528). That's what the messy space of the Caribbean we experienced as children allowed: the possibility of many ways to be.

I argue that my aunts were refusing the colonial imperative to cover oneself as a condition of being recognized as civil, not primitive; human, not animal. My mother, my aunts, Makeda Silvera's Jonesy, and the Guyanese seven are people who often had to abide by, and sometimes reaffirm, the rules of the colonial and neocolonial order to survive. They often negotiated a better deal and lived with the best of circumstances. Sometimes, they faced down the colonial demand to prove themselves human, to make themselves human, and often powerfully replied with a notion that has become the mean beat of my creative and scholarly projects over these past five years: "We are animal; so what?"

The most telling refutation of the use of clothing to mark human from animal, I think, is Petti's experience at the Ministry offices in Trinidad. At the passport office in Port of Spain, after one security guard pointed out the problem with the length of her hem, others present set out to try to help Petti subvert the code so that she could access the service she needed. One worker brought a scarf out they keep at the office for just this kind of occasion, and

Petti was allowed in after she wrapped it around her offending knees. At the Ministry of Legal Affairs, no workers could locate a scarf among themselves, but another woman in line offered the wrap that held her baby, and once again Petti, knees hidden from view, was allowed in. At both offices, Petti explained, it seemed like almost everyone, even the security guard, wanted her to access the services she needed. Most people seemed to view the code as absurd even as everyone felt sure that regardless, it had to be upheld. We have to pretend to be invested in the notion of respectability as rescue from our own savagery even if we don't recognize ourselves as savage.

The Father, a Godfather, and the Specter of Beasts Old and New

3

TWELVE YEARS BEFORE Father Larry interrupted math class to orient me to homosexuality at Presentation College, Colin Robinson was a student at another Catholic high school, St. Mary's, in Port of Spain. "St. Fairies," he dubs it. "You were at Pres*hen*tation," he adds, noting the prevalent, lighthearted stereotype of gender-segregated Catholic schools as hotbeds for homosexual activity. Robinson was the more precocious learner. By age twelve, in 1973, Robinson had already presented himself as a homosexual to a number of people. "I remember I woke up in my mother's bed," he recalls. "I broke down in tears and told my mother, 'I think I am a homo.'" Robinson is not certain what chain of events unfurled this pronouncement of his desire, but he was, he says, "sure of it. The desire was there, manifest, and I had a name for it." His mother's response was to blame herself, believing that her separation from Robinson's father must have caused the transgression. Robinson shared the news that he desired men sexually with others. "I told a priest in the confession booth, and this old, white British man replied that it wasn't a sin (to desire men)." At fifteen, he expressed his "serious, solid crush" to the object of his affection, a teacher, who in turn reported the news to Robinson's mother, and off he was sent to see a psychiatrist, who, it turned out, was also gay. "Because I was a bright boy," Robinson surmises, "I was protected and had people around me who were invested in my welfare. It was very much about protecting me because I was a bright boy." Schools like St. Mary's and Presentation College were expected to produce the *new* leaders of the nation, after all. Of Trinidad and Tobago's seven prime ministers, two were graduates of Pres*hen*tation, Patrick Manning and Basdeo Panday.

In 1980 Robinson's academic prowess resulted in a national scholarship to Yale University. A few psychology classes and one particularly brutal theater course later, however, he dropped out. Robinson moved to New York City and remained there for the next twenty-five years, most of that time as an undocumented immigrant. The heady world of the city's art and activist scenes of the 1980s and 1990s would become his training ground and included work with organizations such as Black and White Men Together, the Committee of Black Gay Men, the Black Hearts Collective, Other Countries, and the Gay Men's Health Crisis. He also cofounded the Audre Lorde Project. "Moving in Caribbean communities in New York in the Reagan/Bush era, during the rise and demise of the Grenada Revolution, violence against Marxist governments in Latin America and southern Africa, and the struggle against apartheid," Robinson says, "also gave me a political grounding" (Sanatan 2019). In 2006 the death of his longest-term partner and his growing frustration with New York politics made him begin to think about leaving the city. "George Bush had been reelected and I had no idea what I was doing in these people's country." It was also around this time that his migrant status was finally legalized. Though he has continued to maintain his status as a US resident, he laughs when he explains that when he went home to Trinidad for Carnival 2007, he packed a large suitcase. "You get a green card so you can go home," he joked. "[My ex-partner] Nene and I used to talk about how we would never go back to live in Ghana or Trinidad. But after he was gone, I wasn't sure what I had in America anymore."

Over the next decade, Robinson (figure 3.1) remained in Trinidad for longer periods and would become the country's most visible gay activist. There is a much larger group of activists that precede, work alongside, and follow Robinson, including but not limited to Jason Jones (figure 3.2), the UK-based plaintiff whose court case forced the decriminalization of sodomy in the country in 2018; Rudy Hanamji (figure 3.3), the lead organizer of Trinidad and Tobago's first Pride parade; historian archivist Geoffrey MacLean; David K. Soomarie, Sharon Mottley, and Luke Sinette, all of whom cofounded rights organizations; writers Andre Bagoo and Shivanee Ramlochan; feminist academics Gabrielle Hosein and Angelique Nixon; Jeremy Steffan Edwards and Kennedy Everett Maraj of the Silver Lining Foundation; and others, such as the cohosts of the groundbreaking livestream *Queer Corner Caribbean*, Terry-Ann Roy and Cherisse Berkeley (figure 3.4), and social media personality Phillipe Tristan Andre. But through his regular columns for the daily newspapers *The Guardian* and *Trinidad and Tobago Newsday*, his frequent broadcast media appearances and lead organizing work, and his lifelong experience of social justice work, Robinson's position is akin to, as SASOD executive director Simpson calls him, "a godfather of the movement" (2018). Robinson's perspectives and politics have provided and largely comprised the archive of sexuality rights work in Trinidad since his "return" in 2007.

There are uncanny connections between Robinson's role as a "godfather" of the contemporary LGBTQI+ organizing in the Caribbean and that of Eric Williams's project of nation building. The "Father of the Nation," Williams led Trinidad and Tobago's independence movement and dominated the country's politics and development for decades; his influence may have not waned following his death in 1981. Robinson was not yet one year old when Williams delivered a speech ostensibly to the "youth of the nation," on August 30, 1962, the evening before Trinidad and Tobago's security of political independence from Britain. The speech was pitched both as a rejection of colonization and an affirmation of the civilizing project that the British government had started in Trinidad following the end of slavery.

> I have given to the nation as its watch words DISCIPLINE, PRODUCTION, TOLERANCE. They apply as much to you the young people as to your parents. The discipline is both individual and national. The individual cannot be allowed to seek his personal interests and gratify his personal ambitions at the expense of a nation. We must produce in order to enjoy. Wealth does not drop from the sky for any individual or any nation. Reduce production, skylark on the job, take twice as long to do a job and make it cost twice as much, do any of these things and in effect you reduce the total amount available to be shared among the total number of people. You don't pull your weight and you fatten at the expense of others. . . . Some of you have ancestors who came from one country, some from another, others from a third. Some of you profess one religion, some another,

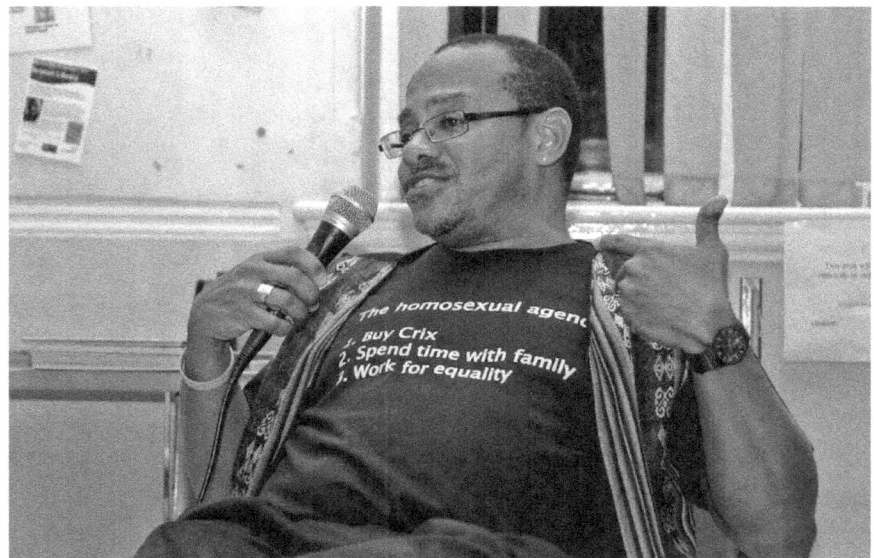

FIGURE 3.1 Colin Robinson, 2013. Photograph by Ajamu.

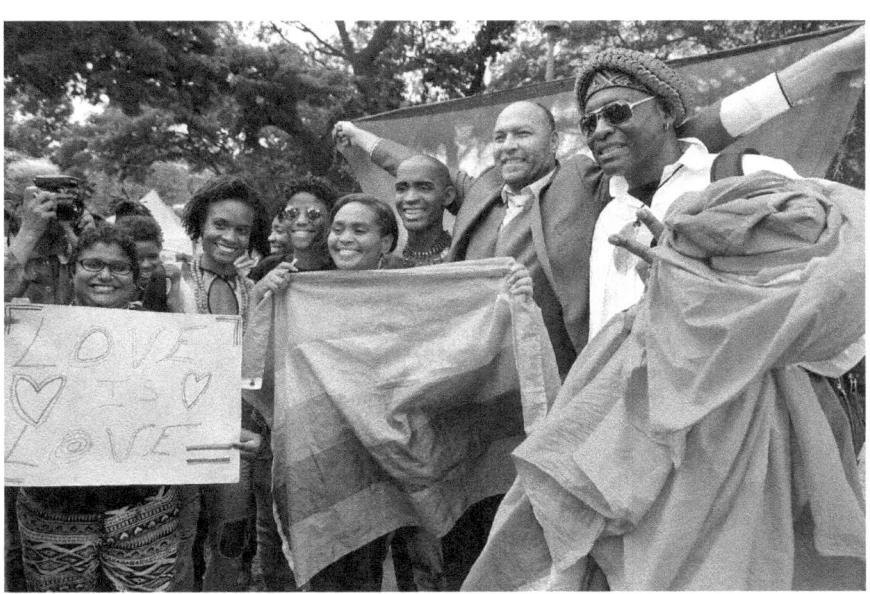

FIGURE 3.2 Jason Jones, 2018.

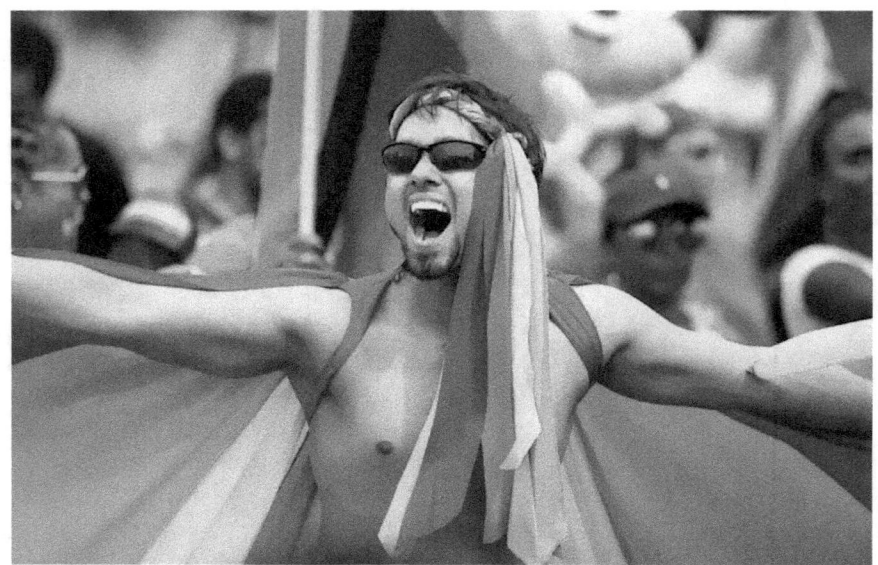

FIGURE 3.4 Rudy Hanamji, 2018.

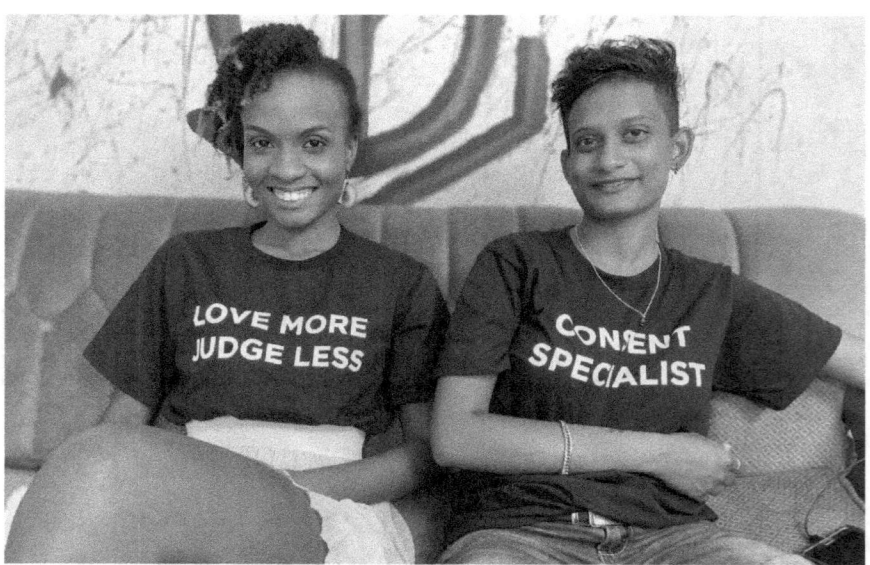

FIGURE 3.4 Terry-Ann Roy and Cherisse Berkeley, 2019.
Photograph by author.

others a third or fourth. You in your schools have, like the nation in general, only two alternatives. You learn to live together in peace or you fight it out and destroy one another. The second alternative makes no sense and is sheer barbarism. The first alternative is civilised and is simple common sense. You the children, yours is the great responsibility to educate your parents, teach them to live together in harmony. The difference is not race, or colour of skin, but merit only—difference of wealth and family status being rejected in favour of equality of opportunities. I call upon all of you young people to practice what you sing today and tomorrow; to translate the ideal of our national anthem into a code of everyday behaviour, and to make our nation one in which every creed and race find an equal place. (Williams 1962)

The closing line of this passage is a refrain from the country's new national anthem, "Forged from the Love of Liberty."

While the "choice" facing the youth of the new nation (and their parents, he says) as being between "civilized common sense" and "sheer barbarism" is framed in specific reference to racial divisions in the country, it may also be read as a reaffirmation of the line between human and animal, with Trinbagonians compelled to show themselves to be the former. Williams's speech is also illustrative of Wynter's argument about the constitution of "Man"/human through the specific European cosmogony that enabled colonization of the Global South and centered the white male subject. Through "discipline," "tolerance," and "production," the once-colonized subject is called to aspire to be like their former colonizers, but that goal is always a mirage since this "Man" can never be fully assumed by him/her/them.

Williams's watchwords were imprinted on my own childhood. "Tolerance" throughout signed a commitment to social equality between the country's various ethnic communities. The notion that the nation was where "every creed and race find an equal place" was always contested, especially from the perspective of the rural Hindu Indo-Caribbean community in George Village.[1] Not in question, however, was the merit and necessity of this goal—that's where we were expected to ultimately end up, and "tolerance" for each other's cultural differences would get us there.[2] "Discipline" and "production" weighed heavier. Williams and Indo-Trinidadian leaders disagreed on many questions, but on this point they did not. Throughout my childhood, I felt compelled to carry this twinned mission. At home, my father, a very hardworking man who had a very humble start in life—he was the youngest and the only one of his ten siblings to complete high school—often repeated his version of one of Mohandas Gandhi's quotes about productivity, most often summarizing it as "there is dignity in every kind of labor."[3] To this day, I have never heard my father elaborate any other piece of philosophy but this one. The "motto" of my primary school still hangs over its most senior, and therefore most important, classroom: "Labour Conquers All" (figure 3.5). The only text plastered on its exterior echoes the same message. "There are no secrets to success," it explains. "It is the result of preparation, hard work and learning from our mistakes" (figure 3.6).

Over my entire life, I am sure I have never labored as much as I did during my final two years at Robert Village Hindu School. Our almost full concentration was on passing the much-feared "Common Entrance" exam, a standardized test that then determined if and which high school we could attend. We ten- and eleven-year-olds would start our day at 7 a.m., usually work through the lunch hour, and stay past the end of the school day until 5 p.m. From then, there was usually homework until 10 or 11 p.m. I fully dedicated myself to it all, understanding that failure to excel would alter the rest of my life. The pressure didn't end with success on the test. Once I did get in to my top choice of school, we were issued report cards every fortnight, and at age fourteen were again ranked and separated by our grades. The highest praise that could be mustered from Form Master Conrad Mercer was "Quite good work"— available only to the boys who finished at the top of the class. Forsaking all play and spending every lunch hour in the library—I had more conversations with school librarian Lucyanna Moy Hing than with any classmate—I had just been ranked first in my class when my parents pulled me out of school and moved us to Canada. All that effort, it seemed then, had been for naught.

The imperatives of *discipline* and *production* carry, with ambivalent effect, the civilizing drive inherited from European colonizers. Labor and self-control are colonizers' promise of "rescue" from the stain of animality. They are, however, no match for sex. The very raucousness of sexual desire injects—perhaps demands—a confrontation with the truth of nature's wildness, and the inevitability of the failure of these watchwords to contain real humans. In this chapter, I put the father of the nation and godfather of the (queer) movement in conversation with each other, thinking through some of the continuities and departures between the men in their pursuit of postcolonial projects of autonomy. I am especially interested in their shared primary concern with external colonizing forces under which the Caribbean is seen to be under siege. Each is haunted by the specter of beasts old and new. For Williams, it is the old beasts of the colonial imagination that his speech has in its sights: the uncivilized African and Indian. They cast a shadow over

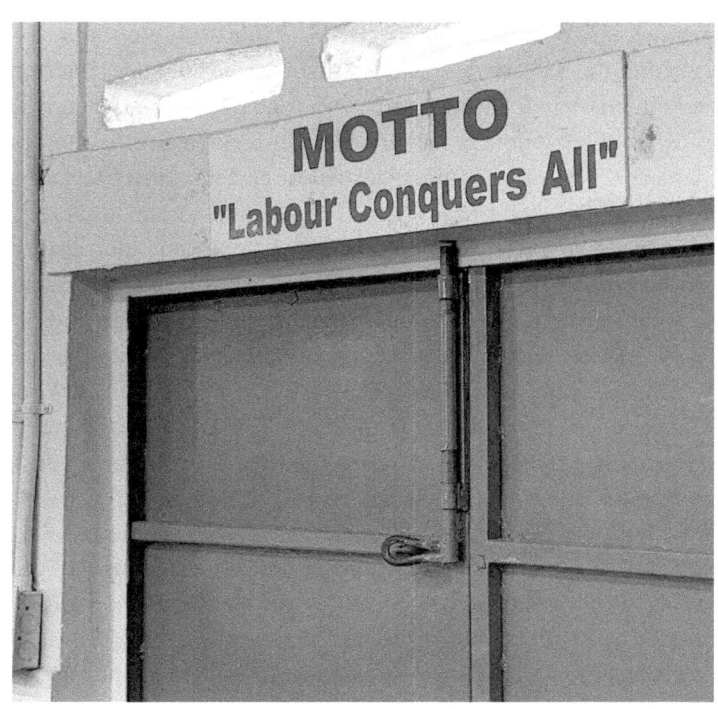

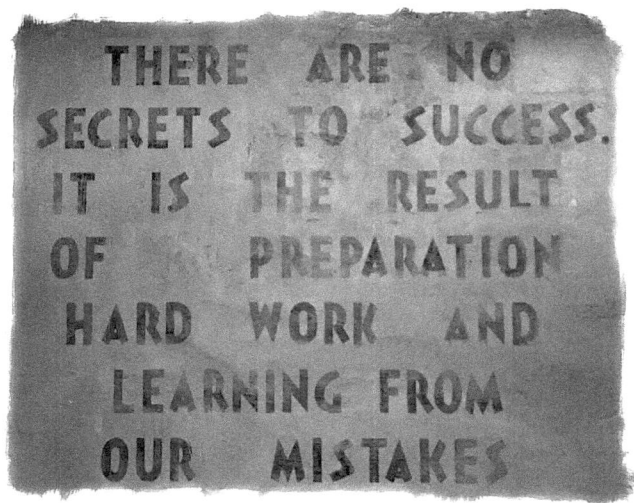

FIGURES 3.5–3.6 Signage at Robert Village Hindu School, Trinidad and Tobago, 2019. Photograph by author.

the national project he imagines and charts ahead. For Robinson, the new beasts emerge from the reiterated racializing imaginations of queer internationalists. The latter have redefined barbarism, replacing the once-denounced Black/Brown/Red/yellow sodomite with the Black/Brown/Red/yellow homophobe. But where Williams called upon his fellow citizens to rise toward a Euro-centered conception of civilized "Man," Robinson takes a different tack. In an echo of anticolonial independence movements, Robinson rallies against Global North–based activists who, as I outline here, operate on assumptions about the incapability of LGBTQI+ actors to understand, speak for, and organize themselves, since we/they are not fully human. He pushes against the notion of a civilizing national project and insists that *we are (already) not animals*. This insistence cuts across his battles with both contradictory pressures faced by sexuality rights activists across the Global South: nationalist, state actors that, mimicking colonial discourse, decry homosexuals as "worse than dogs and pigs"; and Global North saviors that span a wide range of actors, including even Donald Trump, for whom gay liberation affords the continued reproduction of racism (Rodriguez 2019).[4] While Robinson is clearly deeply committed to similar notions of citizenship and nationalism as espoused by Williams, the specific ways in which he incites these categories, I believe, present opportunities to "reimagine" "Man," in the spirit of Wynter's call. Hopeful glimmers of these possibilities are evident in how he has shaped and led the work of CAISO, including in his consistent emphasis on attention to a class analysis. There are also important questions to raise about his approach, which appeared to misread, for example, the consequences of the lawsuit that led to the decriminalization of sodomy in Trinidad and Tobago. Nevertheless, the articulation and practice of his politics, I argue, may be read as efforts at effective and promising refusals of the onus put upon marginalized people to prove themselves human.

THE NEW BEASTS

Williams's call for Caribbean people to prove themselves civilized—that is, *more human, less animal*—may well have been unavoidable in his 1962 context. As demonstrated in the previous chapters, colonization rested in part upon the animalization of conquered, enslaved, and indentured peoples, and a major part of the argument made by anticolonial nationalist leaders like Williams was that formerly colonized peoples could be trusted to govern themselves. That required, for example, the banishment of bestial acts like sodomy. In addition to the antisodomy legal statutes put in place by Britain, figures like Father Larry were enrolled in the project of civilizing Trinbag-onians like us young men attending Presentation College. Christian evan-gelicals from North America remain engaged in this project, and in some cases they have ratcheted up heteronormalization. Representatives of orga-nizations from other religions have also sometimes joined them in this mis-sion. But following the decline of the Church's authority and the embrace of rights for LGBTQI+ people in Western Europe and North America, queer internationalists have taken up missions as new civilizing agents. For them, homophobia has become a definitive marker of civility, determining which people are more human and which are more animal. In a turn of Father Lar-ry's phrase that employs one of Williams's civilizing watchword imperatives, these groups say, "Prove to me that you *tolerate* homosexuals," a demand that is made seemingly without awareness of the ways in which it repeats colo-nial control of self-constitution among Caribbean and other people of the Global South. And where "oppressed gays" in need of liberation are sought out and "discovered" by such global actors, villains must also be brought to light. In the colonial era, people in the Global South were commonly imag-ined as monstrous figures who were bestial, homosexual, or both, but fol-lowing the normalization of homosexuality in Western Europe and North America, a new kind of animal has been produced: the nonwhite, heterosex-ual homophobe.

Narratives of homophobia from LGBTQI+ people from the Global South are also recruited toward the animalization of the nonwhite heterosexual homophobe. Faith Smith describes this dynamic in reference to the critical acclaim showered upon and popularity of Jamaican writer Marlon James, whose tome *A Brief History of Seven Killings* has become the most circulated and celebrated literary meditation on Caribbean queer life internationally. "James himself—despite himself, I imagine," writes Smith, "is gaining legi-bility as an openly gay writer who barely escaped annihilation in the global South, and this is a narrative that irritates people who live in the Caribbean because they understand how his legitimate fear stokes first-world fantasies of rescue and primitivism" (2017, 240). This rendering, she explains, "sees sexuality first, or even solely, marking it off from the totality of quotidian Caribbean experience, and also how it implicitly or explicitly imputes the Caribbean subject's self-narration to the supposed emancipatory project of the North; the tensions within the Caribbean about what or who ought to constitute authentic Caribbeanness; the ways sexuality is at once part of a vigorous debate about 'who we are' but is marked off from such discussions; the dominance of biological men, masculinities, and male sexualities in public debates about sexuality" (240). Work within the Caribbean also becomes shaped through this lens. "Many in T&T's GLBT communities are quite enamoured of the visible manifestations of North American or European GLBT political advocacy," Robinson observes. They "see these forms as the standard to emulate, against which local performance should be judged, and show limited imagination about how to practice an indigenous politics on sexual orientation and gender identity." The effect of this "queer internationalism," he says, is that it "makes the Global South an important target of Global North GLBT concerns—and fundraising; codifies differences in 'freedom' between North and South, representing one as advanced and the other as primitive; and positions the North in a missionary relationship and one of pity with regard to the South" (n.d.).

It also reverses the use of sex to advance racism and colonization. Now that anxieties about sodomy have eased, and representations of homosexual male life in particular are more prevalent and viewed as "acceptable," in more Global North countries, no longer does sodomy as forcefully carry the weight that it had throughout the colonial era. No longer, as it has been for most of the past five centuries, is it rendered an act of bestiality. Instead, in a reversal that nevertheless keeps racial hierarchization intact, the queer internationalist work criticized by Smith and Robinson reappraises sodomy as a respectable sexual act, once more assuring the constitution of "human," as Wynter has argued, as a white "Man." Where their anxieties about sodomy underlined the humanity of colonists up to just a few decades ago, now those same anxieties expressed by governments in the Global South—mostly as a consequence of European antisodomy laws that were adopted in the colonial era—render nonwhite people bestial.

For invaders like Cortés, and the states that colonizing invaders represented, proof of Indigenous peoples' animality was their participation in sodomy and/or bestiality. In the *De Orbe Novo* text, Balboa is represented as a heroic figure who saves the other Cueva people of Panama from their indulgent homosexual king, an act through which Balboa installs himself as their leader. As Jonathan Goldberg observed in *Sodometries*, "in this post facto rewriting, Balboa is not only the righter of sexual wrongs, the restorer of proper gender, he's also the universal liberator of the underclasses" (1992, 183). His ascension to power is made possible through the dehumanization of the sodomite king. This dynamic is not entirely unlike that of contemporary LGBTQI+ activists based in Europe and North America, who have often inserted themselves into sexual rights struggles in countries of the Global South. Interest in—and the resultant extension of resources toward—the rescue of nonheterosexual people from homophobia in Global South countries has multiplied exponentially over the previous decade, including from international development agencies and multilateral institutions like the World Bank and the European Commission. Using the mirage of funding and potential paid work as bait for capital-poor local groups, these actors have often assumed a directive role, working under the premise that people of the Global South need to be trained by them in order to achieve more acceptably modern "human" societies. This phenomenon has been substantively attended to in different ways by scholars such as Jasbir Puar and Joseph Massad. In *Terrorist Assemblages* (2007), Puar linked rising support for same-sex marriage in the United States with militarism and demonstrated how queer bodies were being used to incite and support racialized violence. Massad took a similar position in his critique of what he terms the "Gay International." He views the work of LGBTQI+ organizations engaged in North-South transnational advocacy as an attempt to fulfill Western imperialism's unfinished tasks. In the Middle East, this Gay International lobby, Massad says, proposes that Arabic societies become educated to "catch up" to metropolitan Euro-American norms: "they must take on sexual identities, name themselves 'gay' and 'lesbian' (as conferred, for instance, by the 'Gay and Lesbian Arabic Society'), mimicking the more enlightened and civilized occident" (2007, 173). This charge, it must be noted, as described by Massad, is the rhetorical mirror image of the enduring colonial charge to people of the Global South to prove themselves heterosexual to earn inclusion in sanctioned, colonial communities.

Underlying this demand to conform to certain norms of LGBTQI+ identity, I argue, is the persistent anxiety about the divide between animals and humans: animals have sex, but humans have sexual cultures. The patterns Massad identifies can be seen in a wide range of popular publications; in various lists in online and print publications, countries and whole cultures are marked as animalistic by being tagged as homophobic. For example, in 2014 *Newsweek* listed twelve of the "most homophobic countries" in the world. Jamaica made the list (Strasser 2014). A 2017 article in the British *Guardian* revised the focus to ask, "Where are the most difficult places in the world to be gay or transgender?" (Banning-Lover 2017). The travel site Kayak has developed an "LGBTQ Travel Index" that goes from good to "the 9 deadliest countries in the world" (Sullivan and Hegenauer 2017). No Caribbean countries made the cut on their lists. Even a more credibly serious news source such as *The Independent* proves unable to resist the beck of a scandal, and in a 2017 headline declared, "One of the world's most homophobic countries is about to have a transgender model appear at fashion week" (Batchelor 2017). The country in question is India; my question in reply is: How does a transgender model get to be on the stage of one of the most homophobic countries in the world? Supporters of what Massad terms the "Gay International's missionary tasks" (2007, 162) have produced two kinds of literature on the Muslim world to this end: "an academic literature produced mostly by white male European or American gay scholars 'describing' and 'explaining' what they call 'homosexuality' in Arab and Muslim history to the present; and journalistic accounts of the lives of so-called 'gays' and (much less so) 'lesbians' in the contemporary Arab and Muslim worlds" (162). "The former is intended to unravel the mystery of Islam to a Western audience," Massad says, "while the latter has the unenviable task of informing white gay sex tourists about the region and to help 'liberate' Arab and Muslim 'gays and lesbians' from the oppression under which they allegedly live" (162). In this context, LGBTQI+ activists from the Global North see themselves as having responsibility to take on the burden of freeing LGBTQI+ people from their heterosexual, homophobic societies. Massad observes, "While the pre-modern West attacked the world of Islam's alleged sexual licentiousness, the modern West attacks its alleged *repression* of sexual freedoms" (37).

In this flip, with homophobes trading places with homosexuals as the target in need of training and policing, LGBTQI+ activists replace Christian priests to spread a new gospel of human ethics and morality. Neither party wielded as much power as the states that govern and facilitate their involvement, but they nevertheless play a crucial role in the execution of imperialism. In the past decade, Canadian taxpayers have funded some Canadian LGBTQI+ people to do antihomophobia training in the Caribbean.[5] One Toronto-based project that has acted as a kind of repository for the horrors of Caribbean homophobia is Nancy Nicol's "Envisioning Homophobia," a million-dollar research effort that generated films, books, and multiple public events, and which has included the participation of several Caribbean scholars and activists. Describing one exhibition resulting from the project, Nicol reproduced a familiar refrain: "this body of work speak[s] to profound discrimination and violence: random violence in public places; police harassment, extortion, custodial rape; 'corrective rape' against lesbians 'to make them straight'; exclusion and violence perpetuated by friends, family and community" (Nicol, Mulé, and Gates-Gasse 2014, 8). Video shorts of stories from Botswana, India, Uganda, St. Lucia, Kenya, Belize, Jamaica, and Guyana streamed at the exhibit reaffirmed the characterization of these societies as violent and animalistic, in need of the expertise of Canadian LGBTQI+ specialists to become capably human. This development training approach to North-South LGBTQI+ solidarity activism, which is very often welcomed by activists in the Global South, operates in a strikingly parallel way to the postslavery "civilizing" projects mentioned in chapter 1, both similarly invested in the notion that nonwhite people cannot govern themselves.

Savvy about managing the optics of their emergent international work, Canadian organizations such as Egale and the Canadian HIV Legal Network have also paraded a stream of Caribbean native informants who have fled to "safe" Canada from the "homophobic" Caribbean across the stages of their events and in the media. In considering these facts and trends, it is important to note that the goodwill of the actors advancing these issues is not in question, nor is the truth of anyone's experience of homophobia in any of these places; rather, the question that needs to be asked is: What is the effect of this flattened form of representation of Caribbean people and imaginations of, and impact in, the societies in which they live? Asylum claims by LGBTQI+ people based in Global North countries demand the production of claimants' home states as violently homophobic, so expatriates have to comply with this narrative in order to qualify for immigration. Trinidadian activist Nikoli Attai argues that the financial incentives offered by Canadian LGBTQI+ organizations, including actual employment of them in most cases (Caribbean expats Akim Ade Larcher, Gareth Henry, David Soomarie, Karlene Jones, and Maurice Tomlinson have all been employed by gay organizations in Toronto), "[have] also greatly influenced the positioning of token native informants as authentic cultural voices with seemingly expert knowledge, whose views are upheld as sacrosanct" (2017, 104). It is important to recognize and consider the effects of this process, which reproduce Caribbean people as homophobic beasts.

Such was the case at "Defending LGBT Rights in Barbados," a 2018 event organized by veteran Jamaican activist Maurice Tomlinson, perhaps the most visible of Caribbean expatriates working with Global North groups to train Caribbean societies. The event's description on the Facebook page set up by Tomlinson stated, "Often viewed as a tourist paradise, Barbados also has a troubling secret: the worst anti-gay law in the western hemisphere, with the possibility of life imprisonment. This draconian law encourages homophobic attacks that force many LGBTQ Barbadians to flee to Canada and other places of refuge" (Glad Day Bookshop 2018). It was also a fundraiser for Barbados Pride, one of a few Prides Tomlinson has taken up as his mission to manage and produce, including in places like Barbados, where Pride festivities were already in existence. He has drawn upon a large network of financial sources for his Prides; Attai found that, "by 2017, this alternative pride had also garnered increased technical and financial support from international groups such as the [Canadian HIV/AIDS] Legal Network, the AIDS Healthcare Foundation (AHF), Toronto P-FLAG, Rainbow Alliance and the Ontario Public Service Union (OPSEU)" (2017, 103–4). The emcee's introduction of a drag queen performance at "Defending" perhaps best illustrates the purpose and effect of this kind of narrative. A drag show, she announced, could never happen in Barbados, and she suggested that violence would certainly befall people like the performer. The fact that the emcee had actually not been to the island for many years may explain why she was unaware of the fact that drag shows have happened in Barbados for many years, and one of them has been a particularly popular draw. The founder of United Gays and Lesbians against AIDS in Barbados, Darcy Dear, had actually owned and managed a bar for "queens, gays and lesbians" in Brockton since the 1980s, and s/he and another activist, Didi, had regularly performed in drag at various venues on the island (Murray 2009). These facts appear to matter less than the intended production of the Caribbean as a place rampant with wild homophobes and in need of a civilizing/human-making hand. This narrative became an anchoring point of a much-circulated radio documentary produced by Acey Rowe for the Canadian Broadcasting Corporation in 2019. In it, a lesbian couple from Barbados, using the pseudonyms "Jane" and "Patricia," recall their enduring difficulties with homophobia in their home country. "Early one January morning, a neighbor's son had thrown a Molotov cocktail into the couple's home in the Caribbean country," the documentary begins, "where hate crimes against LGBTQ people are common and being gay can be punishable by life imprisonment." Chapter 154, Section 9 of the Barbados Sexual Offences Act does indeed include the possibility of life imprisonment for buggery (between men or between a man and a woman), but it has not been enforced in the contemporary Caribbean. Other instances of homophobia cited by the couple include Jane's description of dressing like a tomboy, which was hard in her family. "Barbados is a very, say, Christian upbringing," she says. After a family member walked in on her being intimate with a friend, Jane said she had to leave her home and move in with her grandmother—"the only relative at the time who was OK with her being gay." At age sixteen, she was also arrested for having sex with a younger teen girl, she said, thus raising questions about whether the charges were levied because of homosexuality or child abuse.

Shortly after its release, the claims in the documentary were challenged by Roann Mohammed, director of Sexuality, Health and Empowerment (SHE) Barbados and codirector of Pride Barbados. In an interview with *Loop News*, Mohammed said she supported the right of people facing harsh marginalization to seek out a place where they can live a life with dignity: "Everybody deserves to want to be in a space where they can live their lives safely and not worry about the threat of violence all the time" (quoted in Ellis 2019). However, Mohammed points out, "there are [LGBTQ] people who live full and happy lives in Barbados and don't experience any of this persecution. But it is also a case of privilege, and those that are afforded the most privileges are the ones that are most secure." The article's representation of Barbados, she says, "lacks nuance. It's not illegal to be gay in Barbados. It is not illegal to be gay in any Caribbean territory. What is illegal is a particular sex act and that was criminalized in 1868 by British colonizers, and while the particular sex act is criminalized across the board, it is something that is used to legitimize discrimination and marginalization against LGBT people." But, as the title given to the promotional article about the documentary makes clear, its driving purpose is perhaps less about truthfully representing queer life in Barbados than in reassuring the superior civility of Canadians and Canadian society: "'I'm Free': How Canada's Rainbow Railroad Helped a Barbados Couple Fleeing Persecution Find Peace" (Rowe 2019). This is another savior story of the good Canadians saving the poor Caribbean folks. Rainbow Railroad received more than 1,300 requests for relocation and assisted nearly 200 people from sixteen countries. Most were from the Caribbean, and many came from the Middle East, North Africa, Eastern Europe, sub-Saharan Africa, and Latin America.

In response to the release of the documentary, Colin Robinson expressed his frustration with the continued reproduction of this narrative and the fact that those responsible "don't even try to be factual!" He added, "My main issue is with the homonationalist narrative [that] groups outside the Caribbean seem to need to bring to asylum work. Our NGOs do lifesaving work with asylumseekers, but we don't make our beneficiaries posterchildren for our virtue or make the work into something mystical we are providing access to, or need to paint our countries into unlivable places of horror" (personal communication, January 1, 2020). The production of Global South countries and peoples as bestial is a major and persistent concern of Robinson's, and his opposition to this dominant tenet of queer internationalism has in turn shaped his work as a local activist in Trinidad and Tobago. He has been the principal figure leading Trinidad and Tobago's main sexuality rights organization, CAISO, since its foundation in 2009. In many ways, the organization operates in the mold of Williams's imagination of an autonomous Caribbean people. However, unlike Williams's moralistic call to citizens to rise to new/old forms of civility, represented by European "Man," CAISO has strived to foreground, through anticlassist and feminist politics and values, those figures most rendered animalistic, including the poor.

Kennty Dave Mitchell's victory had pushed sexuality rights issues to the main in a way that had not been previously done, and certainly not with the broad positive affirmation he had received. Activists were encouraged to meet more often and push further. But it was anger with the government that emboldened their activism. Despite years of work that made advocates believe sexual rights protection would be included in a new National Policy on Gender, the minister responsible for it, Marlene McDonald, had decided against it. Robinson recalls: "It was the June 25, 2009 words of the minister of community development, culture and gender affairs at a post-cabinet press conference, quoting the gender-policy-for-some green paper's commitment to 'not provide measures dealing with or relating to the issues of termination of pregnancy, same-sex unions, homosexuality or sexual orientation'" (2019). On June 27, activists including David K. Soomarie, Sharon Mottley, Geoffrey MacLean, and Luke Sinette decided to officially form the Coalition Advocating Inclusion of Sexual Orientation (CAISO). The name was MacLean's suggestion. The "Sexual Orientation" part of the title was less a statement about an understanding of sexuality as being a fixed entity than it was a direct reference to the terms used in McDonald's press release. Activists represented a range of groups working on sexual health and rights issues, including Friends for Life, 4Change, and the Trinidad and Tobago Anti-Violence Project; as one diplomat joked about this abundance of organizations in a small population, "Trinidadians don't like to follow, one person is an NGO."[6] The immediate plans of CAISO included a website, monthly meetings, fundraising, educational activities with public and religious officials, and intentions to pursue collaborative work with local and international research groups, advocacy and human rights groups, and religious organizations. As the group developed a more autonomous structure, the "Coalition . . ." element of the title was dropped but the acronym kept. "We wanted something that had cultural resonance," Robinson recalls. The choice of the name CAISO—a play on "kaiso," the name given to the precursor of Trinidad and Tobago's musical art form, calypso—would foreshadow the centering of Robinson's and CAISO's work in the local cultural context. The word *kaiso* has been traced back to the African language of Hausa, where the word is used as an exclamation of approval ("Bravo, bravo!"), another telling indication of the organization's approach. The name CAISO, Robinson says, connotes "a native tradition of speaking out and holding our leaders accountable as we describe the art, wit and poignancy that characterize the political speech of calypso" (2011). In 2012 CAISO was formally incorporated as an NGO with a board, and with Robinson as its executive director. His preferred title is "Director of Imagination."

A year after denying sexual rights protections in the National Gender policy, McDonald boasted about the position of her party, the People's National Movement (PNM), on the election campaign trail. According to Robinson, "Marlene's classic moment was on the PNM's women's May 19 platform in Bournes Road, St James, at which fashionably red-clad candidates rallied to support the criminalisation of women's reproductive choices, and Marlene crowed that a PNM gender policy provided no measures related to homosexuality, calling the People's Partnership 'a sorry bunch of mamapoules'" (2019). "Mamapoules" is a reference to a feminized man, though its specific use is in a heterosexual context: "a man who is ruled by his wife." The "poule" is derived from the French term for chicken. On the campaign stage, McDonald further clarified that "the opposition may flirt with these ideas if they wish, but this PNM government will not. We have stated our case quite categorically. This nation has always been and will continue to be guided by the highest principles and standards of ethical and moral behaviour" (C. Robinson 2019). Indeed, an apparent openness to enshrinement of sexuality rights by the then opposition coalition, the People's Partnership (PP), led Robinson and others to become the first LGBTQI+ organization to become involved in an election, with CAISO generating the election document "6 in 6," which included six suggested policy and leadership steps on sexual orientation and gender identity for a new Trinidad and Tobago government to take in the first six months of their term. The proposals focused on a broad range of social welfare issues, including education, crime, and health. Missing was the issue that had most defined LGBTQI+ initiatives in North America and Europe: rights to gay marriage.

As Robinson explained in an interview, CAISO showed up at election rallies for both parties throughout the campaign. "The idea was to distribute the '6 in 6' brochure to the crowds. We were trying to create visibility, to show that we are part of the nation" (2019). But as one of the candidates for the PP was a strong ally, their hopes rested with her: "Because Verna St. Rose Greaves was running for the PP, we were able to have conversations with her that we didn't have with the PNM." He says that the group asked her to say something about the issues laid out in the "6 in 6" document, and "she challenged us, but she went to a rally and did in fact say something affirming about it" (2019). When it seemed clear that the PP was going to win the election, Robinson wrote a blog entry that didn't endorse the party directly but stated that while the PNM was clear in its communication of homophobia, the PP was not. Robinson and others ended up near the main stage of the new government's victory celebration on election night; however, hope had turned to disillusionment by the next election cycle.

I first met Robinson in Port of Spain in February 2008, just before the workshop "Sexualities in Conversation" would be convened by Tracy Robinson, Trinidadian Jamaican activist and cofounder of the Caribbean Vulnerable Communities (CVC) coalition Robert Carr, and I in Barbados. Invited guests included Anthony Lewis from Jamaica; Joel Simpson, Stacy Gomes, and Natassia Rambarran from Guyana; Kenita Placide and Akim Ade Larcher from St. Lucia; and Sharon Mottley from Trinidad. I invited three Toronto-based academics to participate—Kamala Kempadoo, David Murray, and Rinaldo Walcott—and two Trinidadian scholars from UWI also joined: gender studies professors Michelle Rowley, who chaired part of the meeting, and Gabrielle Hosein. As organizers, Tracy, Robert, and I shared some apprehension about the meeting, convinced that the work of situating the sexual rights discussion more formally and centrally into the public conversation would have to be very carefully pursued, and Colin Robinson was excluded.[7] But I independently reached out to him and we met up one week before "Sexualities," and when I guest edited papers from it for a special edition of the *Caribbean Review of Gender Studies*, I also invited him to contribute work to the issue. In his coauthored piece with Akim Ade Larcher, the two debated the merits of the Stop Murder Music campaign that Larcher had organized in Toronto (Larcher and Robinson 2009).

In the decade that has elapsed since we met, Robinson has become its most visible face and the somewhat official spokesperson for the LGBTQI+ movement in Trinidad and Tobago. He regularly appears on television news programs and at community and political events in the country and has written regular columns for two of its daily newspapers, *Trinidad and Tobago Newsday* and *The Guardian*. Notably, while he will sometimes write about sexual rights, and his own experiences as a gay man, Robinson's columns tend to speak to a variety of issues, ranging from government policy to intimacy, thus providing both a complex portrait of himself and a multidimensionality to representations of queer life. His meticulous upkeep of the CAISO Facebook page has also created an expansive and suitably animated public archive of the LGBTQI+ movement's contemporary history. Additionally, just as Williams influenced the politics of the whole region and informed anticolonial and postcolonial projects internationally, so too has Robinson become a major influencer and, often, a critical public voice on the most significant legal cases and political strategies deployed in the Caribbean and across the Global South. A key reason is his challenge, both discursively and in practice, of a dominant paternalistic and racializing international gay gaze upon the Caribbean and, more broadly, the countries and peoples of the Global South. Significantly, he has steadfastly refused and resisted the production of Caribbean people and others in the Global South as too animal—either monstrous homophobes or incapable, undercivilized queers—by a world of LGBTQI+ activists, academics, and literary writers, complicit expatriates from the Global South, and the powerful national and multilateral organizations that have supported them. As further explained later in this chapter, this approach is illustrative of his, and CAISO's, general demeanor, which has been to present itself as akin to a child in search of parental approval, represented by both the instruments of the state and the wider public. Echoing Williams's view, Robinson's most consistent message is that LGBTQI+ people just want to be recognized as part of the national family.

Like Williams's, Robinson's politics are haunted by the threat posed by external colonizing forces to Caribbean autonomy. He has often spoken up, and directly, to activists and organizations making incursions in the region. In a circulated email to Richard Elliott, the executive director of the Canadian HIV/AIDS Legal Network, in 2015, Robinson challenged him about some of his organization's activities.

> I was surprised earlier this year to read accounts that your Network was embarking on LGBTI work that targets the Caribbean. No one I work with based in the region reports being offered the opportunity to guide that work or ensure it complements and advances the political goals of our regional or domestic movements. Our past struggles with the Network's Canadian counterpart EGALE over murder music and cruise ship boycott threats are still clear in my mind. I know some of our allies in Toronto and Trinbagonian activists and academics living and spending time there have attended presentations of your vision for this Caribbean work. But I have seen reports of questions raised by them, particularly about the limited understanding displayed of the Caribbean movement and the rich presence of organisations with strategic visions and politics, voices and campaigns. So I know you are personally aware already of some of these concerns.

Robinson was particularly incensed about a protest that Jamaican expatriate Maurice Tomlinson, as part of his work as a senior analyst for the Legal Network, organized at the Toronto Consulate General of Trinidad and Tobago to, organizers stated, "draw attention to the fact that after 53 years of independence, the country still retains colonial-era laws that ban the entry of LGBTI people, and threaten up to 25 years imprisonment for consensual sodomy" (email forwarded by Robinson). In his message to Elliott, Robinson explained:

> The Toronto event blindsided us a bit, as we learned of it first from Facebook reports, after it took place. In accounts of the activity on 76crimes.com and in Facebook groups, I learned that the event was also timed as T&T "prepares to select a new national government on Sept. 7" and that, as a result, "copies of the election manifesto prepared by local TnT LGBTI groups entitled: '12 Initiatives to Improve LGBTI Lives & Options for Decision Makers'" were distributed as part of the event. . . . That manifesto seeks to focus T&T decision makers on two *postcolonial*—not colonial-era—laws as our top priorities; and that in the case of imprisonment for consensual sodomy, we are not focused on government decision makers, who appoint our diplomats, but on an independent prosecutor. I shared my frustration as well at how hard it has been in the current election campaign to domesticate conversations about LGBTI issues and focus on the initiatives prioritised in the manifesto that we find most productive and fruitful, and noted how the issues international voices deem important continue to distract attention from what is politically feasible here.

In his reply, Elliott defended the Canadian incursions, saying that the Legal Network had decided to develop more "proactive" work, which included "activities in solidarity with activists internationally, in response to troubling new legal developments in various parts of the world, as well as opportunities identified for advancing human rights (via litigation, of course, as one strategy, but also via other, complementary efforts)." "I think it's fair to say that litigation is a *necessary* part of a larger overall strategy for LGBT rights," he nevertheless concluded. Rebuffing Robinson's invitation to come to Trinidad and meet with local activists, he remarked, "I suppose by law I'm banned from entering the country." It's worth noting that Tomlinson's lawsuit against the Trinidad government failed. The Caribbean Court of Justice ruled that the laws against the entry of homosexuals never applied to him as a Caribbean Community (CARICOM) national and did not prevent his free movement.

Perhaps the most striking aspect of Robinson's disagreement with the international organizations and complicit diasporic "native informants"—and how, as he put it, they "*houseniggah* for the international LGBTI movement" (Sanatan 2019)—is his refusal to take an antagonistic view of the broader Caribbean society. Robinson's insistence on a locally led movement that does not demonize Caribbean people and cultures was evident right from the first event CAISO organized. Titled "Patricia Gone with Millicent? The Ingenious Imagination of Homosexuality in Calypso," it took the form of a listening party held on July 30, 2009. Set in Windrush-era Great Britain, "Patricia Gone with Millicent" was the name of a calypso written and performed by the calypsonian Terror about a woman who had left her husband for another woman. The event's flyer acknowledged the historical visibility of homosexuality in Trinidad and Tobago's national art form with a World War II–era image of a popular calypsonian cross-dressed on stage and the following text: "Believe it or not, in sharp contrast to dancehall, homosexuality is one of the topics that calypso has handled with some of its sweetest ingenuity and subtlest imagination. Not all the time, of course. But surprisingly often." When the call went out for attendees to the event, it was this national affection for calypso that the group drew upon, not merely some presumption of ties to shared gay or lesbian identity: "Whether you simply love the calypso art form and Trini culture or you have a personal or family connection to the topic, join in a tent-like atmosphere where we will take in some two dozen recordings of fascinating calypsoes from the 1950s to the present that display surprising wit and intelligence in their treatment of same-sex love. Share your own thoughts and calypsoes in the following brief discussion on calypso, soca, dancehall and sexual orientation in regional music and society and some ideas about next year's Carnival. Lime afterwards" (C. Robinson, personal communication, 2009).[8]

The announcement made clear that "this is a free event in honour of Pride month and in support of CAISO's mission to promote a 20/20 vision of sexual orientation in sweet T&T," but CAISO still framed it as an offering for all Trinidadians and Tobagonians.[9] "Let's use the national artform for which the coalition is playfully named to bring folks together in fun," the organizers suggested. Both this language and the approach of the event mimic one of Williams's most celebrated initiatives. Shortly after Trinidad and Tobago assumed independence, Williams began a Meet the People Tour in which he met communities across the country. Its conclusion was his implementation of the Better Village Program, in which locals would share their cultural performances for a national audience and compete for a trophy. Williams's and

Robinson's concepts align, both examples of the *negritude* championed by Aimé Césaire. They appear to be very differently executed projects, however.

Following his study of Williams's Better Village Program, Teruyuki Tsuji concludes:

> Williams's narrative was not a denial of the then-current explanations of the colonial society. Rather, having accepted cultural pluralism and the Anglo-conforming moral community accounts for colonial Trinidad, the political leaders and colonized intellectuals projected the liberation from the mimicry of "things English" and the development of a medley of people into a single "moral community." And what would make this transition was, for Williams, the designated application of political technology to tame traditional folk cultures for sociopolitical needs based on the transcendent authority of the state and its political ideology. The political intention and intervention would be able to deflect the inter-cultural dialogue from cultural pluralism and to bring about interculturation, eventually evolving into the moral community defined by "Creole authenticity." (2008, 1168–69)

Tsuji turns to Fanon to shed light on Williams's perspective:

> According to Fanon (1963), colonial stigmatization of folk cultures produced a "psycho-affective equilibrium" (210) among the colonized intellectuals, which was responsible for their late obsession with the past. In their response to the colonialist theory of pre-colonial barbarism, the colonized intellectuals became desperate for indications there was nothing in their past to be ashamed of—much as Williams looked for as many putative folk traditions as possible and for them to be as close to their original forms as possible. Yet, the claim to national culture was beyond the "rehabilitation" of cultural origins. The traditions selectively extracted from the past must be "collected, indexed, and archived" (Braithwaite and Elder 1) so that they could contribute legitimatization of the nation in the making. (1169–70)

Consequently, Tsuji says, the "national" culture imagined as the legitimating symbols of the nation was becoming less and less attached to the ever-present reality of the people.

The focus of CAISO's work, however, has been to foreground "everyday experiences" of at least some Trinidadians. In executing "Patricia Gone with Millicent," Robinson's approach, as is communicated in his casual invitation to a listening party, is not to civilize his fellow Trinbagonians in the way that the Better Village competition emphasized authoritative validation. "Patricia" simultaneously contrasted with the kind of consumption of outrage over "wild homophobes" paraded in the West. The jouissance that marries calypso etymologically with its African roots, the fusion of an exclamation of approval and a type of music that becomes a name for a group behind a movement, is a model that listens to the people living in the Caribbean, those raised on its rhythms and complex histories. Indeed, the act of listening as the form of sensory engagement encouraged by the event reflects a genuine and practical desire to hear buried stories, whether ingrained in calypso lyrics or brought out by inclusive, open-ended events. Such stories can only be heard through listening. They are quickly drowned out by speaking about or decrying monstrous oppression, which is the cornerstone of international antihomophobia events; as we have seen, in contrast to the listening party, which brings out strains of historical LGBTQI+ experience in music, Western models of advocacy produce stories that, for instance, omit and efface the reality of Barbados's rich drag scene, in their haste to decry the impossibility of drag being performed in a monstrously homophobic Barbados.[10] "Patricia" instead recognizes the rich lived history of LGBTQI+ experience in the Caribbean and fosters broader engagement, bringing out the supposedly homophobic general populace outside the queer community. In his opening remarks at the event, Robinson commented on his pleasure that it had drawn a diverse audience: "I joked, 'Surprise: you're at a gay pride event!'" There were two key objectives of organizing an event like this: to situate CAISO as a local group, and to communicate its demeanor as one of potential allyship with, not antagonism toward, "heterosexual" Trinbagonians. "What the event did," Robinson remembered in an interview in 2012, was that "it opened up a frame for people to come together."

This attitude of working with people from outside the LGBTQI+ community stands in contrast to international gay narratives of a Caribbean rampant with unfettered homophobia. "It's not all about horror," Robinson says. While critical of and working against forms of sexual discrimination, they have not tended to be as aggressively dismissive of their fellow, heterosexual nationals. Indeed, it was Kenny Mitchell, in an interview done in the midst of general elections in the country, who perhaps first flagged the notion that heterosexual Trinidadians might be supportive of LGBTQI+ people. The Trinidad *Guardian* newspaper's Sascha Wilson quoted Mitchell, commenting on this after his successful 2007 decision. "We might not be able to tip the scale in the next election because we are a minority," Mitchell said, "but we belong to a family, we have friends and they all support us so it will be more than just the gay votes" (Wilson 2007). Against the call by gay internationalists to identify themselves as part of a global gay community first, CAISO allies Trinbagonian LGBTQI+ people with heterosexual people, thus undercutting the animalization of Caribbean homophobes. It's an approach that has also influenced—and been influenced by—the operation of neighboring SASOD in Guyana. Joel Simpson, SASOD's executive director, credits Robinson with helping their organization take a similar position to involve themselves in other campaigns by marginalized groups in Guyana. Consequently, he says, most people think of SASOD as a "human rights" organization first rather than one exclusively interested in promoting LGBTQI+ issues. As well, he has learned from Robinson on how to negotiate relationships with international organizations and funders. "Any decision making about the Caribbean has to come from people in the countries who live, breathe, and work in these countries," he said in 2018. "People in the diaspora, people controlling funding, can't be running our show. They can't be speaking for us and making our decisions that affect our lives and well-being without us. Those are our decisions to make" (Simpson 2018).

BUY CRIX

One CAISO campaign that cleverly underlined this attitude was its class-conscious design of an amusing T-shirt (as worn by Robinson in figure 3.1) in response to the visit of Evangelical American pastor Phillip Lee, an advocate of gay conversion therapy. Against a black background, the white text reads:

The homosexual agenda:

1. Buy Crix
2. Spend time with family
3. Work for equality

"Crix" is the name of a local plain biscuit. It is cheap and ubiquitous. Every Trinbagonian household will be stocked with Crix, because, as the company motto goes, "Crix goes with everything." But more important, Crix is a critical household staple for working and lower-income families. Cheddar and guava jam on Crix was a mainstay at my home. By making "Buy Crix" the first priority of "the homosexual agenda," the T-shirt humorously defines CAISO's aspirations as meeting basic needs, whether that means food to eat or rights to sex and freedom to love. But in naming Crix, it is very clearly invoking a notion of class that entwines sexual and class liberation, a very

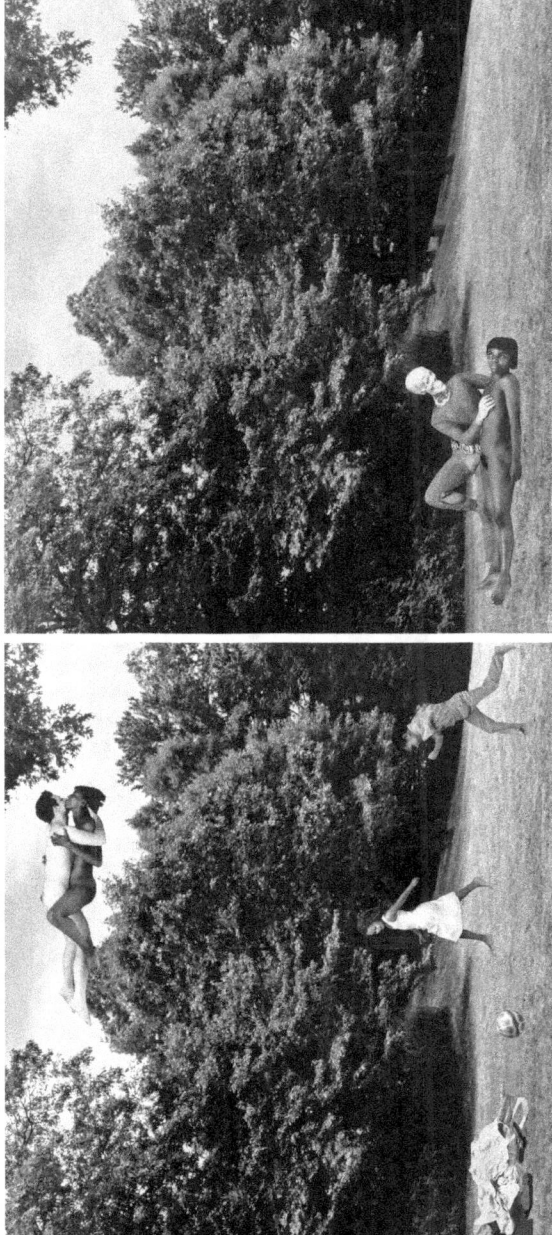

PLATE 1 Lorraine O'Grady, *The Clearing: or Cortez and La Malinche, Thomas Jefferson and Sally Hemings, N. and Me*, 1991/2012. Courtesy of the artist.

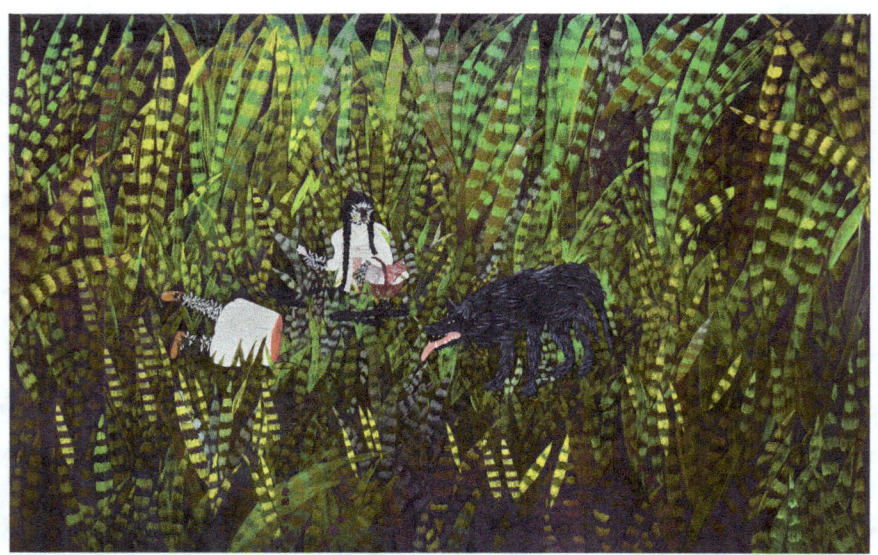

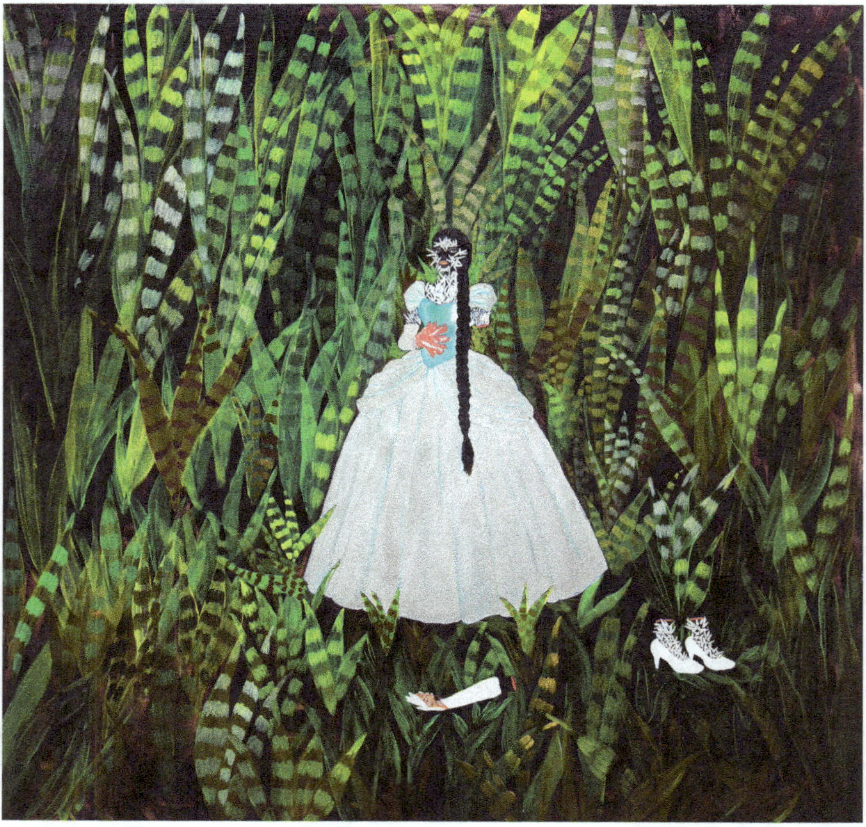

PLATES 2–5 Kelly Sinnapah Mary, *Notebook of No Return*, 2018.

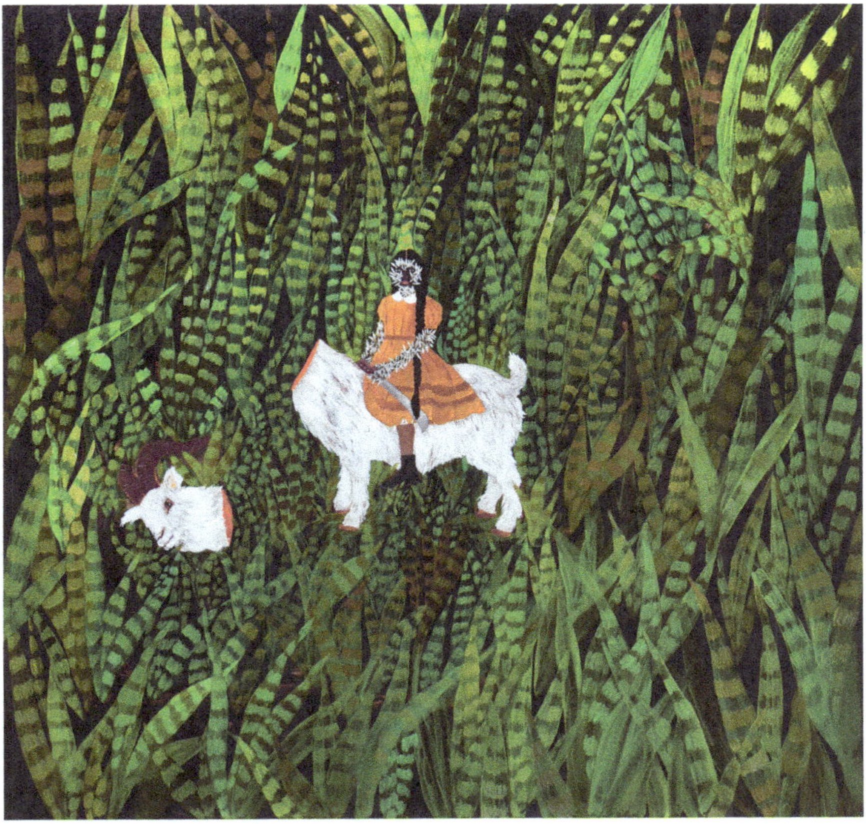

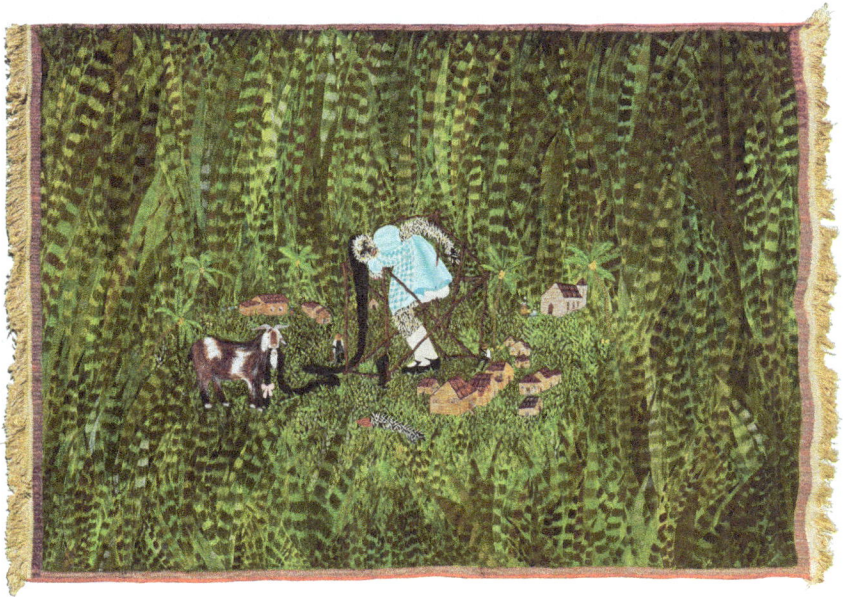

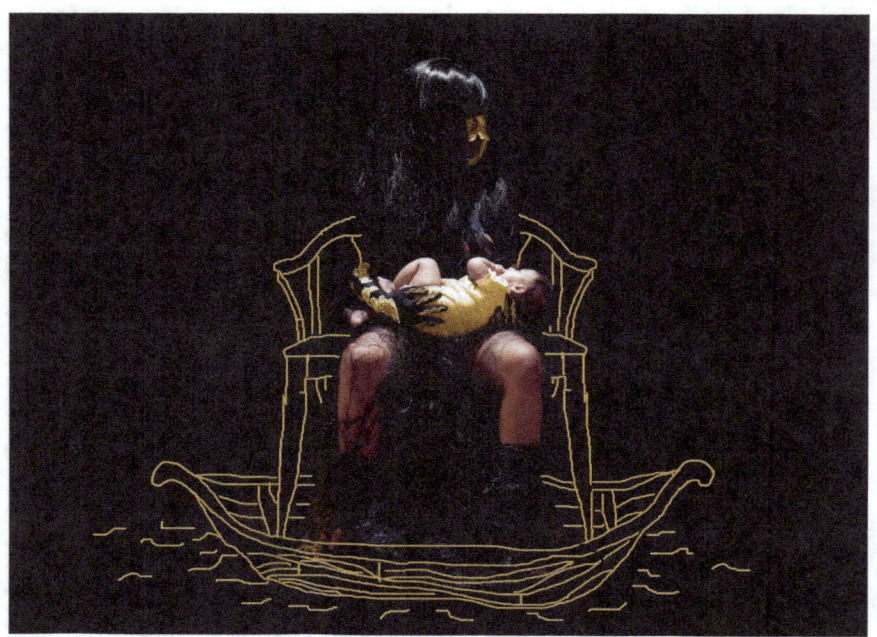

PLATE 6   Kelly Sinnapah Mary, *Hotmilk*, 2016.

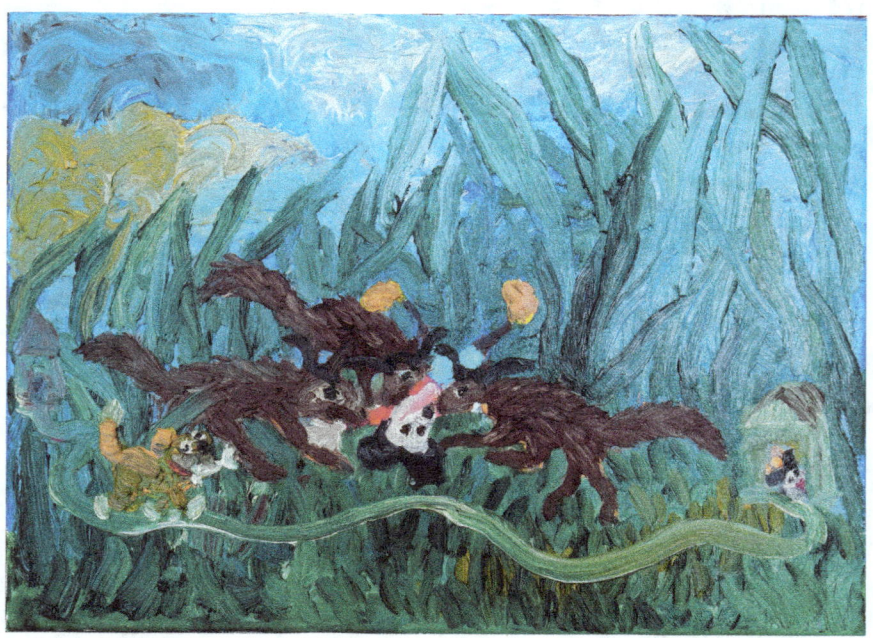

PLATE 7   Kelly Sinnapah Mary, *Notebook of No Return: The Fire Next Time*, 2020.

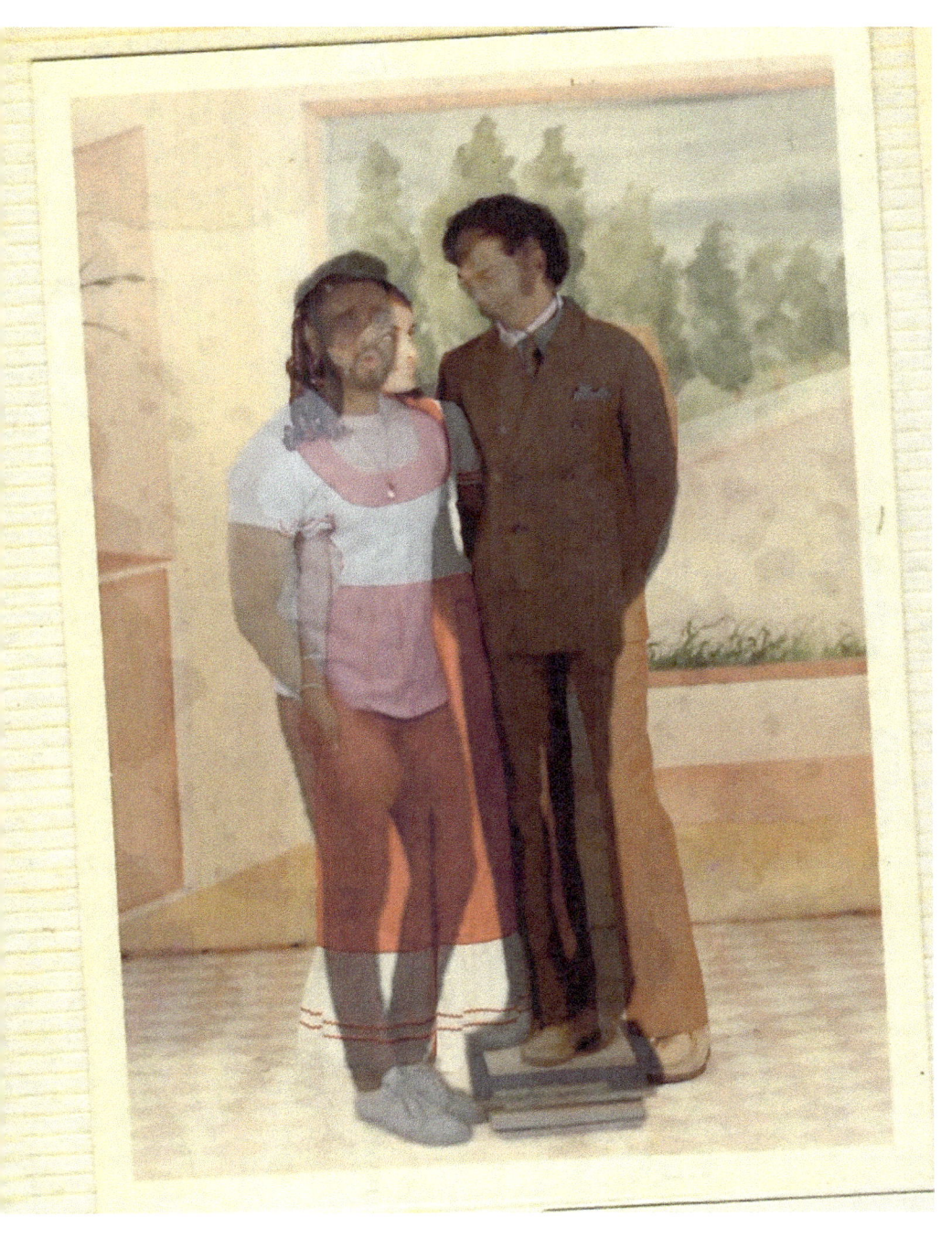

PLATE 8 Andil Gosine, *(Made in Love)*, 2014.

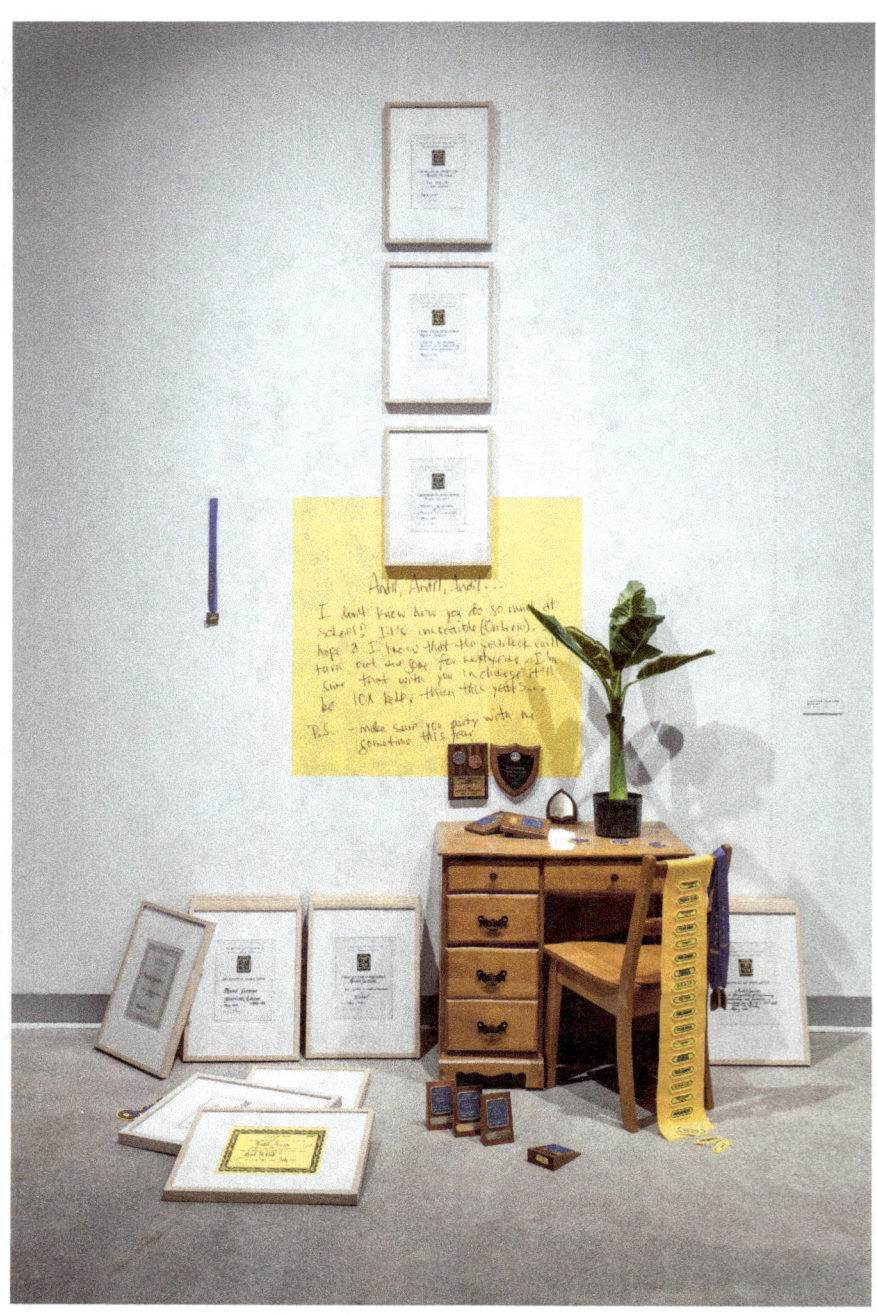

PLATE 9 Andil Gosine, *Caution: Will Bear No Fruit*, 2018.

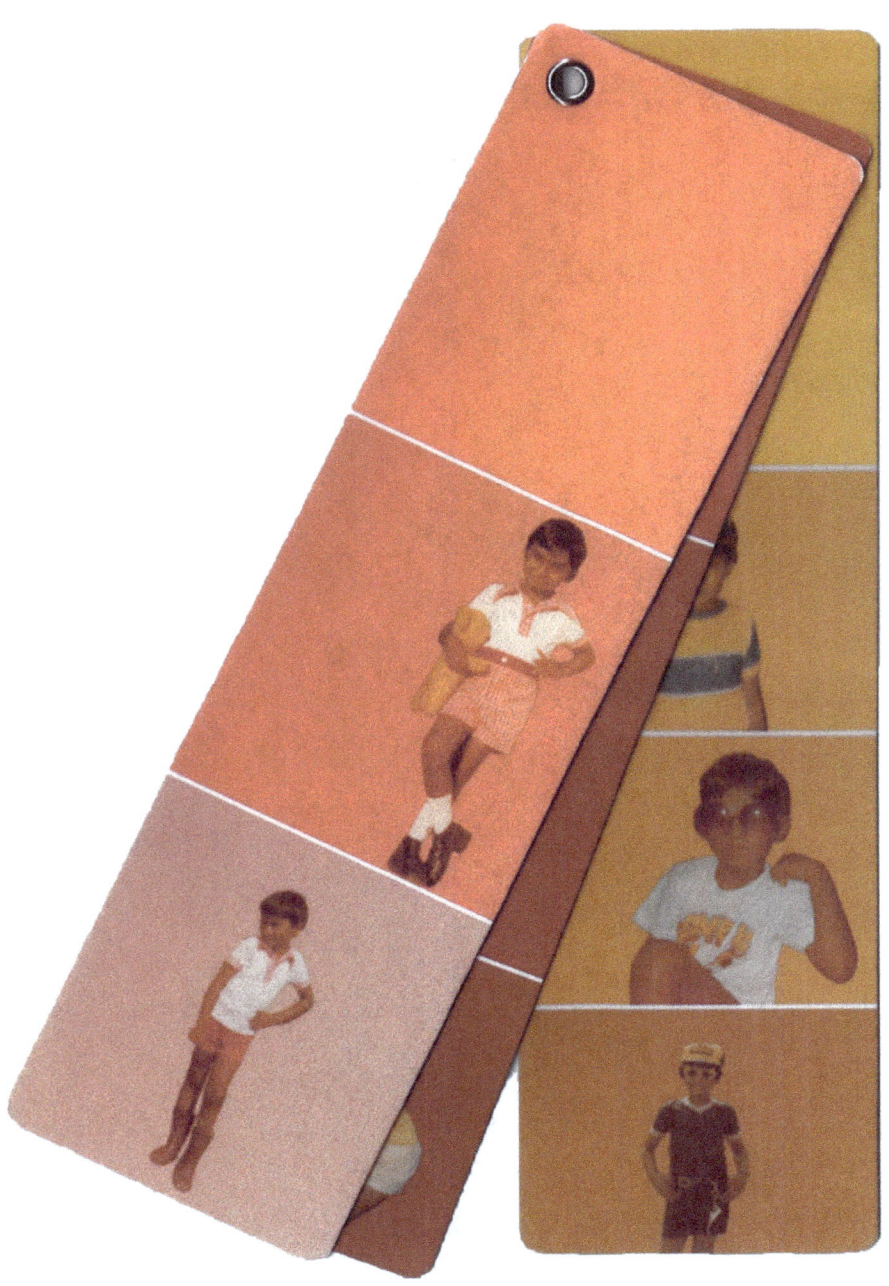

PLATE 10 Andil Gosine, *Coolie Colors* (detail), *I Could Have Been Fabulous/ But Then We Moved to Canada*, 2016. Installation, pantone fan with digital photographic print, Robert McLaughlin Gallery, Oshawa.

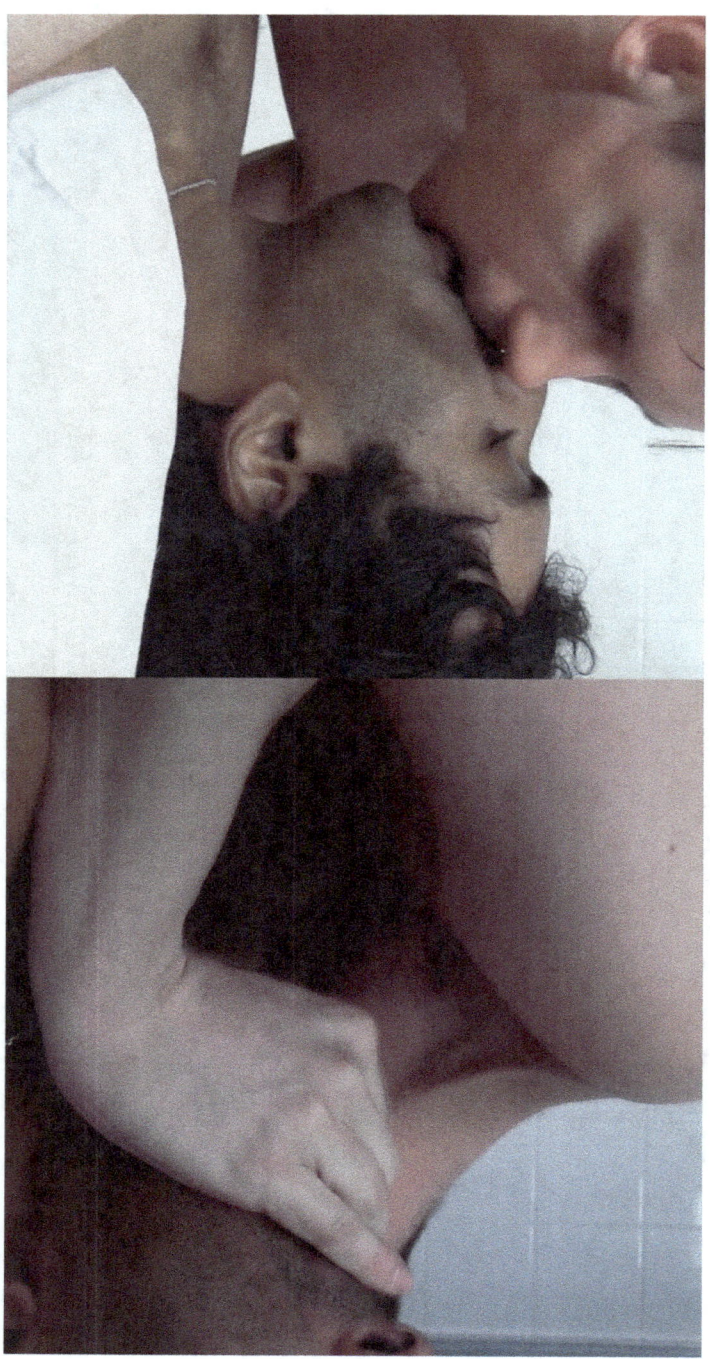

PLATE 11 Andil Gosine, *Natures: A Guerrilla Girl Story*, 2015.
Video still, McIntosh Gallery, London.

significant posture given the representations of queer life, including those in the Caribbean, as both emergent from economic privilege and antagonistic toward lower-class people. Writing about the United States, Amber Hollibaugh and Margot Weiss point out: "The LGBT movement's laser-focus on marriage equality propagates the myth of gay and lesbian affluence as political strategy, leaving aside any analysis of class or economic inequality or poverty—much less an analysis of capitalism. LGBT people are typically depicted as affluent consumers with high disposable incomes" (2015, 18). Research has shown, however, that "the majority of LGBT/Q people are poor or working class, female, and people of color, who struggle to get a job or hold on to one, to pay their rent and care for themselves and the people they love" (18). Because representations of queerness are defined as affluent, those from lower-income households see dissonance. From her fieldwork with women loving women in Trinidad, Krystal Ghisyawan concluded that class was a major factor in whether women identified themselves as "lesbian." Those who saw themselves as belonging to a privileged class claimed the identity and believed it was not available to others (2016). Class disparity was also a noticeable tension and attended-to concern in the organization of Trinidad and Tobago's first public Pride parade, which was largely dependent on the financial charity of, and often reflected the tastes and interests of, economically privileged gay men. Organizers showed consistent sensitivity, however, to issues of accessibility and committed to making all events free.

The "Buy Crix" shirt positioned its wearer squarely within the LGBTQI+ community, against the incursion of a pastor from outside the community who had come to try to dictate or erase ways of life. Williams's speech to "Youth of the Nation" similarly invoked class consciousness within the nation as a response to external forces of division, calling for "difference of wealth and family status being rejected in favour of equality of opportunities." The T-shirt situated LGBTQI+ people alongside and with, not against, other Trinbagonians; all homosexuals want to do is what other Trinbagonians want to do as well: spend time with family, work for equality, and "Buy Crix." The references to spending time with family and working for equality might appear on the surface to be reminiscent of the normative organizing poetics of dominant gay and lesbian movements worldwide, but another reading that takes better account of the Trinidadian context is possible. As scholars such as Christine Barrow have pointed out, the Euro-American nuclear family model has never characterized the majority of Caribbean families (2001, 423–24, 436–37). Instead, "family" connotes much broader and looser networks of attachment than that confined model. Where LGBTQI+ movements in the north have focused on marriage rights as a way to emulate the heterosexual nuclear family (cf. McCaskell 2016), the T-shirt's "spending time with family" goal is much less narrowly defined and structured. Similarly, "working for equality" in another context might be read as mimicry of heterosexual forms of relationships, but here it is a direct reference to the central positioning of social justice in formulations of Trinbagonian nationalism. The country's national anthem closes with a repetition of the refrain "Here every creed and race find an equal place" to emphasize the centrality of this multicultural ethic to the nation.

Robinson further elaborated attention to class consciousness in his column about the CCJ's ruling on the McEwan case. In a suitably titled column, "The Small-Man Court," Robinson calls the verdict a win for all "small people"—that is, people who were not upper/middle class (C. Robinson 2018b). He writes: "McEwan was an enormous case brought by small people. The first constitutional challenge to Caribbean anti-LGBTI laws, it's been overlooked in the international gaze. Its litigants weren't the lightskinned, world-travelling, in-your-face gay male activists in the Orozco or Jones cases people want to film and make heroes. This wasn't about sex. It was a case about a petty-offence arrest of four working class Black and Indian 'crossdressers.' From Guyana." Robinson goes on to declare, "The court's clearly-worded main opinion . . . shows its incredible self-confidence in itself and its Caribbean-ness." He also underlines the judgment's contextualization of the case as a strike against the demands of colonization to prove ourselves human:

> For the CCJ—and the advocates—McEwan wasn't just an LGBTI case. The judgement locates the "crossdressing" offence within a suite of Caribbean "vagrancy laws" "passed in the post-emancipation period . . . to cope with the paradigm shift in the mode of production from slavery to free labour. The laws were designed to regulate and exercise control of both the ex-slave population and, in places like Guyana, the newly imported indentured labourers. . . . The laws . . . also regulated gender and religion." They were law officers' "go-to response against anyone who threatened . . . to move 'out of place' socially, culturally, politically, racially, sexually, economically, or spatially." In both the June hearing and judgement the justices acknowledged how unfriendly justice systems lead unrepresented people like the litigants to plead guilty.

Robinson concludes, "McEwan isn't a 'transgender rights' case. It's a ricocheting decision about justice for the Caribbean small-man, brought to him by four courageous transwomen. And a Caribbean court."

Against the near-universal condemnation of the state among Caribbean sexuality scholars, Robinson also chuckles at the idea of the all-powerful hand of government. "I was like, 'What fucking state?' This is a tiny ass little country where everybody knows everybody else, where institutions are run by people you see in the supermarket. What *state*?" (personal interview, 2011). His deliberate exaggeration is of course made just to emphasize his main point: "this rarefied notion of the state is just not real." It's not that he denies the critical work state branches do in institutionalizing homophobia. Rather, he points out that in most Anglo-Caribbean countries, "you have relatively reasonable traditions [and] some ability to build a future." Against the idea that nonheterosexual people have no rights at all, historical experience as well as the rapidly changing context of sexual rights regulation across the region, once demands were actually made, suggest otherwise. "Especially in a place like Trinidad and Tobago," Robinson adds, "where you have prosperity." Thus, there is the possibility for all people—including gays and lesbians—to "construct and refashion." In speeches, interviews, and columns, he tends to emphasize this possibility. At a forum held on March 22, 2010, in Trinidad and Tobago, to launch "Sexual Rights: An IPPF Declaration," Robinson said, "I am proud to live in Trinidad and Tobago and to be part of this wonderful legacy of a 53-year-old Family Planning and sexual health movement. Of a feminist movement that has demonstrated leadership on gender and sexuality issues not just for women but for men and gay, lesbian, bisexual and transgender persons" (2010). In the speech, he invokes feminist discourse and Trinidadian nationalism together, to make a call for rights:

> Our nation of Trinidad and Tobago . . . was forged in the fires of overcoming several forms of domination and repression: *Colonialism*, that says your land and decisionmaking do not belong to you. *Imperialism*, that says your resources do not belong to you and you do not think for yourself. *Indentureship*, that says your labour does not belong to you. And *slavery*, that says your *body* does not belong to you. And, as we know well from the history of miscegenation during slavery, when your body does not belong to you, neither do your sexuality nor your reproduction—they belong to the master.

Robinson also referenced Williams's perhaps most stirring and influential 1961 speech in making his.[11] "Now that 'massa day done,'" he said, "we cannot replace massa with husbands; or political leaders; or the state; or laws and policies that say: yes *you* are free, but we will still tell you what you may do with your free *body*, with your sexuality, with your reproduction." Referencing several revered national holidays observed in Trinidad and Tobago around this commitment to anti-/postcolonial nationalism, Robinson also commented on

> the bloody struggles to win respect and compensation for the value of the efforts of our bodies and the right to come together in union that our unique Labour Day symbolizes, in its commemoration of the 1937 oilfield riots. (Which Spiritual Baptist figure was at the centre of those riots? Uriah Butler—you see how these struggles are indivisible.) Emancipation, which memorialises the triumph of one of the most epic of human rights projects, to restore ownership of our very bodies to ourselves. Independence and Republic Day, that mark our stepwise maturity at political autonomy and self-determination as a people. And Carnival, the mother of national festivals, in which the nation comes together along so many axes in traditions that flow from multiple geographies in a celebration that is so profoundly corporeal.

This discursive framing recognizes Caribbean people as capable actors, not homophobes in need of the training hand of outside experts. Robinson's more engaged approach is not really possible in those more common representations in Caribbean critical scholarship of the state as a punitive actor. In contrast to much-circulated heresy about rampant Caribbean homophobia, Robinson concluded his speech by saying, "Let us be honest. . . . No one has been jailed for joining CAISO. Indeed, Government technocrats have been directed to meet with us (though the politicians are still afraid to sit down with us). And our views are often aired fairly in a relatively free press. Our nation is *not* a place where no sexual rights exist." Robinson's remark speaks to the actual lived experience of LGBTQI+ people like Kenny Mitchell, who are certainly oppressively targeted in the country's legal code and risk its violent application but who nevertheless are able to access redemptive justice through the country's court systems. The lived reality of LGBTQI+ people in Trinidad and Tobago, as it is elsewhere in the Caribbean and across the Global South, is more complex than the reductive discursive framework advanced in dominant gay internationalism. That Robinson chose a calypso listening party to launch CAISO underlines the lack of careful attention in the more heretic forms of activism that use the human/animal divide to mark freedom as belonging to the civilized, and challenges us to engage the kind of invested and more open-ended analysis that cultural criticism demands.

Given his politics, it was no surprise that Robinson did not support the decision by Jason Jones to bring his case against the government of Trinidad and Tobago over its antisodomy legislation. On February 23, 2017, Jones filed a lawsuit against the government challenging the constitutionality of the Sexual Offences Act of Trinidad and Tobago. Section 13 of the act set out that "a person who commits the offence of buggery is liable on conviction to imprisonment for twenty-five years." It further clarified that "'buggery' means sexual intercourse by a male person with a male person or by a male person with a female person." Section 16 stipulated an imprisonment sentence of up to five years for "involving use of the genitals for the purpose of arousal or sexual gratification" between, among other persons, consenting same-sex adults. Jones's lawyers, comprising British counsel Richard Drabble and local lawyers Rishi Dass and Antonio Emmanuel, argued that the "very existence of these sections continuously and directly affects the claimant's private life by forcing him to either respect the law and refrain from engaging—even in private with consenting male partners—in prohibited sexual acts to which he is disposed by reason of his homosexual orientation, or to commit the prohibited acts and thereby become liable to criminal prosecution." The lawsuit claimed the legislation infringed on Jones's rights to privacy and freedom of thought and expression and contravened his human rights. Jones further claimed those sections of the act opened him up to ridicule and persecution because they criminalized consensual adult homosexual acts. The court heard arguments in January 2018 and Justice Devindra Rampersad delivered a strong judgment in the plaintiff's favor on April 12, 2018. Explaining his decision, Rampersad touched on several issues, including the right to privacy, colonialism, and Trinidad and Tobago's cultural diversity. The two sections, he said, had "everything to do with homosexuality and the colonial abhorrence to the practice," likening their impact to major historical forms of violent oppression globally. "The experiences of apartheid South Africa and the USA during and after slavery," he wrote, "have shown the depths that human dignity has been plunged as a result of presupposed and predetermined prejudices based on factors that do not accept or recognise humanity." Rampersad concluded, "We should not continue to imprison ourselves in colonialism."

Justifiably, Jones's name has now gone down in history as a permanently significant figure in the history of sexual politics in Trinidad and Tobago and the wider Caribbean (as should Rampersad's, one would think, given that he made the ruling). The impact of the case and the decision has been formidable. As I write, the front page of the national paper *Trinidad and Tobago Newsday* is an affirmative story of the birth of a child to two queer women, a direct consequence, I believe, of Jones's lawsuit as well as of Robinson's activism. In honing in on their rearticulation of Williams's concerns about civility, barbarism, and nationalism, however, I identify and consider how anxieties about the demarcation of human from animal haunt the specter of erotic autonomy. There have been international repercussions from it as well, as the decision was cited in the decriminalization of sodomy that would follow in India. The day after the verdict was delivered, Jones was given the space in *The Guardian* to record the story of his legal victory. In the column, he drew upon the popular imagination of Caribbean people as homophobes, opening with these lines: "I am a gay Trinidadian. Until three days ago, making that statement could have landed me in prison. Before Thursday, it was a crime for adults of the same gender to have sex. Our 'buggery' law imposed 25 years' imprisonment. All other intimacy between two women or two men risked five years' imprisonment under the demeaningly named offence of 'serious indecency'" (Jones 2018a). Despite the emphasis on jail time to convey a severe and archaic system, Jones's lawyers did not cite for the courts any cases of persons having been charged or imprisoned for consensual homosexual conduct. Drawing on the specter of a ravenous homophobic society, Jones's essay also gave the impression that he was forced to flee to the United Kingdom.

> As a teenager, it was obvious to others that I was gay. The bullying was incessant and cruel. In the 1980s I left Trinidad for London, unable to cope with the daily homophobia. In 1992, I returned home but the persecution had not changed. In 1996 I was forced away again. I came back between 2011 and 2014 to try to progress on this issue through engagement and advocacy but the homophobia remained intolerable. In the end, this saga of suffering won me my case. My having to leave—effectively forced into exile—was submitted as evidence to the court of how vile these laws are.

Being "forced into exile" is the standard argument of refugee claimants, although Jones himself was not one. His migration to London in 1985 was prompted by his desire to pursue a singing career there and facilitated because his mother was a British citizen. One of his statements is especially telling of Jones's representation of Trinbagonians for the international audience. As if to underline his expectation of uncivil behavior and suggesting his investment in a "politics of respectability," Jones writes, "The religious groups who supported the retention of the laws were polite opponents, as much as we disagreed." In a video posted on YouTube in 2017, he had characterized religious conservatives in Trinidad as "foaming at the mouth" and "disgusting" (OutRight Action International 2017). Jones concluded: "Last year I said enough is enough and sued my country to change the law." He estimated that "on a rough count, there are about 100,000 LGBTQ+ people in Trinidad and Tobago." "Finally," thanks to his case, "each of us is free from the fear of arrest, prosecution and imprisonment simply for living our lives" (2018a). In one of his last (public) Facebook posts at the end of 2018, Jones acknowledged, "What an amazing year for me and my small team of lawyers. They all said NO! But we battled for 3 years and came out victorious, and literally changed the lives of OVER 50 MILLION LGBT PEOPLE!" (2018b). Jones has remained upset about the lack of support from local groups and CAISO in particular. In a thinly veiled attack that he has many times since reiterated, Jones noted, "The shock to me was that those who should most support decriminalization most disrupted my challenge. My only support from any NGO—in Trinidad, the UK or internationally—was some funding from an HIV-prevention charity" (2018a).

There is some disagreement about whether Jones invited the participation of local NGOs to support his case. Although based in London for years, he had been visiting Trinidad with great frequency and regularly attending events. When he organized a forum in February 2017 to publicly launch the case, activists there recall he stated that his effort was going to be singularly his, but in statements following the verdict, Jones has made a point of calling out LGBT groups for not supporting his effort. Records show that both prior to and on the day of the case, a coalition of groups including CAISO had been involved in both lobbying public support for decriminalization and countering the homophobic narratives that the case prompted some religious leaders to produce. In fact, soon after Jones's case was filed, groups comprising the Alliance for Justice and Diversity (AJD) continued to mobilize support for sexual rights. Friends for Life, Womantra, Silver Lining Foundation, Women's Caucus of T&T, and I Am One, which Jones himself founded but with whom ties had been cut, formed this alliance in an attempt to influence Trinidad and Tobago's national 2015 elections. Over several months, they met, strategized, and took various actions. For example, they created infographics explaining the issues at stake in the case, conducted media briefings, publicized pro-LGBTQI+ rights statements by a range of public groups, responded to the Evangelical demonstrations leading up to the judgment with counterprotests; and on April 9, 2018, staged the largest pro-LGBTQI+ rights demonstration outside the Parliament prior to the judgment. They also gathered outside and inside the courthouse on the day of the judgment and appeared in and spoke to media consistently about the judgment and responded to case reports of backlash following the judgment. Arguably, it was these NGOs that were doing the groundwork to both encourage a supportive decision and prepare for the fallout from a negative one. Notably, the official statement issued by the AJD following the verdict stated, "Jones returned from London to file the case. No local LGBTI NGOS were invited to join." On the morning of the judgment, in fact, several LGBTQI+ activists gathered early to await the judgment and counterprotests by Evangelicals and the Muslimeen outside the courtroom. A flag-waving Rudy Hanamji skipped work to take his perch across the street from the Hall of Justice, at the city's historical home of protest, Woodford Square, and soon he would be joined by dozens of friends and fellow activists, including Cherisse Berkeley, Andre Bagoo, Kennedy Everett Maraj, and popular drag artist Miss Jinnay, among many others.

Robinson arrived earliest, at just past 9 a.m. He wanted to get to the Hall of Justice early, expecting that he would have to fight for a seat in the courtroom before Evangelicals claimed most of them. He knew the verdict, regardless of which way it went, would have major ramifications, but he was not supportive of bringing the case to court. Robinson's first impression of Jones, in 2012, was that he was an impressive figure with a critical lens. One statement Jones made early on has stayed with Robinson ever since: "He had said 'change required a catalyzing moment.'" Jones's comments about the lack of support from quarters where he might expect to find it are no doubt directed at Robinson and CAISO. After lively internal debate among its Board of Directors, CAISO opted not to try to intervene in Jones's challenge. "It wasn't a priority," Robinson said in a 2018 interview, "to change a law that was not being enforced." Avoiding the costs of challenging legislation seemed to outweigh potential benefits to joining the case: "As we saw in Belize, litigation can be very polarizing, threatening to create or deepen divisions." He also worried that for the duration of the case and its appeals, it would stall legislative action in other areas, like employment and domestic violence law, where there was hope of progressive changes being made, which decriminalization would neither deliver nor guarantee. For decades, groups like Friends for Life were laying the groundwork to calm anxieties about homosexuality. While Jones worked on the case, activists from the AJD were engaging the larger public.

Robinson came up with the theme "Keep Calm. We can share the nation" as an antidote to his expected fears of a backlash to a supportive decision. The phrases were used to headline a press release put out on March 16, 2018. "CAISO's moral responsibility around this case is bigger than cheerleading for either side," it stated. "It is to make sure all of us living here continue to share the nation after the judgment. That is what our commitment to universal human rights is about." The CAISO statement criticized homophobic opposition without characterizing all Trinbagonians as raging homophobes. The statement pointed out that "a small group of Evangelical Christians, including pastoral leaders, has been vigorously protesting the impending court ruling outside the Parliament. They have also shared in the media's extraordinary claims that repeal of the unenforced laws will increase both crime and cancer, and force churches to perform homosexual weddings. US and UK gay media have also published imaginative interpretations of the case. CAISO fears that the laws themselves, the impact of the upcoming ruling, as well as basic facts and civics, are being misrepresented to the public and wildly misunderstood" (Douglas 2018). Robinson further argued that these expressions of homophobia were limited to a smaller population and un-Trinbagonian. "I can't say why the protestors seem so panicked, or why they are trying to hold politicians accountable for a judge's decision. I do notice larger religions aren't as threatened." He reassured "concerned Christians that we can share the nation with them, if they share it with us" (Douglas 2018). Reflective of his longtime position and in a possible allusion to the McEwan case, which was being tried at the time but not yet adjudicated, the statement also noted that "CAISO defends faith groups' right to protest, and to hold moral views about grooming, clothing, diet, sexuality and marriage. But the role of the law, protected by the Constitution, isn't to enforce any faith group's teachings" (Douglas 2018).

The media release also revealed members' anticipation of a loss in the courts. Angelique Nixon, CAISO board member and a feminist scholar at the University of the West Indies, appealed to CAISO's stakeholders, as well, not to exaggerate the weight of a potential loss. "If the judge upholds the law," she was quoted as saying, "it won't mean Government will suddenly come marching into our bedrooms. Plus, there are two appeals ahead" (Douglas 2018). Nixon noted that a win in the case still leaves people unprotected against discrimination or bullying, and politicians would need to pass new laws to do so. While preparing for the loss of Jones's case, they nevertheless pushed for a win. The biggest victors in the case, the statement concluded, would be "all the Trinidad & Tobago citizens who would now be able to use the Constitution to challenge unjust laws, including laws like those that outlawed Spiritual Baptist worship and Carnival drumming," once more linking the decriminalization of sodomy to other struggles toward decolonization. "It would also be a celebration of our local courts and democratic institutions. But there is absolutely no cause for moral panic if Jones wins," Nixon said.

To quell anxieties about marriage, they pointed out that although the national Parliament in the Bahamas had decriminalized sodomy twenty-seven years earlier, same-sex marriage rights did not immediately follow. They reminded the country that religion is protected from discrimination in the constitution and that in all places where same-sex marriage was legal, no religious institution was being forced to marry same-sex people. The AJD also sought to scale back the rhetoric generated in the international media that a positive decision in the Jones case would automatically invalidate sodomy laws protected by savings clauses in other Caribbean jurisdictions. In a statement put out by the AJD following the verdict, Robinson sought to calm fears: "Our sodomy laws do not prevent or punish us having sex. What they do instead is deny people dignity, entrench the idea that either we do not deserve human rights protections or the state is constrained from extending them to us" (AJD 2017). But, sitting in court as Justice Rampersad delivered his ruling, Robinson says he began to wonder if the laws had also denied him something else—"the ability to imagine that a T&T institution could deliver as humane a judgment as this Court did" (AJD 2017). As the AJD groups turn away from the courtroom to the less imaginative work of supporting Trinbagonians to manage the uptick in hate speech and threats of violence, and the fear and evictions in the immediate days after the historic ruling, they have called on political and religious leaders to join their public appeals for "sharing the nation."

The story constructed of Jones through most international reporting of the case, including in Jones's own written reaction to the ruling, casts a clearly identifiable hero (Jones), victims (LGBTQI+ people in Trinidad and Tobago), and villains (heterosexual Trinbagonians and their government, which is consistent with dominant tropes of gay globalist initiatives headquartered in Europe and North America). But this rendering oversimplifies the more complex historical reality and contemporary diversity of experiences and dynamism of the country, the region, and its peoples. Asked by a journalist to describe how the Rampersad ruling would affect his life, law student Josh Ryan replied, "I've always been comfortable. The High Court just changed that there's a recognition on a legal level to some sort of progression toward human rights [and] equality."[12] Not just in Trinidad, but my own glimpses of queer life in the twenty-first century in different Caribbean spaces confirm that being "comfortable" was not a feeling unique to Ryan. In 2003 I went to a queer dance party in Paramaribo where the house floor was filled with sand to activate the beach theme, and to the cutest gay bar on the edge of the city that was frequented that night by many a handsome French *Guyannais*. A

Carifesta event at the Surinamese president's house opened with a confidently gender-defiant performance by an Indo-Surinamese dancer that referenced Indian *hijras*. On a weekend stopover in Trinidad that same year, my hairdresser aunt decided I needed subtle purple highlights, but two washes later, that purple turned neon pink—the kind of hair that gets you asked questions like "Are you a boy or a girl?" by primary school children in St. Lucia and cruised by a closeted schoolteacher-pastor who was to marry a churchgoing Trinidadian woman the next week; when my shirt came off, he complained, "I thought Indian guys were supposed to be hairy." Though I forget how, I made two new queer friends in St. Vincent—writer William Abbott and photographer Nadia Huggins. Gay men seemed to be everywhere in Barbados: artists, lawyers, bed and breakfast owners, drag queens, beach bums. Though my movements were heavily guarded by my employer in Kingston, I didn't need to go far—just as far as the hotel lobby and the bookshop—to encounter flirtatious men. Trinidad and Tobago, however, was clearly the pink pearl of the Caribbean. There were gay *bars* (plural) and multiple *parties* from which to choose on the same night. Even outside the busy pre-Carnival period, the nightlife scene always seemed to buzz with queer energy. In my work as a development consultant to the World Bank between 2003 and 2006, I dealt with senior bureaucrats, members of Parliament, and even a couple of prime ministers across the region. Not a homophobic slight was ever suggested. My then-partner sometimes accompanied me for parts of these trips. We were always read as a couple. Only once did we encounter a gesture of disapproval, from a cleaner in St. Vincent who insisted on pulling apart the twin beds we pushed together every night.

The repeated representation of Jones's lawsuit as a singular, all-powerful act internationally not only oversimplifies the richly layered, complex experiences of LGBTQI+ people in the region. It also undermines and invisibilizes the years of work and effort of activists that may have produced the context that enabled the judgment in Jones's favor. Although many local activists were not enthusiastic about Jones's filing of a lawsuit, the court victory surely would not have been secured without them. Tracy Robinson's detailed consideration of sexual regulation legislation led her to conclude that "Caribbean courts seem to make judgments based on their sense of what the society wants" (Bulkan and Robinson 2018). In Trinidad and Tobago, would the Rampersad decision have been possible without the previous decades of groundwork done by NGOs and activists, and without the cultural impact of Robinson's weekly columns, speeches, and protests, as well as others by feminist allies at the University of West Indies in particular?

When Robinson took the stage to address Pride parade participants at Queen's Park Savannah, on the same grounds where every major Trinbagonian festival is held, on July 28, 2018, he commended, rather than condemned, his fellow countrypeople. "Are you proud today?" he asked, twice. "Are you proud of our judiciary? Are you proud of the decision they made on April 12? We may not always be proud of all of them, but we are proud of the judiciary as a whole." He also claimed pride in "the Equal Opportunity Commission, the one state institution that keeps saying we belong, that we ought to be protected," and praised incoming president Paula-Mae Weekes, "your President, who even before she took office told you that you were equal to everybody else in the nation, and your country should protect you." Trinbagonians were not framed as the homophobes as in Jones's speech but as compatriots in a shared task of decolonization, including from punitive colonial sexual regulation. Robinson closed his Pride remarks with a familiar refrain of collective interest: "We want to build stronger families. . . . We are creating spaces for your parents and your families to learn and live and how to embrace you on their own terms." Robinson's conditional "pride" in the country's judiciary also extended to the police. "We are not always proud of the police," he declared, "but we are very proud that they are protecting and serving us today." More important is the break this discursive strategy makes from what often seems like the rest of the LGBTQI+ rights world, in refusing to swap out homosexuality for homophobia as a means through which to measure the human condition. Neither ought to facilitate the dehumanization of nonwhite Caribbean and other peoples of the Global South.

As for Williams, national patriotism is a central drive of Robinson's political discourse. "The idea of nationalism and nation building motivates my organizing," Robinson acknowledges. But familiar with criticisms of nationalist politics, especially feminist critiques of the patriarchal stance of most forms of nationalism historically, he further acknowledges "the notion of a postcolonial, feminist nationalism, one that is generative, not Old World and patriarchal—a visionary idea of being part of creating a nation that all can share" (Sanatan 2019). He likens this work to that undertaken by his former writing group Other Countries in creating Black gay consciousness and community. Critics of this approach warn that such nationalism risks masking homophobia, and Robinson himself has been critical of Afro-nationalism. The difference between Robinson's and Williams's understanding of nationalism is perhaps most evident in a comparison between the former's speech at the country's first Pride parade and the latter's "Youth of the Nation" address. Both shared an air of celebration and hopefulness about the autonomy of their constituencies. But where Williams draws from colonial imaginations of civility that center European "Man" and makes a plea for transformation, Robinson's aspirational call does not impel his fellow Trinbagonians to become better. Instead, he is focused on issues of social equality. There is no anxiety about a threatening, wild animality.

"MAN" BEYOND THE METROPOLE

In her interview with David Scott, Wynter expressed her frustration with the continuity of colonial epistemes in postcolonial states as represented in Williams's "Youth" speech: "What had earlier been a hands-on direct political and militarily enforced imperialism, with its back-up ideology based on the premise of white superiority/Black inferiority being carried by the curricula of the elementary and secondary school system," she explains, "is now going to become a properly epistemological imperialism. Because by the time your colonizer flag goes down you have already trained your 'natives.' Trained them . . . so you will therefore continue to legitimate your dominance by means of your ruling ideas, even where cast now in new sanitized terms" (D. Scott 2000, 158). Williams's centering of "European Man" and implicit commitment to colonialism's civilizing project are especially evident in his expressed disdain for rural Indo-Trinbagonian culture. The passage most cited as evidence of Williams's animosity toward Indo-Trinbagonians is from his *History of the People of Trinidad and Tobago*, published on August 31, 1962, to mark the country's achievement of independence from Britain and Williams's inauguration as its first prime minister. With the aim of defining the "people" of Trinidad and Tobago, the book presents a thorough list arranged according to putative cultural and racial differences and chronologically by settlement. In its conclusion, the listed groups of immigrants are integrated as a single family under the guardianship of the one and only "Mother":

> There can be no Mother India . . . and the Trinidad and Tobago society is living a lie and heading for trouble if it seeks to create the impression or to allow to act under the delusion that Trinidad and Tobago is an African society. There can be no Mother England. . . . There can be no Mother China . . . and there can be no Mother Syria or no Lebanon. A nation, like an individual, can have only one Mother. The only Mother we recognize is Mother Trinidad and Tobago, and Mother cannot discriminate between her children. All must be in her eyes. (1962, 279)

While Williams's statement might be read as a counter to tribal ethnona-tionalism, Indo-Trinbagonians saw it as an affront to their cultural religious practices and continued connections with India. Williams's fundamental investment in the civilizing logic of "European Man" continued to produce anti-Indian rhetoric. In his 1969 autobiographic collection of essays, *Inward Hunger: The Education of a Prime Minister*, Williams emphasized how the distant class and geographic location of Indians in Trinidad made them less civilized. "There was no question that the Indian occupied the lowest rung of the ladder," he wrote. "Cribb'd, cabin'd and confin'd in the sugar plantation economy, from which other racial groups had succeeded in large in escaping, the few who did escape to the Mecca of Port of Spain were concentrated on the outskirts of the town in a sort popularly known as 'Coolie-Town' . . . a bustling suburbs capital, which tourists interested in Oriental scenes and ceremonies were advised to visit in order to see 'the Son of India in all of his Oriental primitiveness'" (21). This framing of civility as a measure of proximity to the metropole largely held. In his 1975 dissertation, "Coolie and Creole: Differential Adaptations in a Neo-Plantation Village," John O. Stewart recognized a strong predisposition among urban residents in Port of Spain to emphasize how their "civilized" lifestyle was distant from the "culturally backward bush-dwellers" (1973, 67–68; cited in Tsuji 2008, 1160). Indeed, even though Williams viewed the Better Village Project as a civilizing endeavor, it was met with disdain from artists and intellectuals. Joyce Wong Sang, a founding member of the project, recalled, "Several well known artists [at the inception of the competition] were offended that Williams did not see cultural exercise with them at the forefront. Instead he went to the lowly villages. Imagine, culture for the peasants! Many stayed away, feeling that if these artists condemned it, it was below their station" (Tsuji 2008, 1160).

Little, then, had shifted in the colonial logic that placed those closer to the center as more human and those further away as more animal. Wynter describes how an encounter with Myrtle, a house assistant she employed, helped her to recognize the deep investment of metropolitan Caribbean "middle-class" people in racialized and class measures of one's humanity: Myrtle "told me about the ceremonies in which she took part. . . . She opened up for me the realities of this underground alternative reality, of whose existence I had no clue" (2003, 162). Describing her discovery, Wynter observes, "We have hitherto turned away in shame from our . . . folklore. But . . . in doing so, we are turning away from the evidence of the most moving history in the world, that of a people who, coming as chained slaves across the middle passage, in the worst possible condition, had arrived in a strange land, and humanized its landscape by means of their transplanted folklore, in order to 'snatch their place among men.' So this was a moment of discovery" (162).

Similar to Wynter's experience of distance from more rural forms of culture, what we often see as a result is the Port of Spain elite replacing the colonizing classes in relationship to others outside its cultural norms, akin to Wynter's description of how Rastafarians are treated in Jamaica: "The negation of their human dignity is not just because of their blackness. It is also because of their jobless status, their institutional poverty and joblessness, their always-discriminated-against deviant status. The fact that as they assert themselves with their revalued symbols they become the objects of suspicion to the police, who, although black themselves, were always anxious to secure their middle-class status by putting visible distance between themselves and the black and poor Other of the Rastafari. In Jamaica, middle classness cancels out the negativity of the sign of blackness" (D. Scott 2000, 173). As a product of that privileged group, Wynter admits, "I knew nothing about my own historical reality, except in the negative terms, that would have made it normal for me, as Fanon points out, both to *want* to be a British subject and in so wanting, to be anti-black everything I existentially was. I knew what it was to experience a total abjection of being" (D. Scott 2000, 188).

But what about those more removed from this experience of colonial disciplining? What can be learned from consideration of the experiences of those from outside the metropole who might have been less instituted into the hegemony of "European Man"? Robinson himself has rarely traveled outside the capital city, and while activists like Hanamji have made special efforts to connect with people in other parts of the country, local gay culture is still primarily defined through Port of Spain. As various ethnographic projects about rural LGBTQI+ life outside the dominant metropolitan forms have demonstrated, alternative cosmogonies of sexual identity, relationships, and family exist. Gloria Wekker's comprehensive study of *Mati work* in Suriname, a relationship that pairs women, is perhaps the best-known example (2006). Jasbir Puar's dissertation (1999) similarly highlighted her complex encounter with a couple in Trinidad that left her challenged to characterize using categories of gender and sexuality. Newer projects such as Krystal Ghisyawan's (2016) analysis of same-sex relationships between women in Trinidad and Priety Kumar's (2018) ethnography of Indo-Guyanese women also produce examples of understandings of sexualities and relationships that are not the same as those defined by dominant Euro-American narratives put forward by LGBTQI+ activists, and which come to define the outlook and politics of groups like CAISO. Similarly, in poetry and autobiographic prose, Rajiv Mohabir has been exploring how particular aspects of Indo-Caribbean cultural forms open up space for queer explorations. In his 2021 memoir *Antiman*, for example, Mohabir looks to the space for him to exercise erotic autonomy by the choices made by his grandmother as she negotiates the aftermath of indentureship. These initiatives may provide alternate possibilities to the Euro-American model of gay sexual identity that remains centered even as an object of (Robinson's) critique. In the final two chapters, I explore creative outputs from two spaces of rural, Indo-Caribbean experience that, because they were perhaps not as forcefully disciplined by colonial and postcolonial authorities, perhaps offer renderings of "human" that break from the mold of European "Man." The unsteadiness—one might say the wilder-ness—of these spaces may potentially embrace, rather than reject, animality.

The intentional racial divide purposefully set up by colonial administrators between Indians and Africans has continued to structure present-day conditions of life in Trinidad and Tobago, Guyana, Guadeloupe, and other places. Then, as now, alliances between Indo- and Afro-Caribbean people were viewed as a threat to established networks of power, and it was imperative that each group be kept distant from and suspicious of the other. Nearly six decades after official independence, what is explicitly structured, especially in governance, as a racial divide in Trinidad and Tobago is really, I think, a way to keep class in check—particularly to prevent intimate and political alliance between economically marginalized Afro-Trinidadians, who are mostly urban based, and Indo-Trinidadians, who remain mostly rural based. I wonder: What might become possible if Robinson's class-conscious politics is stretched to also consider and include the engagement of rural-based Indo-Caribbean people? How could more deliberative engagement between them challenge and produce alternatives to European "Man"?

4   *Désir Cannibale*

"HAPPY 'WE DRANK the blood of the colonizers from their skull as we feasted on their entrails' day!'" texted one sister to another in 2018 about Haitian Independence Day, celebrated every January 1 since 1804. "Happy 'we danced as their plantations burned and made them believe we signed a pact with the devil' day and happy new year!" replied the younger sister, my friend and sometime collaborator, Mélissa Laveaux, a Paris-based, Haitian Canadian singer. The demands of respectability weighed heavy in the Laveaux household. Their parents were well-educated, upwardly mobile Haitian professionals who migrated to Canada, and Mélissa in particular has paid a high price for choosing an artistic path over the security and status of a medical profession, and for declaring herself lesbian. Their exchange, which has become an annual rite, is a kiss-off not only to colonial fantasies of Caribbean people as cannibals but also to the way in which postcolonial subjects, especially colonial elites, have assumed the burden of proving themselves human, not animal. No, reply the Laveaux sisters, we don't need to prove *anything* to claim our worth. The quips about blood drinking and devil cavorting were actually passed on to them by their parents. The legacy of colonial pressure on Caribbean people to prove themselves human endures among the Caribbean diaspora; this sisterly exchange dramatizes, names, and subverts the dynamic's lingering hold, reimagining the meanings of simple holiday greetings, recharged with buried colonial histories that continue to make themselves felt. In their letters, the midsections of Independence Day and benign New Year's tidings are split open to reveal the messy insides—the violent struggle for dominance, over both literal space and the space to imagine one's relationship to humanity and to power.

Of the many strategies European colonizers deployed to justify their invasion of would-be colonies in the Americas, a prominent one, as I have touched on in previous chapters, was the circulation of narratives alleging cannibalistic practices by its Indigenous peoples, usually presented as evidence that their condition of being was less human, more animal. In a journal entry dated November 4, 1493, one week after landing in Cuba (at which point he still believed that he had arrived in Asia), Christopher Columbus wrote that "there are men with one eye and others with dog snouts who eat men. On taking a man, they behead him and drink his blood and cut off his genitals." Encountering resistance by the Cigüayos peoples in Quizqueia (Hispaniola), he speculated that "without doubt, the people here are evil, and I believe . . . that they eat men" (quoted in Fuson 1987, 102, 173). A much-circulated 1493 letter by Columbus that would come to define the Caribbean in European imaginations further described the renamed "Caribs" as "very fierce" people "who eat human flesh" (quoted in Jane 1960, 200). This characterization became so deeply institutionalized that by 1503, Spain's Queen Isabella issued an order protecting Indigenous peoples of the Americas from capture or injury except "a certain people called Cannibals" (quoted in Sauer 1966, 161). Those who refused to accede to Spanish invaders were man-eaters and, as "eating human flesh always erases any other possible ethnic or national identification," cannibalism negated consideration of them as *human* beings (Hulme 1998, 22). Cannibalism became a justification for the enslavement of Indigenous peoples. "They may be captured and are to be taken to these my Kingdoms and Domain and to other parts and places and be sold," announced Isabella's declaration (quoted in Whitehead 1984, 70).

The word *cannibal* became etymologically rooted in *Carib*. Scholars, artists, and colonial officials would continue this narrative reproduction of In-

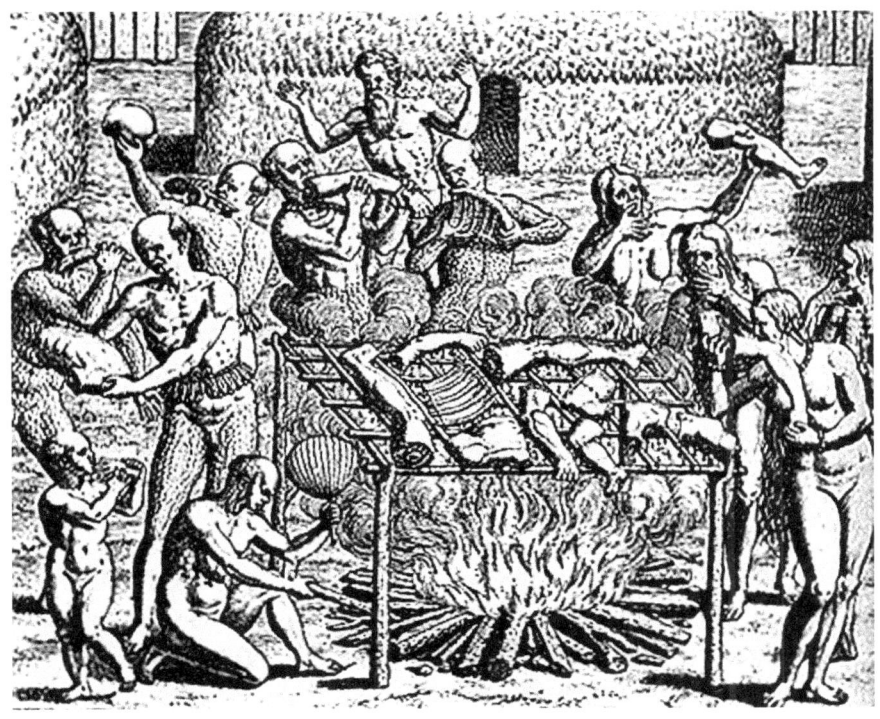

FIGURE 4.1 Theodore de Bry, *Cannibalism in Brazil*, 1557.

digenous peoples as cannibals over the next five hundred years. A 1557 gravure by Theodore de Bry depicted "cannibalism in Brazil" (figure 4.1). In 1897 Puerto Rican historian Cayetano Coll y Toste wrote that "The Island Carib, eaters of fresh meat, of adventurous and warlike instincts, blood-thirsty, cruel man-eater is the antithesis of the Arawak, the aboriginal occupant of the Antilles, eater of cereals, peaceful, hospitable, charming and indolent," and in 1912 Martir de Angleria accused Amerindians writ large of cannibalism (quoted in Whitehead 1984, 70–71). Debates over the "truth" of accusations of cannibalism have continued to the present. Research projects continue to test the veracity of claims about cannibalism in the Caribbean in the present day. A recent newspaper story in the British *Guardian* reported, "Archaeologists say Caribbeans were not 'savage cannibals,' as colonists wrote" (Handy 2018). "For centuries," runs its opening sentence, "historians have held that the earliest inhabitants were peaceful farmers who were wiped out by the ferocious man-eating Carib people." The article reported on new findings from

Désir Cannibale

an excavation at a twelve-acre site in Antigua, which includes the conclusion reached by one researcher that "far from being cannibals, they largely lived on shell animals and fish." Meanwhile, in January 2020, the newsletter of the American Association for the Advancement of Science reported the findings of a joint research team from North Carolina State University and the Florida Museum of Natural History, which deployed face recognition technology to defend Columbus's writings. When the story was picked up in mass media, the resulting *Daily Mail* headline trumpeted that "Columbus' CANNIBAL claims may have been true after all" (Morrison 2020).

That the Caribbean's Indigenous peoples were either "peaceful" Arawaks or "warlike" cannibalistic Caribs was a principal fact of precolonial history I learned in my Trinidadian classrooms, a lesson that is still widely taught across the whole region today. Through the entirety of my schooling in Trinidad in the 1980s, no other understanding of Indigenous peoples would be presented except as simple primitives who lacked any kind of human cultural sophistication. Outside the classroom, the only other example of precolonial society I would be exposed to came in the form of Westerns, a film genre that my father enjoys to this day, and which I do not. This production of Indigenous peoples as bestial, coupled with similar narratives about African slaves and Indian indentured laborers, collectively located nonwhite Caribbean peoples in a liminal space between human and animal, a position that endures. Cannibalism was "the absolute marker of savagery and primitivism," Njeri Githire concludes in *Cannibal Writes: Eating Others in Caribbean and Indian Ocean Women's Writing*, "a trope upon which the resulting narrative of quintessential Caribbean and Indian Ocean alterity was constructed." Githire further contends that the accusation of cannibalism against the Kalinago people (Caribs) is as definitive of the Caribbean experience as the Middle Passage, calling it "the incipient moment" of the region's history (2014, 5, 14).

Honor Ford-Smith further explains how the production of the region's Indigenous people as cannibalistic was key to the making of the European "Man." Wynter's argument, Ford-Smith reminds us, "goes roughly as follows":

Columbus' voyage demonstrated the weakness of medieval epistemes by revealing inaccuracy of its representation of the world. Columbus' journey and the process it began led to changes in medieval systems of knowledge production and ultimately ushered in a new secular based epistemology. At the centre of this new system of knowledge was man rather than God—but man emerged in contrast to others defined as lesser beings—people of colour, women of all colors, children, the disabled and homosexuals. Man became "us"—middle class, white able bodied men—and everyone else became "them." (2007, 10)

Columbus's description of his first voyage to the Caribbean, for example, characterized Indigenous people by what they *lack*. "Early European male colonizers could not understand difference without linking it to superiority or inferiority," says Ford-Smith. Taino men, for example, are described as *mancebos*, "adolescents," or less than grown men. "They are marked by weakness or cowardice or ignorance or by their animal sexuality." This rendering of early contact, Ford-Smith says, "suggests that the region and its peoples are from a place where European civilization can be devoured and excreted into savage nature—that it is a site where Western culture is so threatened that it might revert to unmediated nature for the pleasurable nourishment of all that 'man' is not resulting of course in the overthrow of civilization" (2007, 11).

Yet as Mimi Sheller asks, "Was the Caribbean truly a place where Europeans were at risk of being eaten? Or were they in fact the ones who posed a threat to the bodies, health, and lives of the indigenous people of the region, and later to the enslaved and indentured workers who were consumed in the system of plantation slavery and colonial capitalism?" (2003, 143). Were they also perhaps projecting fears about themselves and their own societies onto Others? In 1979 William Arens published *The Man-Eating Myth*, a detailed repudiation of Europeans' claims of cannibalism, which itself produced several challenges. Weighing Arens's position against his critics, Neil Whitehead concluded: "Nevertheless, since it appears that the Spanish were usually quite indiscriminatory in their accusations of cannibalism, and that such accusations tended to be levelled most particularly at Amerindians as yet unconquered, one must agree that political expediency, rather than an attempt at objective reportage, was the most influential factor in Spanish chronicling of this question" (1984, 81). Whitehead's closing sentence in that article, however, is its most telling: "It was the European pre-occupation with this subject . . . rather than its overall sociological significance for Carib peoples that necessitates such a detailed treatment of the topic" (81). Indeed, mirroring the history of sodomy, Europeans' fascination with cannibalism may have been a projection of anxieties about its existence in their own societies. In a 2013 article for *Smithsonian Magazine*, Sarah Everts calls out Europe's "hypocritical history of cannibalism," drawing attention to research that showed the world's first cannibal incident took place during the Crusades, in 1098, when after the capture of the Syrian city of Ma'arra, Christian soldiers reportedly ate the bodies of conquered Muslims (see also Rubenstein 2008). In some stories, the bodies were consumed in private at "wicked banquets," while others characterize it as a deliberate military strategy, believing the stories of the barbaric act would work as a psychological fear tactic in future Crusade battles (Everts 2013). The accusation of cannibalism against an enemy was invoked in the medieval era, and by the sixteenth century, "cannibalism was not just part of the mental furniture of Europeans; it was a common part of everyday medicine from Spain to England" (Everts 2013). In *Medicinal Cannibalism in Early Modern English Literature and Culture*, Louise Noble concludes, "it's a big paradox," since the term *cannibal* was being used to inferiorize and authorize power over a people while the "civilized in Europe were also eating bits of the human body" (quoted in Everts 2013).

This long history and its myriad provocations are the necessary backdrop to introduce *Désir Cannibale*, an exhibition of works by nine young Guadeloupean artists presented at the Fondation Clément in Martinique between July 27 and September 19, 2018. In his instructions to the participating artists, curator Jean-Marc Hunt asked the artists to "think of the world as predators, to swallow all the cultures of the world and then to be better distinguished by their practices" (Romero 2018). His provocation appears to draw from the sensibilities of Brazilian poet and one of the founders of modernism, José Oswald de Souza Andrade, whose polemic *Manifesto antropófago* (Cannibal manifesto) attempted to usurp and shift its colonial intentions. Its opening lines—"Cannibalism alone unites us. Socially, Economically. Philosophically."—reference both the historical production of peoples as cannibals and claiming it, foreshadowing a turn on its head. "We want the Carib Revolution," he writes. "We were never catechized. We live in somnambulistic law. We made Christ to be born in Bahia. Or in Belém do Pará" (Andrade and Bary 1991, 38–39). Hunt's directions to the commissioned artists seemed to incite this spirit of resistance, redeploying old terms of violence to new ends. The promotional press release for *Désir Cannibale* explained that the result was a collection that "responds to powerful impulses, desires and fantasies of violence from another time." Hunt proposes that "the impulse of cannibal desire then becomes a state of consciousness . . . a way of thinking and thinking about the world" (Brebion 2018, author's translation).

KELLY SINNAPAH MARY

In this chapter, I offer a close reading of the works of one of the nine artists featured in Hunt's exhibition, Kelly Sinnapah Mary, examining how she "thinks and thinks about" her world in relationship to this shadow of cannibalistic accusation. Born in Guadeloupe in 1981, Sinnapah Mary is a descendant of Indian indentured workers who were brought to the island to work on plantations in 1861. About forty thousand indentures had traveled to Guadeloupe, but poor treatment and living conditions resulted in a very high mortality rate that quickly reduced the Indian population by as much as 25 percent. Today, the population of Indo-Guadeloupeans numbers around thirty-six thousand, comprising 10 percent of the total population (this count excludes a number of multiethnic people with Indian roots). Except for the years she trained in Visual Art at the University of Toulouse in France, Sinnapah Mary has continued to live and work from her hometown of Saint Francois, the southeasternmost point of the island. Her practice, I suggest, operates in a similar way to that of puhngah—the joke and the game—as well as some elements of Colin Robinson's politics and the Laveauxes' celebratory toast, as an answer to accusations of animality not with a demonstration of "civility" but with a refusal to take on this burden of proof. Arguably, her works boldly embrace her animality.

NOTEBOOK OF NO RETURN

Sinnapah Mary's installation of paintings and objects created for *Désir, Notebook of No Return*, conveys her reflections about the history of her ancestors, Indians brought to the Caribbean as indentured workers by the British to Guadeloupe to replace Africans on plantations following the abolition of slavery in the mid-nineteenth century. *Notebook of No Return* is titled after Aimé Césaire's epic 1939 poem *Cahier d'un retour au pays natal*, although the artist notably drops the "native land" portion of the Martinican French philosopher's title. Taking Hunt's proposition seriously, Sinnapah Mary's work offers a compelling response to the historical animalization of Black/Brown Caribbean peoples. Refusing the common postcolonial practice of having to prove ourselves "not animal" in order to claim our condition as human, she instead boldly affirms her—and by extension our—animality in a visual historicization of her own existence in Guadeloupe and that of her indentured ancestors, evident in both her representation of the Indo-Caribbean body in relationship to and continuous with those of animals and in her demand for a more complex rendering of her (and our) subjectivity, turning both colonial violences of dehumanization and racist essentialism on their head.

Notebook of No Return is a continuing series of installations composed primarily of oil paintings on canvas and cloth. In its first exhibited iteration at *Désir Cannibale*, the project comprised two large painted textile tapestries, three oil paintings, and a mixed-media sculpture formed on a small rug. The dominant colors of the paintings are dark-green, brown, and black hues, with smaller and pointed details in bright red. The human protagonist in each work is recognizable as the artist herself, with her signature plaited hair, dark skin, and facial and body structure. This form of self-representation is consistent with others made over the course of Sinnapah Mary's practice, whether in photography and video or in drawings and on canvas. Consistent with the organizing theme of the exhibition, dismembered bodies appear in all three of the paintings in *Désir*. Throughout the different components of *Notebook of No Return*, Sinnapah Mary refuses the colonial demand to prove oneself not cannibal, not wild, and therefore not animal, and instead evokes cannibalism, often jarringly, to acknowledge her animality and disrupt the violent intentions of the colonial slur.

Two of the paintings in the series reference well-known children's stories. In one, Sinnapah Mary restages the children's tale "Little Red Riding Hood" (plate 2). On the canvas, a large black wolf faces the lower half of a corpse that is painted to resemble a pork chop. The setting is dark, thick jungle grasses. A figure recognizable as Sinnapah Mary carries a basket, like Red Riding Hood, and is holding a machete—perhaps an allusion to the type of cutlass that indentured laborers used to cut sugarcane—and is staring at the wolf. The continuous wardrobe and thorn markers covering both halves of Sinnapah Mary's figure indicate that the split body is hers. The background plant in this and other paintings from the series is *Sansevieria trifasciata*, also known as "mother-in-law's tongue," "Saint George's sword," "snake plant," or "tiger's tail." Native to West Africa, the plant is now ubiquitous worldwide.

Prior to the completion of the works for *Notebook of No Return*, Sinnapah Mary explained (in an interview with me at her studio in Pombiray, Guadeloupe, in May 2018) that the inspiration for this painting was a traumatic encounter she experienced as a young girl at school. The elementary school she attended in Pombiray was composed almost entirely of Indo-Caribbean students. In the memory recalled in her painting, a group of Indo-Caribbean girls was ostracizing the only Afro-Caribbean student in the class. She recalled feeling scared and confused, unsure what made the girls different from one another, and finding herself identifying with both the predators and the victim in the scene. In her review of *Désir Cannibale*, critic Dominique Brebion characterized this representation as "a disconcerting reversal of the fate generally reserved for the Indian fraction of the population" (2018, author's translation). Brebion's comment and Sinnapah Mary's story of the painting's inspiration reveal an important detail about the political context in which

Chapter Four

descendants of Indian indentured laborers exist: at once marginalized from dominant representations of the Caribbean, particularly as evidenced by the near absence of Indo-Caribbean artists in recent surveys of Caribbean contemporary art and its institutions, as I have discussed; and, as Shalini Puri has shown in *The Caribbean Postcolonial*, also complicit with and sometimes productive of its forms of anti-Black racism (Gosine 2016b; Puri 2004).

The "confusion" Sinnapah Mary experiences in the traumatic encounter is typical of the perpetual tensions of belonging that characterize Caribbean life in general, pulled between reproduction and rejection of colonial violence and contemporary American imperialism, and demands of formations of ethnic, racial, religious, and cultural belonging. Less common, perhaps, is how Sinnapah Mary contends with them in this painting, engaging the very colonial tools used to dehumanize Indigenous peoples, Africans, and Asians. Sinnapah Mary is both the split human corpse and the carnivorous animal in the painting, and both are linked to violence. Reading the work through her explanation of its source, we find everyone in Guadeloupe implicated in a confusing tribalistic war—who is the predator on Sinnapah Mary's canvas, the knife-wielding woman or the wolf? If we read the wolf as representational of her classmates, is Sinnapah Mary suggesting that ethnic tribalism is a feature of our animal instinct? That is not to say that racial tribalism is itself natural (or unnatural) but that racial identification perhaps provides an available and easily accessible means through which the natural need for group belonging—like that of all social animals—can be exercised. Perhaps what we witness on Sinnapah Mary's canvas is not so much a "reversal," as Brebion suggests, but a statement about the tribalistic drive of humans, which will always result in the ostracization of the less powerful by the more powerful, regardless of which kind of human is in the position of power. If the wolf in Sinnapah Mary's painting stands in place of her Indo-Caribbean classmates, is the artist alluding to the corruptive impulse in everyone to claim the privileges of being in the dominant group in any setting? Is it possible to also read the scene as a critique of ethnocentric Indo-Guadeloupean politics? The figure in the painting has likely mutilated herself, because the cut is so sharp and clean and, I would suggest, clearly not the result of an attack from the wolf (which is nevertheless ready to devour her). Is she contesting the usefulness of an ethnocentric response, one that is certainly not unique to the Francophone Caribbean?

References to the history of Indo-Guadeloupeans are also visible in the second painting, which was used as the poster image to promote *Désir Cannibale*, and in which Sinnapah Mary casts herself as Cinderella (plate 3). Set in the same jungle background, this Cinderella's dismembered feet are still inside her iconic glass slippers, and set aside from her lies one of her arms, severed from her body. The figure's face and arms are covered with thorns, and the Hindu/Indian conch is visible in the hand at the end of the severed arm. In the third painting (plate 4), which echoes common representations of Hindu gods and goddesses riding on animals, Sinnapah Mary is riding a large ram, but the machete/cutlass in her hand suggests that she has decapitated it.[1] Because the mutilation in each of these three works appears to be inflicted by Sinnapah Mary, we might read her practice as self-interrogative. In separate interviews with myself and literary scholar Lisa Outar, the artist expressed her own sense of deep fracturing from her Indian heritage and culture. Her paternal and maternal grandparents practiced two religions, Catholicism and Hinduism. Her paternal grandfather was a Hindu pundit (priest), but when she was a child, her father became a Jehovah's Witness, as did, eventually, her (once-reluctant) mother: "My brother and I grew up in this religion, which formed a bubble around us that, by and large, cut us off from Indian culture in Guadeloupe. The Indian ceremonies were forbidden for Jehovah's Witnesses. My parents were interested neither in cultural events oriented to the Indian diaspora nor to the languages spoken by our ancestors" (Outar 2016, 196). Sinnapah Mary indicates that her parents' conversion cut her off from "Indian culture," a relationship that parallels the French state's suppression of Indian languages, religions, and practices, and its structured assimilation of descendants of indentureship. The literal cut in her paintings, as she explains, is an apt visualization of her feelings about her sense of her culture. Enacting Hunt's call for artists to view cannibal desire as a catalyst for self-reflection, Sinnapah Mary observed, in our interview in Guadeloupe prior to her exhibit, that "becoming aware of my story and my misunderstanding about my identity made me feel uncomfortable. . . . It was as if I had awakened one day from my limbs. . . . I was missing pieces of me." As she is holding the machete in the images, however, it adds an element of suggestive self-mutilation: Is it the Indo-Guadeloupean community's ethnocentrism that is self-destructive?

The artist says she also feels cut off from other forms of Indian community established in Guadeloupe, which, she believes, are stuck to an essentializing form of identity. For example, at the first International Festival of Coolitude—organized as a celebration of the histories and stories of indentureship in the Caribbean and its diaspora—held in Guadeloupe in May 2018, representations of often-imagined "authentic" Indians were circulated despite the stated foundational theoretical commitment of festival founder Khal Torabully's conceptual framework against cultural essentialism. Demonstrating

Chapter Four

the persistence of an essentializing ethnic identity politics, festival organizers even brought in "authentic" Indians who lived in neighboring St. Martin
to cook "authentic" Indian food, believing that their own creolized, Asian-
influenced local cuisine would somehow be lesser, much to my disappoint-
ment, and to some other conference-goers. Similarly, no Indo-Guadeloupeans
were permitted space as speakers at the event, and deference was again given
to French citizens and continental Indians—many of whom had never before visited the Caribbean—to pontificate about "the coolies." Rather than
inviting artists from the region—who are grappling with the afterlife of colonialism, slavery, and indentureship—to share their work, the event's gallery
space was allotted to a Mauritian British artist instructed to paint specific
scenes of arrival. The self-immolation in Sinnapah Mary's paintings may be
read as an interrogation of her family's and her own acts of distancing from
certain cultural forms of Indianness. They may alternatively or simultaneously be read as the self-inflicted wounds of cultural essentialism to the Indo-
Guadeloupean community as a whole, whereby the creolized Indian is considered "lesser" than "real" Indians, resulting in the kind of dynamic that was
observed at the Coolitude festival.

Other works in *Notebook of No Return* allude to these tensions around
the representation of authentic identity, including the two large embroidered
tapestries occupying its center wall. Their gold lines and tassels, and the presence and placement of European figures (possibly Greek maidens/goddesses),
convey a classical European sensibility and, thus, colonial heritage. In one,
Sinnapah Mary, recognizable again through her plaited hair, morphs into a
figure that is part crab, part conch. The conch is a common symbol in representations and rituals of Hinduism. Hindu gods are often depicted with the
item, and Hindu pundits (priests) will often loudly blow a conch shell during
ceremonies. Again, the bodies shown in the work are dismembered. Through
this image, the artist pointedly situates herself in the heritage of colonization
and the fracturing of cultures. But through her representation as part conch,
part crab, part human, she also gestures toward creolization and its perpetual re-creation of culture through the narrative of Hindu reincarnation. The
image in full can be read as neither celebratory nor condemnatory: she presents *what is*. The second tapestry shows a severed head against a backdrop
of goats and (possibly Greek or European) maidens. The dark head is covered
in thorns, but the mouth is open, as is one visible eye. Through this image,
Sinnapah Mary seems to allude to the impossibility of colonialism's total victory and the conviction that its destructive intent will never entirely succeed.
The piece seems to suggest that the colonizer is the cannibal, performing the

act of removing the head, but then the head returns to life, in an afterlife of its own, to return in a zombielike fashion and a gaze trained on the colonizer, recognizing the violence through the act of looking back.

At the foot of the tapestries and paintings, Sinnapah Mary installed a sculpture in which a bag made from seashells rests on sand in the middle of a carpet. This sculpture ties the work to both the sea journeys of indentured laborers and the contemporary existence of their descendants, signaled by the modern design of the bag. She offers no ready answers or directions, preferring instead to emphasize irresolution. The playful positioning of an element on the floor, below the paintings and tapestries, stresses the sense that the works can be viewed from multiple perspectives, that the ground of her work is unstable, sometimes on the wall, sometimes below, undermining the traditional placement of art. In its literal use of a carpet, the work grounds and brings into the everyday and the domestic the kinds of dynamics depicted in the seemingly floating, fantastical engagements of the wall-mounted pieces.

Enhancing the drama created by the positioning of the works across different surfaces, the situation of *Notebook of No Return* within a three-walled room plays with the tension of the "fourth wall" in performance, a reckoning with its constitution and/or destruction. The bright-pink walls echo elements of the tapestries but also provide an emphatic contrast with the harsher tones of the artist's paintings. The space of *Notebook of No Return* is at once tragic and tender, dangerous and hopeful, suggesting the kind of ambivalence that necessarily runs through any creolization process: the losses that pile up and the mourning that endures must be inflected with hope and a sense of the new possibilities that emerge from re-creation. In Guadeloupe, Sinnapah Mary says, the commonality between the descendant of the African slave and the Indian indentured laborer "is to be found in the destruction of the self during the crossing which is symbolic of a deconstruction which leads to a reconstruction" (Outar 2016, 202).

A year after *Désir Cannibale*, Sinnapah Mary created a new version of her *Notebook* series for the exhibition *Present Passing: South by Southeast Asia* at the Osage Foundation in Hong Kong. The paintings were again shown in an adjusted installation format in Miami at the end of 2019, as part of the Art Basel program. In Hong Kong, *Notebook* comprised a three-walled installation of paintings and objects. On the right wall were two small paintings, one depicting a large, decapitated fish that is swallowing the artist whole—the skirt and shoes identify the figure as Sinnapah Mary—and the other of a miniature version of the artist facing a large decapitated, bloodied head that appears to be, we read from the hair, of an African figure. On the left wall, a satchel hung from a wooden rack. Beneath it was a wooden bench. From the top of the bench flowed a set of locks of her signature braided hair, and beneath it, a pair of decapitated feet. In the middle hung the large defining painting of this set, which also carries the title *Alice & Goliath* (plate 5). Another self-portrait, this time it takes on the two personas indicated in its title.

Returning to the same moment that inspired the *Désir* paintings, Sinnapah Mary says she sees parallels between her experience navigating her identity in Guadeloupe and the characters in the two referenced works, Lewis Carroll's *Alice's Adventures in Wonderland* and the biblical tale of David and Goliath. The white rabbit appears at the beginning of Carroll's novel as the figure who initially lures Alice down the rabbit hole into the mystical Wonderland. Similarly, Sinnapah Mary says, *Notebook* is meant to "arouse curiosity" and lead her audience to examine their history. In her installation, the form of White Rabbit lies on the floor, sewed from the blue gingham of her school uniform—a "half apron," the artist says—and next to it are the rabbit's bloodied, decapitated feet. White Rabbit in this sense, says Sinnapah Mary, "is a metaphor of the passive teacher" that she had in primary school, one who did nothing to interrupt the scene of interethnic violence that traumatized and continues to haunt her. But this Alice is also David *and* Goliath. Explaining the personal significance of the story, the artist recalls:

> When I was a child, my father often told me the story of "David and Goliath." I found [it] interesting to confront these two characters from the Bible and the other from [a] children's story. The story of David and Goliath is extraordinary because it tells that David was a young shepherd. One day, his country was invaded by the Philistines, a people of giants that measured about three meters high. David was enlisted in the army but the Philistines offered them a singular fight, to face off against Goliath, the best warrior on the other side. David had a bag of six pebbles and his opponent was heavily armed. As the fight began, David threw three stones at Goliath's head and one against his belly. Goliath fell dead. The Philistines were defeated and departed. David became king.

After he told the story, Sinnapah Mary's father would end with its message: "We must not trust appearances because even the smallest can triumph over the strongest." In her practice, the artist transposes this tale to convey the parallel fight of the colonized against the colonizer. Her father's emphasis on the "smallest" might also be read as an allusion to the minority status of Indo-Guadeloupeans on the island.

There is thus an interesting inversion of David and Goliath with Alice at play in Sinnapah Mary's work. In a smaller painting, the artist appears as Alice/David facing the large head of the decapitated (and African signing) Goliath. In the main, central painting, however, she is Alice/Goliath, as indicated by the largeness of her figure, looming over the small village. In this painting, Alice/Goliath is the defeated victim, trapped in a fishing net and giving the appearance that she is pulled in many directions as she struggles to free herself from captivity. Sinnapah Mary's braids are caught in the mouth of a goat, but we are not sure if the animal is help or hindrance. One of Alice/Goliath's legs is also missing and not even making an appearance in the painting.

This scene also echoes the part of the *Wonderland* plot where young Alice is stuck in a house after drinking the drink that makes her grow. "Alice is a very curious little girl," says the artist. "I found myself in her, in the sense that at one point in my life, I had the need to know more about my identity, I wanted to see a little further than this village where I grew up, to learn my story, the history of my ancestors, of the indentured workers." Notably, the stories she has turned into in her attempt to communicate this longing are replete with animal characters that are connected in complex and ambivalent ways to the artist, and neither human nor nonhuman animal can be marked as hero or villain in Sinnapah Mary's visual storytelling.

HUMAN ANIMALS, ANIMAL HUMANS

The determined equation of human life, in terms of not only its "value" but its capability of violence and destructive harm, is further underlined in *Notebook of No Return*'s challenge to a culturally dominant human/animal dichotomy. "Not animal" is the defining quality of humanness, and among humans, hierarchies of worth have been predicated on the degree of one's animality. In colonial and even contemporary discourses, nonwhite people have often been located somewhere between animal and human, and therefore have struggled for and prioritized recognition as the latter. A frequently cited case demonstrating the violent animalization of nonwhite people is that of the caging and exhibition of Sara Baartman by Dutch settler-colonists. In the early nineteenth century, Baartman was taken to Europe, where she was caged, put on display, and later sold to an animal trainer and examined as the potential "missing link" between humans and animals. After her death, her corpse was split into pieces and exhibited in parts at the Sorbonne, a suitable location since Paris was also home to an actual "human zoo" of colonized peoples from around the world. Colonizers' investment in animalizing others was tied to anxieties about their own animalistic desires, especially sexual expression. Consequently, as previously discussed, laws about bestiality, interracial mixing, and sodomy were bundled together, with the onus on colonized subjects to prove themselves not perverse, not homosexual, not animal. Fears about the hypersexuality of Asians (particularly Asian women) would become expressed as hysteria about overpopulation (cf. Gosine 2015). Given this history of animalizing nonwhite people, representations of us/them as animals in contemporary popular culture are loaded. In recent years, controversies that have been circulated internationally, such as clothing brand H&M's advertising image of a young Black boy in a "monkey" sweatshirt on the store's online site for its European markets (Bever 2018), actress Roseanne Barr's tweets calling Black women apes (Koblin 2018), and the persistent representation of Barack and Michelle Obama as primates (BBC News 2016), have understandably generated much public outrage (cf. Joseph 2011). Indeed, the animalization of Black people by characterizing them as primates is a persistent device that remains popular in American right-wing culture (Chapman 2018).

Sinnapah Mary's choice to animalize humans and show continuity between human and animal is, therefore, a contentious one. Importantly, the veracity of racialized animalizing strategies may likely not register as violently to Sinnapah Mary as they would if she were Black/Afro-Caribbean, although she is often read as such. But it is also true that the animals she uses in her work are not the ones that have been deployed to advance racism. In making lateral comparisons, however, Sinnapah Mary undoes the hierarchical placement of us, as humans, above and separate from other animals, including those with which we share no evolutionary ties. The mythologizing Western world order dictated by the Christian patriarchal construct of the "great chain of being" organizes all organisms into a complex hierarchy, with man above woman, animal below human, fish below land animal, plant below fish, and stone below plant, so as to allow no object in existence to escape ranking and evaluative categorization, an exertion that suggests anxiety about what might happen to those at the top of the chain if the relative worth of all other creatures were to be left undefined—betraying a similar anxiety rather than a lateral, nonhierarchical comparison, as engaged by Sinnapah Mary's depiction of nonprimate animals. For example, the black wolf in the painting from the story of Little Red Riding Hood is not racially marked. In fact, it's not clear from the image whether the wolf represents Indo-Guadeloupeans, Afro-Guadeloupeans, or, as I believe, potentially all humans. The artist's elaboration of the inspiration behind the painting supports this conclusion, as she seems to be drawing an equation between the way Indo-Guadeloupeans are marginalized and the violence inflicted on the Afro-Caribbean girl in her childhood classroom. The image of the wolf is used in her work to characterize human survivalist and tribalist drives across ethnicities. Pairing the image of the wolf with her self-mutilated body may then be possibly viewed as a criticism of ethnocentrism, as she might characterize the strategies of some Indo-Guadeloupean organizations as a response to racism. Similarly, her painting with the ram does not draw upon any historical racist tropes, but a careful observer will see that it perhaps responds to the colonial fabric of the tapestry, which features goats next to the Greek maidens. In the painting, which mirrors the form and style of Hindu drawings of gods and goddesses, Sinnapah Mary is riding the goat, and has severed its head, but it is a complicated cut. As she rides the decapitated goat, she also implicates herself (and possibly all Guadeloupeans) as complicit with France's continuing colonization.

Sinnapah Mary's works also feature intriguing human-animal hybrids. The Hindu belief in reincarnation is a clear reference point in her aesthetic, a belief that is in notable tension with the hierarchical Western "great chain of being," in its suggestion that there is metamorphic fluidity between beings, but which also comes with its own ordering functions, albeit an ordering that teaches acknowledgment of other life-forms as worthy of respect. In my own community, this belief powerfully structured our lives. Reincarnation was used as a disciplinary tool at my Hindu school. And the only commandment I can recall from Sunday school is to not hurt other living beings: *God is in them as they are in us*, I was told, and I took it to heart. There were, of course, contradictions and selective applications of this philosophy—the same person might be very passionate about the value, care, and protection of one animal but comfortably consume another. Although she was raised as a Jehovah's Witness, this Hindu heritage likely informs Sinnapah Mary's practice as well, but in her renderings of human/animal hybridity, I see a powerful rejection of the animal/human divide that simultaneously underlines the instinctive animality of humans. The crab/conch/human hybrid pictured on one of the tapestries, for instance, uses animals to allude to human anxieties. We might read the conch head/body as a symbol of concealing or protecting our human vulnerability, while the crab/human legs symbolize a kind of wild animalistic freneticism.

Sinnapah Mary has also produced hybridized human-animals in other work. In 2016 I invited the artist to collaborate with me on *1, 2*, "a children's book for adults" that narrated a story in which "Joshna," a young Caribbean boy, faces sexual overtures from his older cousin. This situation is not unique. Nobel laureate V. S. Naipaul recalled his own experience of such a scenario as a child growing up in Trinidad. "I was myself subjected to sexual abuse by an older cousin, Boysie. I was corrupted, I was assaulted," he told his biographer Patrick French in *The World Is What It Is*. "I was about six or seven. It was done in a sly, terrible way and it gave me a hatred, a detestation of the homosexual thing. I never went through a period of liking the same sex" (2008, 36). French doubts Naipaul's denial that he was a willing participant in the exchange, "given the similarity in age of the two boys" (36). When Naipaul insists that the encounter constituted assault, French undercuts the author's claim with the observation that "he feared *the idea* that he was a participant in sexual experimentation between male cousins" (36; my emphasis). Revisiting French's text a decade later in his essay "Naipaul's Nightmare," Trinidadian writer Andre Bagoo raises more questions: "Could Naipaul himself have had a more complex relationship with the idea of same-sex desire? Is it possible that his own homophobia was to some extent the expression of internalized conflict, directed at nascent tendencies, tendencies which then triggered shame and self-loathing and the desire to violently squash the legitimacy of such feelings?" (2020, 20).

Joshna's story in *1, 2* sits in the "gray space" between sexual awakening and sexual abuse that often occurs in this period of adolescence and in both its form and content references the myriad ways in which it is socially considered. While large-scale drawings from *1, 2* have been exhibited at galleries, none of the written text was publicly shared. The book came packaged as a sealed book coated in plastic, and its content is intended only for its 108 purchasers, referencing the deafening silence that surrounds the topics of incest and adolescent sexuality. A 2010 UNICEF study of child sex abuse in the Caribbean found that "incest was viewed as prevalent throughout the society but it was felt that such acts were commonly concealed under a 'cloak of silence'" (15). The shame and disgrace that followed revelations of incest were cited as the main reasons for keeping incestuous relationships hidden or unacknowledged. Naipaul himself never mentioned the episode to anyone in his family. Whereas Naipaul is clear about characterizing his experience as assault, however, Joshna's experience in *1, 2* leaves the question more open, since no assault happens. The dissonance between Naipaul's and French's evaluations of the laureate's experience on the one hand seems ridiculous; if Naipaul says he was molested and that the sexual experience with his cousin was unwilling, why should we doubt him? Why is French so cavalier in his dismissal of Naipaul's insistence that the experience was unwelcome and traumatizing? Yet French's reaction is not so surprising because he is aware and he knows that *we* are aware that sexual experimentation does in fact happen between adolescents. At the same time, the paucity of research resulting from the silence surrounding incest and other forms of adolescent sexuality makes that reality difficult to contend with. For example, in "Breaking the Silence: A Multi-Sectoral Approach to Preventing and Addressing Child Sexual Abuse in Trinidad and Tobago," a 2011 report on the to-date largest research and educational initiative on child sexual abuse in the country, the authors explain that "this project focuses primarily on [child sexual abuse] in the home, which may be carried out by relatives, primarily male relatives—fathers, stepfathers, older brothers, cousins etc. Commonly referred to as incest, preliminary explorations using newspaper sources, information from schools, social workers and other research suggest that this comprises a significant component of [child sexual abuse] in Trinidad and Tobago and the region" (Reddock, Reid, and Parpart 2011, 4). While the report condemns child sexual abuse throughout, it also notably continues to list the study's key focus as "CSA/Incest," thus distinguishing the latter from the former and perhaps leaving space for contending with experimentation that does not easily accommodate dominant notions of consensual choice.

To produce *1, 2*, I sent Sinnapah Mary the French translation of the English text, described a few key components of images I would like to see, and left it to her to determine their ultimate representation. I was floored by her choices. Chickens appear in the background of *1, 2*. While chickens do appear in the story, they take center stage in Sinnapah Mary's reimagination of them, becoming indivisible from the human characters (figure 4.2). The central story in *1, 2* is about the encounter between two male cousins, but Sinnapah Mary muddies gender identification in the story. Perhaps playing the characterization of gay men as "hens" (as in Pres*hen*tation College), she puts high-heeled shoes on some of them (figure 4.3). As well, she puts herself in the scene as a hybrid hen/woman figure marked by her trademark plaited hair (figure 4.4). Was this addition an interruption to the male-dominant figuration of the story? Her images appear to place her hen/woman figure as potential protector/rescuer of Joshna (figure 4.5). Sinnapah Mary's commitment to the storytelling, perhaps heightened by the fact of her own mothering of a

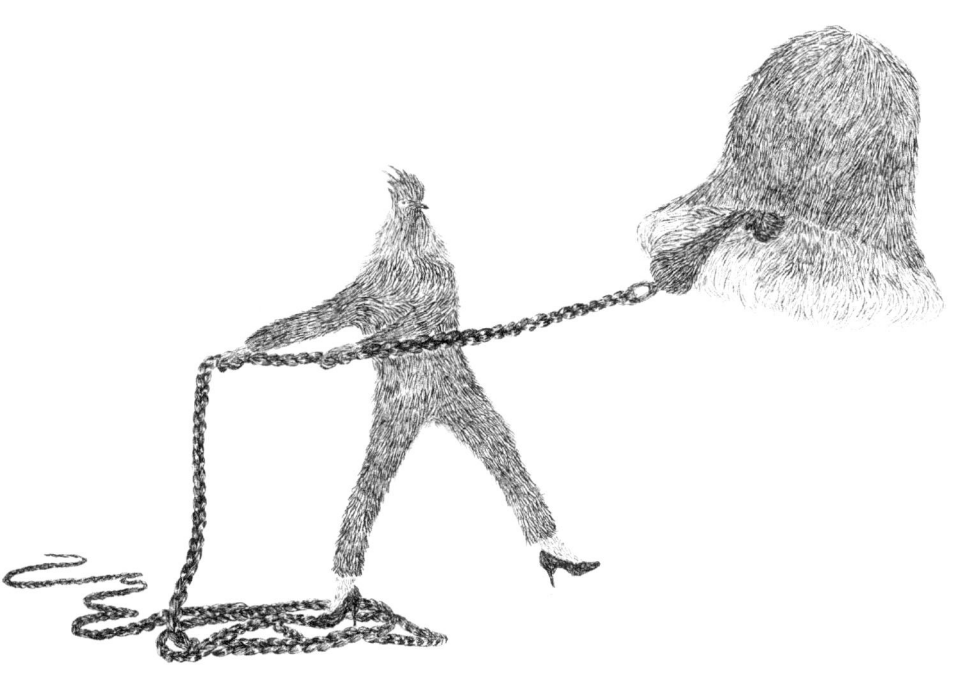

FIGURE 4.2 Kelly Sinnapah Mary, *1, 2*, 2016.

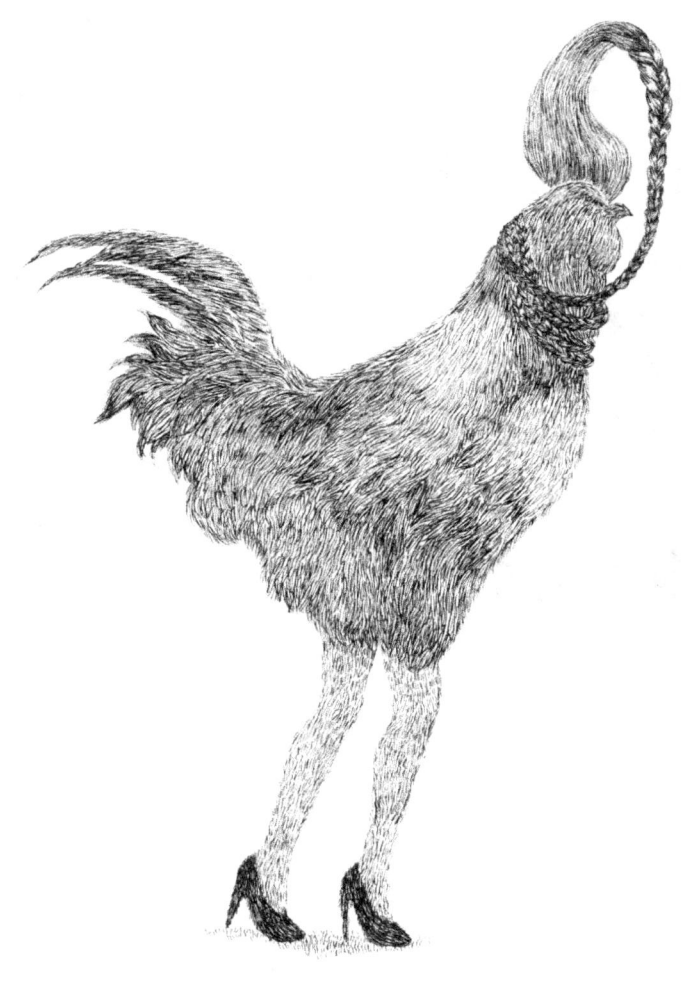

FIGURE 4.3 Kelly Sinnapah Mary, *1, 2*, 2016.

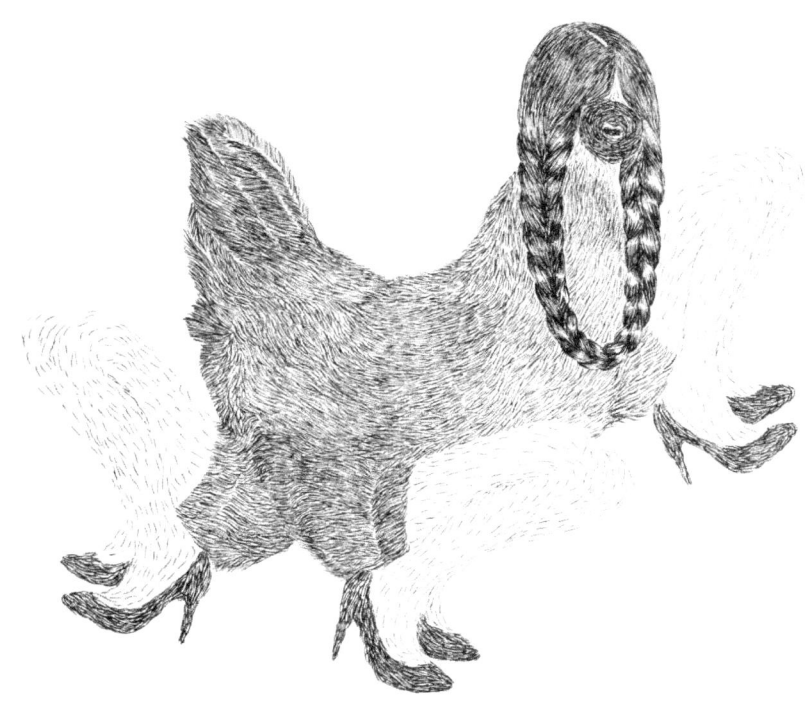

FIGURE 4.4 Kelly Sinnapah Mary, *1, 2,* 2016.

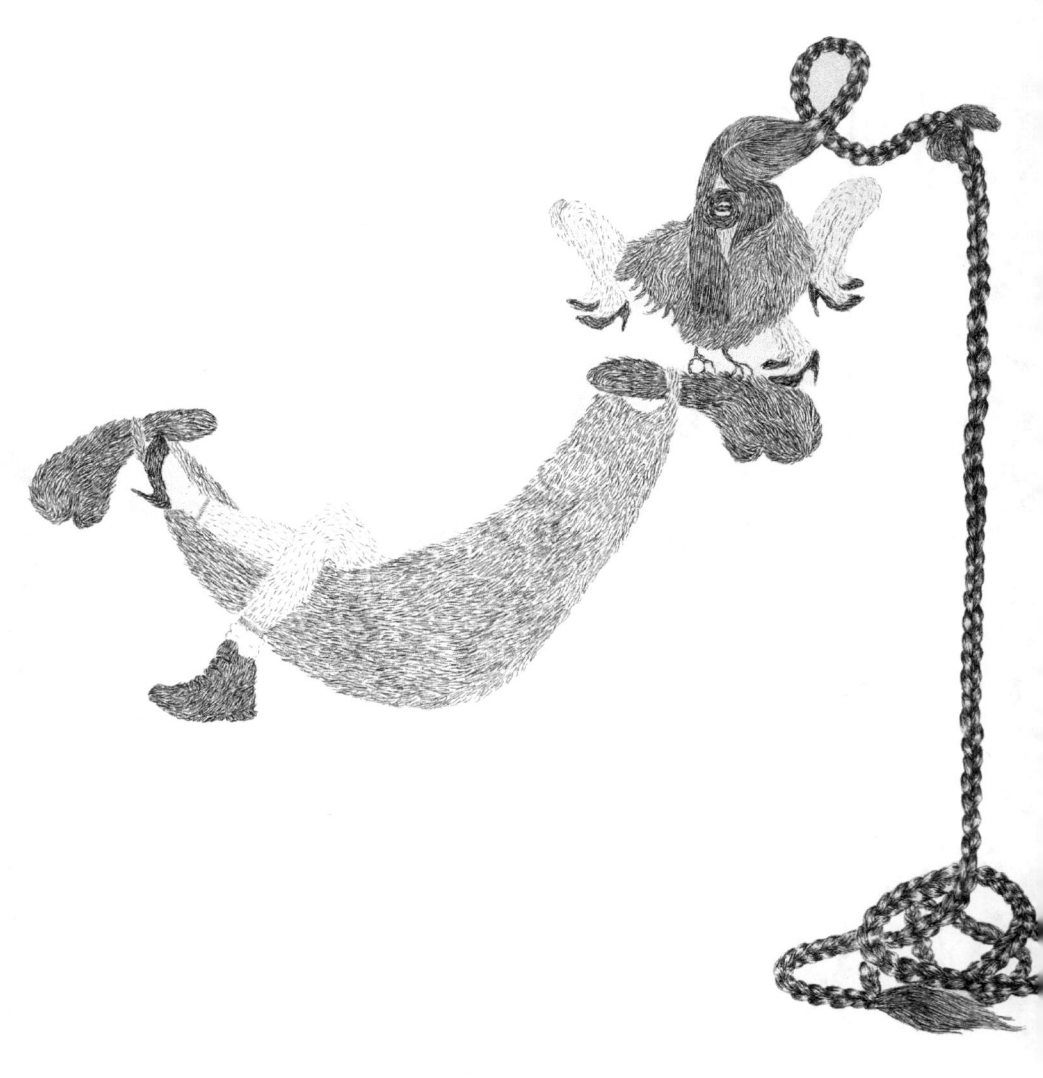

FIGURE 4.5 Kelly Sinnapah Mary, *1, 2,* 2016.

young son that might one day become a "Joshna," meant that she in fact began to raise chickens during the process of making the drawings.

Sinnapah Mary does not just blur the line between human and animal in *1, 2* but appears to reject it altogether. In my story, the chickens take on a protective role against the predatory male cousin. But in Sinnapah Mary's interpretation, the hybridization of the animal and human figures serves to also complicate our understanding of sexual desire as instinctive, animalistic. Similar to Lorraine O'Grady's observation that the sexual act betrays the fiction that humans could civilize themselves out of their animality, Sinnapah Mary links sexual desire and humans' natural animality that neither villainizes nor glorifies nature. Merging the bodies of my story's heroic chickens with those of the vulturine cousin, Sinnapah Mary underlines that both loving sexual desire and violent sexual acts spring from instinctual drive. Recognition of humans' animality is not in itself a solution to any problem but a gesture toward complicated truthfulness.

Human-animal hybridization also features in her 2016 photographic series *Hotmilk*, in which she plays with the myth of Roman twins Remus and Romulus, suckled by a She-Wolf (plate 6). In an interview with the Association internationale des critiques d'art for the Southern Caribbean, Sinnapah Mary explains:

> I took the posture of the wolf for its ambivalence because it takes the image of maternal tenderness and fertility and another side of sexual desire. Legend has it that an altered wolf, descended from the surrounding mountains, rushed to the sound of the wails of Remus and Romulus, and presenting them with the breast, forgot so much of his ferocity that the steward of the king's flock found her caressing her tongue upon his infants. Faustulus . . . took them home and entrusted them to the care of his wife Larentia. According to others, this Larentia was a prostitute to whom the shepherds had given the name of Louve; this is the origin of this wonderful tradition. This new character gives a different vision of the maternal feeling, often very instinctual and unreasonable, bringing the woman closer to the animal. (AICACS 2017, translation mine)

Among the many new works that Sinnapah Mary completed during the lockdown period related to COVID-19 were ones that continued to imagine human/animal hybrids, including one that recalled the scene of bullying of the Afro-

Caribbean student in her classroom that clearly continues to haunt her (plate 7). Here again, there is no line between human and nonhuman animal, with her torturing classmates now appearing as cartoonish, ravenous wolves. In this series, the artist also represents herself as a three-tailed mongoose, as signaled by the figure's feet dressed in her recognizable elementary school shoes. She explains that the main crises that dominated 2020—the pandemic, police violence against Black people, and the US presidential election—made her feel "very mongoose." That is, they produced a kind of distress that resulted in an awareness of her own visceral animality, marked by both feelings of fear and panic and a survivalist instinct. The choice of the mongoose also held specific historical significance. Although she was consciously unaware of its history at the time, the species in which she places herself is the one she is familiar with in her environment. This Javan mongoose was introduced to the Caribbean in the 1870s to control snakes and rats in the sugarcane fields on which her Indian indentured ancestors were working.

VISUAL ART AFTER INDENTURESHIP

In all of these human/animal–animal/human representations, Sinnapah Mary's audiences are asked to recognize and deepen their analysis of Caribbean history, and the complexity of Caribbean peoples' humanness. Rather than depict a familiar and flattened register of circulating Caribbean tropes—the suffering laborer, the violated woman, the innocent child—she instead draws audiences' attention to universally human subconscious drives. It is through this exposure of human animality that she asserts, for example, the fullness of the Indo-Caribbean person. Her self-representation in images and many of the signs and symbols she uses visibilize the historical Indo-Caribbean presence in the region and the community's active shaping of Caribbean history without limiting them to a narrow set of ethnic types.

Sinnapah Mary's embrace of our human animality is a result of her methodological practice as an artist. While she is clearly very interested in and seriously considers the histories of the communities and places that surround her, Sinnapah Mary maintains a deliberately self-interrogative autobiographical posture in her work. This stance has worked to liberate her from the demands of representation that burden nonwhite artists, allowing her to confidently cite—and therefore value—the details of her personal experience, and to enter into more complex sets of questions about identity, justice, and representation. Cultural critic Kobena Mercer's observation about the conundrums facing Black artists in the 1990s is still broadly applicable today: "Artists positioned in the margins of institutional spaces of cultural production are burdened with the impossible role of speaking as 'representatives' in the sense that they are expected to 'speak for' the Black communities from which they come." Mercer further explains that "'representation' concerns not only practices of depiction or textual production, but practices of delegation and substitution such that, at the point of reception, the Black artist is expected to *speak* for the Black communities as if she or he were its political 'representative'" (1990, 65). I would add that this demand for representation is exercised from both scholarly and commercial components of the art world. The former is motivated by an investment in the appearance of fair treatment, coded in the language of "diversity" and "inclusion." Art markets tend to prefer works that can be easily categorized and explained to buyers. In the sphere of Indo-Caribbean visual arts, the most circulated images might be described as "representative" of Indo-Caribbean peoples: images of cane fields and indentures, boats and seas, and references to aesthetics of Hindu rituals.[2]

Many kinds of artistic practice reflect the truth that our experiences are always produced both through the structuring forces of our histories and the individual agency we exercise. But there are certainly variations in how openly and confidently this is expressed. Sinnapah Mary's work registers as confidently embracing the particularities of her life that lend themselves to broader social significance. The artist explains: "I do not separate my artistic process from my own person. Regardless of the action performed, a cross stitch, or a photographic staging, everything in my work can be a hint of my personal life, of my experience. Photography as well as video allow me to stage multiple identities. Using accessories (wigs and hoods), I can assume ambiguous roles" (Outar 2016, 200). Over time, she has repeated the plaited hairstyle she wore as a child, which is both very specific to her experience but also deployed to make statements about historical continuity. This hair is "an extension of identity and a memorial that carries a historic burden, that of the coolies chosen for the colonies who came to replace the former slaves refusing to continue to work on the plantations," she explains. In the video *I'm a Hill Coolie*, the act of braiding enacts

> a process of identity reconstruction by a social class considered low in India. Braiding hair is here seen as a metaphor for the integration of indentured laborers, which was not done without difficulty. The signs are there to indicate that, for example, some of them voluntarily chopped off the parts of their name that sounded very Indian. They also left their mother tongue behind for Créole. This aspiration to integration was a real fight

for dignity because we had to be recognized within the Caribbean community. The various actions in the cross-weaving of the braiding, the assembling in order to form a whole seems to me a nice metaphor to speak of the reconstruction of the identity of Indian indentured workers. (Outar 2016, 202)

Thus, her reference to a very specific detail of her body serves to tell a broader story. Sinnapah Mary has previously permitted herself to share a very intimate sense of vulnerability in one of her first projects to be publicly shared, titled *Vagina*. This installation was constructed as a replica of the artist's bedroom with images of vaginas appearing throughout, including one version made from pins in a cushion beneath the phrase *Touch Me*. This installation simultaneously channeled her own anxieties and experiences as well as acts of sexual violence in the Caribbean and globally. Through her explicit invocation of her own body and sexuality, Sinnapah Mary speaks about the challenges faced by women in general. The intimacy of the subject and the bedroom concept incite a powerful and conflicted response from the audience; is the invitation to "touch" a result of Sinnapah Mary's desires, a recognition of our violent impulse, or possibly both?

Her human-animal-hybridizing and human-animal-equating work reaches even more broadly. While her interest in animals has been shaped in part by telling children's stories to her young son over the past two years, as well as to the animals that she encounters in Guadeloupe, this confident pursuit of her instincts on the canvas manages to provide reflection about the human condition in general. Artists from marginalized communities are rarely given space to offer insight into the human condition *in general*. Rather, whatever they might say about the human condition is conditionally framed as relatable to just the "group" to which they belong. Sinnapah Mary's *Notebook of No Return* reflects on the experience and aftermath of indentureship to say something about the human condition: that we are animals, all of us. Furthermore, the animality signed in her work is viewed neither as curse nor promise but as an observation of conditions that *are*. In navigating a path after slavery, after indentureship, perhaps after colonization, it is perhaps better to recognize this condition rather than to actively suppress it.

Sinnapah Mary's practice signals the future of visual artistic practice after indentureship. At the 2018 Coolitude festival, the only dedicated artistic space was reserved for one painter's renderings of the arrival of indentured laborers in Mauritius. The scenes were easily recognizable as dominant tropes employed in the illustration of Indo-Caribbean history: men on ships, workers in the cane field, pious women covered in veils, places of worship. These indentured laborers were indistinguishable from each other, none conveying any kind of specific story that might register them as having a complex human subjectivity to the audience, a consequence of the representational thrust that is unfortunately characteristic of many Caribbean representational projects about Indo-Caribbean people. Sinnapah Mary's confidently self-citational practice, one that registers the intimate contours of her experience, permits her more fertile ground for both examining the aftermath of indentureship and claiming the fullness of indentured laborers and the humanity of their descendants. The allusions to human animality in *Notebook of No Return* radically shift our trajectory, refusing the repetitious anxieties to locate our bodies and identities somewhere, or to subject them entirely to the violences of colonialism. She charges forward instead, assuming our humanity and confident that considerations of our own experiences—as individuals or members of groups—might have something to tell us about the human condition in general. Through its recognition of human animality, Sinnapah Mary's work also refuses the politics of respectability that have demanded that colonized people prove their humanity, *that we are not animals.* Erasing the line between human and animal, and making representations of human-animal hybrids, Sinnapah Mary boldly declares: *We are animal; so what?*

Natures' Wild   5

ARE WE ANIMALS? A brief moment at the end of the short documentary video *I Am Isabella* shows how jarring this question can feel to some respondents.[1] A profile of one of the litigants in the McEwan case that was produced by the Caribbean International Resources Network and Trans United Guyana, the video features principal subject and defendant Isabella (Seyon) Persaud recalling her/his experiences growing up in Guyana, including those of homelessness, drug use, and violence.[2] "We were always treated like trash," she says, speaking against the backdrop of Georgetown Botanical Gardens, a place that police regularly surveilled and from which they historically have pushed out people, like Persaud, marked as transgressive. About the case, which was pending at the time, she emphasizes, "I want to go to court and be treated the same way as a human being should be treated." Persaud adds, "You're dealing with animal, you're dealing with human being." While uttering *animal*, her head shakes as if to indicate, "No, we are not animals," and her strained face suggests that emotions were running high during the taping. She surely meant to say, "You're *not* dealing with animal[s]." This absent *not*—eclipsed in Persaud's speech at a moment of racialized, gendered criminalization experienced as profound trauma as she is charged to prove and perhaps to question what she *is*—demonstrates the irresolution of the conundrum: Are we humans *not animal*?

Persaud's conflicted response corresponds strikingly with Sigmund Freud's characterization of civilization as the product of the repression, sublimation, *or* introversion of humans' animalistic instincts. The Father of Psychoanalysis struggled with the task of discerning how much distance to put between "us" and "them."[3] The intensity of Persaud's absent *not* in the video clip specifically reveals the particular onus placed on people like her in the Caribbean—that is, to disprove our animality. For centuries, Indigenous peoples and descendants of enslaved peoples and indentured workers in the region have been subject to this dehumanization through the historical characterization of them as *more animal, less human*. Laura Facey's 2015 installation *62 Men and 63 Women*, in which she reproduces 1820 ledgers from the holdings at a property in St. Ann, Jamaica, is pointedly illustrative of this process. The ledgers ascribe higher values to some animals than to some humans. That this historical injury remains viscerally felt by Caribbean people, even in banal encounters, speaks to its endurance. In 2017, an Indo-Caribbean friend of mine wrote a Facebook post about being enraged after encountering a white woman who had given her dog the same common Hindi name as his mother. "I was stunned," he confessed. "I wish I could have said something to them. I would have said, 'Do you know what [name] means? That's [a] name we give to people. It's my mother's name [that] you are insulting. There is a long history of white people owning South Asians as laborers by contract. You are terrible people.'" So traumatized are we by a long history of strategies of dehumanization achieved through our animalization that even a seemingly banal gesture such as a woman telling her dog with an Indian name to sit unleashed provoked hurt and fury in my friend. No such panic ensues for people unburdened by a history of racialized animalization. On my apartment floor, one (white, European) neighbor and another neighbor's dog share the same name, and neither Sophie is bothered.

"To be no-Man is to be not-quite-human," Sylvia Wynter wrote. "Yet that plot . . . on which the slave grew food for his/her subsistence, carried over a millennially *other* conception of the human to that of Man's" (D. Scott 2000, 166). Given the fact of their permeable boundaries and entwined histories, especially in the Caribbean, I am not convinced that an*other* conception is entirely discernible from European "Man," but the various examples of social justice activism, artistic interventions, and everyday acts described throughout this project reveal persistent efforts toward alternative cosmogonies. We witness resistances play out in scenes like Shari Petti's encounter at the passport office: on the one hand, the state law demands that Petti civilize/humanize her nonwhite body through conscription to a colonial dress code, but on the other, the attempts by most people around her at the office to help her elide the rules, as well as her own disregard for them, demonstrate a rejection of the demands of European "Man." I can list numerous other examples of this dissonance from Trinidad and Tobago, a country where the bacchanalia of Carnival and evangelical conservatism exist simultaneously and generate dominant and conflicting discourses of morality. These contradictory lived experiences trouble the cosmogony of European "Man": the outright refusal to submit to our measure against that man—without necessitating investment in an alternative one—disrupts its impact. Kelly Sinnapah Mary's paintings, Colin Robinson's politics, and even the puhngah joke and Photography Club game respond to the accusation of savagery with emboldened indifference to anxieties about marking the line between human and animal. They reply confidently: *We are animal. So what?*

Only in the past decade have I become aware of and begun to grapple with the ways in which the demand to show oneself as *human, not animal* has shaped my development. The catalyst for this reckoning was the unexpected torment of my first experience of heartbreak, a moment in which my visceral, subconscious feelings upended my reliably cautious and disciplined conscious. At the time, I began to form friendships with a new community of artists in New York, including Leor Grady, Sur Rodney (Sur), Geoffrey Hendricks, Esther K. Smith, and most significantly Lorraine O'Grady. From these engagements, I found new appreciation for artistic production as a method of analysis. My visual arts practice was an impulsive, unrationalized consequence of these circumstances but can now explain that the appeal lay in art's capacity to channel subconscious knowledge and better express complexity in ways that were not easily facilitated by my toolbox of social scientific practices. Artistic practice became a different kind of search for truth, one that demanded a deeper level of introspective reflection and the confidence both to trust unconscious and subconscious instincts and to publicly share vulnerabilities.

My first effort, *Wardrobes (A Preview)*, was an exhibition of four objects presented at New York's Fashion Institute of Technology (FIT) in March 2011 that signaled some of the shifts that were beginning to emerge in my think-

Chapter Five

ing about the onus placed on Caribbean people to be *human, not animal.* My exploration continued to develop over the next decade, resulting in the works referenced and elaborated in this chapter. Generated from the three solo exhibitions representing my practice over this period (*All the Flowers* at the Robert McLaughlin Gallery [RMG] in Oshawa [2018], *Coolie Coolie Viens* at the Glenhyrst Gallery in Brantford and at the McIntosh Gallery in London [2017 and 2018–19]; and *rêvenir* at Medulla Gallery in Port of Spain [2020]), these works are themselves my analysis of the history, meaning, and impact of the civilizing imperatives that have been placed on Caribbean people since the colonial encounter. Following O'Grady's artistic practice in particular, they entwine the personal and social historical but refuse broad claims of representation. I identify and consider the histories and related networks of power that interact with my own agency in response to the demand to be *human, not animal,* but I do not make the case for universalizing my experience.

(MADE IN LOVE)

A photograph of my parents has featured in my visual arts practice right from the start. Taken in a studio just prior to my mother's pregnancy with me, the photograph features the two smiling lovingly at each other. At FIT, I reproduced the image as a fabric print and from it produced wardrobe pieces. Later, the image was the catalyst for my performance series *Cane Portraiture,* in which I invite subjects to pose for photographs against the backdrop of sugarcane (see M. R. Smith 2020). In *Coolie Coolie Viens,* the photograph was transformed into a scored video projection, *(Made in Love)* (plate 8). But the first time I shared the photograph with a public audience was at my 2010 talk at the University of Cincinnati organized by feminist queer scholar Amy Lind. The lecture, "But I Love," was billed as a discussion of sexuality and international development, and I was expected to report on my research in the area, which included my by-then well-circulated master's thesis (published as Gosine 2004) and a stint working as a sexual rights policy adviser at the World Bank. I used the photograph of my parents to draw attention to and problematize the dominant representation of sexuality in international development policies and analysis. This image, I explained, was anathema to my education in the field, beginning with my Canadian undergraduate classes. In my environmental studies and international development studies courses at York University in Toronto, I learned that people like my parents—like all the people I grew up around, like me, the people labeled "Third World, rural people" or, more commonly at that time, "the poor"—were incapable of the complex emotion of *love*. This doctrine was repeated throughout my subsequent education at the Institute of Development Studies at Sussex University in Brighton. In popular expressions of Euro-American culture, companionship, marriage, and children ideally came about from intimate connections between people with individually wired, complex desires. But in the countries of the Global South, marriage was an enforced tradition and children an economic calculation or a consequence of the uneducated, unfettered desires of undercultured masses who mated "like flies," a once very common characterization of Third World people found in the materials we would be assigned to read for class. They/we were animals who paired and reproduced but who lacked the sophistication to experience romantic, human love. This account did not match the people I grew up around, and it definitely bore no resemblance to the relationship I most knew. My parents have always been and remain as annoyingly, one might say outlandishly, affectionate and into each other as they appear to be in this picture. I would confidently go so far to say that *all* of their life decisions have entirely and often impractically hinged on their lifelong romance. In their nearly fifty-year relationship, they have been apart for no more than two weeks, and through all that time, even today, they go for long walks holding hands; every day, they cuddle on their couch. The last time we were at Ikea, I found them stealing a kiss in an aisle.

The representation of the Global South's "poor" as romance-incapable animals was contiguous with that of the more deviant subject that emerged in the 1980s: HIV/AIDS – spreading "men who have sex with men" (MSM). Where heterosexual couples' pursuit of their raw desires resulted in too many children and poverty, the same pursuit by MSM resulted in death—not only of the sexual actors themselves but also of the "innocent" women and children they would also infect. As I noted when first encountering these representations as a student, and as I have documented in other publications (Gosine 2004, 2006, 2009a, 2009b, 2018), MSM tended to be represented as uncontrollable creatures devoid of the complex emotional experiences and ability to make intelligent choices that are ascribed to and expected of full humans. Whether heterosexual reproduction or homosexual sex, the issue was the same: the flattening out of Third World people, a failure to recognize the possibility of their agency and intelligence. The recuperation of our humanity, in opposition to the racist, sexist, and classist representations of Third World peoples in international development, thus lay in the simple message communicated in the photograph of my parents: *We love too, as all humans do.*

My interest in this image broadened beyond this polemic when I reproduced it as the patterned fabric print at FIT. First, I made a set of surgeon's scrubs from the organic cotton material that connected my personal story to the history of indentureship through the figure of the doctor. My parents and my longest-term partner first met while I was being wheeled into an operating room to have my appendix removed. The scrubs were also a reference to the doctors on ships carrying Indian indentures traveling to the Caribbean. Because doctors were paid by the number of indentures who arrived alive, Indians looked to those doctors for hope that they would survive the journey. Other objects that held some kind of personal significance for me followed, including a kitchen apron, shower curtains, pillowcases and a set of bedsheets, and a soccer uniform, and in 2013, I used the image to name and frame the first of my *Cane Portraiture* performances. These experiments with the image prompted reconsideration of the thesis I presented in Cincinnati. I began to recognize some of its limitations.

I saw that my argument unfortunately hung on centralizing the notion of "romantic desire" (what O'Grady [2010] calls "courtly love") that was key to the civilization of sex in Euro-American culture and on which the separation of animal from human hinged. The claim that only humans are capable of romantic desire is simply untrue. Animals, research has shown, demonstrate a wide range of emotional attachments that may well be described as love. Rats, for example, lead incredibly romantic lives. They like to be tickled; they chirp their laughter and are emphatic with each other. Rats communicate with a variety of vocalizations in ultrasonic ranges, above the hearing capacity of other animals. One of their highest calls (at 50 Hz) is most plentiful when rats engage in rough-and-tumble play together, when they are tickled, and when they are having sex (Fawcett 2016, 460). And humans of course do not need romantic love to participate in sex. Sexual desire, as O'Grady (2010) posits, is the thing that perhaps most demonstrates that there is no daylight between human and animal. Pop singer Troye Sivan's 2018 single "Animal" says it plainly:

I want you all to myself
Don't leave none for nobody else
I am an animal with you
No angels could beckon me back
And it's hotter than hell where I'm at
I am an animal with you.

It's in the height of pleasure, for those who freely pursue pleasure, that we can most recognize and indulge the fact of our animality.

In the fall of 2013, I returned to the photograph of my parents to create a video installation, *(Made in Love)* (see N. Mohabir 2018). The idea was simple enough. I would place myself and another male figure, representing an idealized partner, against a projection of the image. We dressed in the same colors as my parents, and I stood atop a pile of feminist books that both served a functional aesthetic purpose and subtly signaled some of my own political investments. My figure was placed over my father's, and singer Vivek Shraya's over my mother's (plate 8).[4] We wore wardrobes that matched those of my parents. Where the piece departs from the way I had used it in the context of international development, however, was through its score. In the final video, Shraya's figure serenades mine with a cover of one of my father's favorite songs, "A Whiter Shade of Pale," by British pop group Procol Harum. I remember my father blasting this record at our home in Trinidad, and when I gifted Annie Lennox's 1995 cover version of the song to him as a Christmas present that year, he lit up and immediately grabbed my mother's hand for a dance. The instrumentation in this 1967 composition gives the impression of romantic grandeur but the lyrics reveal the song to be simply a story of a one-night stand. The song dresses up what is a quick sexual encounter as an epic romance, offering a kind of parallel to how raw, animalistic sexual desire is reconstituted as romantic love for civilized humans. Adding a layer to the meaning of the project was the irony that while my fading in and out over my father's image speaks to the attempts of homosexual couples to fit the prescribed romantic models of heterosexual relationships and underlines my own failure, the truth of it is that my parents' experience also did not match the dominant conventions of romance. There was no big ceremonial wedding, and I was an unanticipated arrival that likely hastened their nuptials. What may well have driven their pairing and lifelong relationship might simply have been desire itself, bereft of its narrative furnishings. This unfurling of my deep investment in notions of romantic love as a signifier of one's humanity would be followed over the next years by other artistic projects that made me recognize, weigh, and question both institutional and personal investments in denying my animality.

COOLIE COLORS

In 2016, I created a piece that began as a playful experiment with collage but that facilitated my recognition and processing of connections between my experience of migration to Canada and the historical and contemporary uses of animalization to manufacture racism. Shown as part of the *Small Axe* exhibition *Caribbean Queer Visualities* in Belfast (2016) and Glasgow (2017), *Coolie Colors* is composed of two parts: a large clay plant pot filled with dirt and three flags hoisted on short bamboo sticks (*jhandis*), akin to the way diasporic Hindus plant flags after prayer rituals in places like Queens, New York; and a pantone fan (plate 10), with images taken from *Baby*, the album of my childhood put together by my mother that was the starting point for the piece.

Throughout *Baby*, there are few clear markers ascribing a male gender. There are no blue blankets or booties to indicate a boy. My wardrobes feature bright colors, gingham patterns, and hues and cuts consistent with 1970s fashion sensibilities. In the pictures, the color coordination is impressively detailed. As mentioned in chapter 2, I have sharp memories of putting together my outfits from a very young age, paying attention to such things as how the stripes at the top of my socks might correspond with my belt or the collar of my shirt. My clothes are no doubt "boys' clothes," but their investments in signaling masculinity are undercut by my confidently effeminate poses, likely an emulation of the women I most admired, my fashionable aunts. Adding to the gender confusion is the matter of my name, which my mother invented and which in my experience is never gender-ascriptive.[5]

Trinidadian filmmaker Richard Fung has joked that the poses and wardrobes in the original photographs are among the gayest childhood pictures he has seen. John, my research assistant who scanned the images, asked if I had picked ones that show "early evidence of gay." He also said that he had been corrected by his parents for posing similarly in early 2000s western Canada. Audiences who have interacted with the work in the United Kingdom, United States, and Canada react similarly. As obviously as the images appear to convey homosexuality, there were no moments in my first fourteen years of life in rural Trinidad that I was made to feel like there was anything abnormal about how I moved in the world. That all of the pictures were taken by my mother or father or an aunt *and* appear in the album suggests that those people were unconcerned with any deviations from acceptable gender roles that I might have made. Perhaps the transgressions of dominant masculinity I engaged in did not go far enough to warrant a disciplinary response, but I suspect that in another context, gender-related "corrections" might have been forthcoming for a boy who did not play sports; who regularly staged tea parties and picnics with his life-sized gown-and-silk-gloves-attired Miss Piggy; who created and performed choreography for Tina Turner's "Private Dancer"; whose first record was the soundtrack to the campy *Xanadu*; and who gave feedback to his aunts about their wardrobes. I cannot think of a single moment where any of my behaviors or preferences were "corrected" by a relative or teacher in Trinidad.

The very few times that my gender-averse sensibilities were mocked happened in urban space dominated by local elites, at Presentation College in San Fernando. But even there, the confidence with which I was raised to believe in my basic human dignity allowed me to relatively easily dismiss teasing about my higher-pitched country Indian accent, my occasionally flamboyant wardrobe, and my disinterest in sports. As I stated in chapter 2, I tended to view this kind of criticism as evidence of my critics' cultural heathenism. I cannot recall a single moment in which the intended injuries were consciously sustained.

The colors in *Coolie Colors* reference and trouble dominant, teleological narratives of urban space as "progressive" and rural space as "backward," especially in reference to queer people. The reds, pinks, and yellows I emphasized in the piece are drawn both from popular jhandi flags, each representing a different Hindu deity, and my clothing. These colors are often preceded by *coolie*, as in the title of feminist scholar Patricia Mohammed's 2009 film, *Coolie Pink and Green*.[6] The precursor conveyed the point that the aesthetic tastes of Indians were unsophisticated and primitive, a notion I both document and interrupt by using them and bringing them into the space of metropolitan galleries.

Coolie Colors also contests another teleological narrative through the separate, intentionally whimsical title that I have given to its pantone fan element: *I could have been fabulous/But then we moved to Canada*. The title is a blunt refusal of the hegemonic homonationalist (see Puar 2007) framing of sexuality that characterizes the "modern" states of North America and Europe as "more civilized" due to their adoption of same-sex rights such as the right to marry and Global South states like those in the Caribbean as "less civilized." As I outline in chapters 1 and 3, sexuality has long been a powerful trope for gauging civility, but its measuring stick has recently flipped. Evidence of homosexual sex in African, Asian, and Latin American societies was used as evidence of their being more animal than human. Following the fall and/or retreat of colonial powers in the 1950s and 1960s, emergent states did not usurp old and imposed colonial measures of civility, like antisodomy, but aspired to meet them. Taking charge after winning independence required proof of fitness to lead, and postcolonial leaders such as Eric Williams outlined road maps in speeches and in the definition of watchwords. Disciplined sexuality was a key component of civility, as M. Jacqui Alexander observed: "Erotic autonomy signals danger to the heterosexual family and to the nation. And because loyalty to the nation as citizen is perennially colonized within reproduction and heterosexuality, erotic autonomy brings with it the potential of undoing the nation entirely, a possible charge of irresponsible citizenship, or no responsibility at all" (2005, 22–23). Following European and North American states' legalization of particular forms of homosexual expression and unions (primarily ones that mimic dominant heterosexual forms such as marriage), it is now other countries' expressed discomfort with that particular form of sexual expression that makes *them* beasts. This narrative, as I show in chapter 3, underlies dominant forms of contemporary gay organizing, including many efforts by diasporic Caribbean people about the Caribbean.

Through location of the "freer" space in 1980s George Village, over and above, as inferred by the title, present-day Canada, I am of course not making a serious comparative evaluation of the two places, a futile and deeply problematic exercise that offers no real insight into the particularities of social relations operating in each space. I am instead troubling the reliance on a few key indicators like the criminalization of sodomy that are often used to construct teleological narratives. But it is also true that in my case, my claim is not fiction. The images shared in *Coolie Colors* show a child unburdened by demands to prove himself "Man"; following our migration to Canada, however, I was quickly schooled in the powerful advantages of embodying dominant forms of masculinity in a cis male body, and I saw that lowly class status and dark skin were treated as evidence that one was *more animal, less human.*

ALL THE FLOWERS

My experience of gender socialization in George Village might have been freer, but as I note in chapter 3, Williams's watchwords were imprinted on my childhood. The force of *discipline* and *production* did not retreat when I arrived in Canada as a teenager. In 2018, I put together *All the Flowers*, an exhibition that addressed my experience of migration to Oshawa in the city's main gallery, the RMG. The exhibition's strongest piece, I think, was *Caution: Will Bear No Fruit* (plate 9), an installation that underlined this continuity. *Caution* pairs an artificial banana plant with my high school desk, which holds the substantial haul of scholarly and service awards that I received during my teen years in Oshawa. Behind them are scribbled notes on a bright yellow background, a reproduction of a page from my twelfth-grade yearbook. "I don't know how you do so much at school!" it read. A postscript added, "Make sure you party with me sometime this year!" Its author would in subsequent years come out as "gay." Through the juxtaposition of the awards with this note and their placement around my desk, I draw attention to the ambivalent consequences of discipline and production, while the addition of the artificial banana plant whimsically signs my sexuality and tropical origins. Whatever the rewards earned by my labor and good behavior, I argue, the disavowal of my sexual desires during those years incurred terrible losses, including of adolescent experimentation (perhaps with the note's author!), experiences of socialization, and practice with sex. On most days, these losses feel much more devastating than and irrecuperable from the material security that persistently "good civilized behavior" has afforded.

Undoubtedly, as evidenced by Williams's nationalist speeches and as executed on the ground in contexts like my primary school, *discipline* and *production* were mandated under threat of potential animalization and allegations of "slackness." The seriousness with which I took on these imperatives spoiled many pleasures and slowed my sexual maturity. But I was not aware of feeling burdened by them. Instead, I took to all the work and pressure to achieve and perform, and I mostly enjoyed it. The desk in *Caution* is telling about my state of mind at the moment of migration. I remember the cost of the desk ($135) because I used all of the monies I had been gifted from relatives when we left Trinidad to make the purchase. That a desk was the thing a fourteen-year-old boy most wanted and most cherished speaks volumes about the impact of Williams's watchwords. But whereas diligence was forward-looking and generally deployed with joyfulness in George Village, I quickly began to understand that adherence to discipline and production were basic requirements of survival in Oshawa.

Immediately after my family's arrival in Canada, I was schooled about the ways in which adolescent exploration was structured and strictly limited by racism and sexism. The day we moved into our house, I was sent to get milk at the convenience store and was called "Paki" by a neighbor. Since I was unaware of and therefore unintimidated by the word, he frustratedly ordered his fortunately uncooperative dog to "sic 'em." On my first day of school, I had to challenge the guidance counselor's quick decision to enroll me in the general stream rather than the advanced one that would lead to university, simply because I was Caribbean. She recanted after my strong protest. The first days of school would bring easily recognizable acts of racism: the N-word graffitied on my locker, teachers who mocked my accent or habits or who sadistically harnessed institutional power to execute torment. My very first class was Canadian Geography, on the day of a quiz in which students had to identify the provinces of Canada by their shape. I had only ever heard of Ontario and Quebec and had no idea what either looked like, so I remember my strategy to maximize my chances was to answer with either province for all of the shapes we were provided. The teacher not only insisted that I do the test as my initiation into the Canadian system but that my resulting 10 percent score count toward my final grade for the class. (As testament to my diligence, that still did not prevent me from earning an A in the class.) I was told I could not enroll in drama class because "no one would understand my accent."

While I continued to rely on discipline and production as my best gear for survival, I also recognized that they were not requirements for everyone. Some people get to embrace their animality more than others, depending on the context in which they live. In most places, the sons of the elites are generally protected from their explorations with sex and drugs by their socioeconomic status and privileges afforded by patriarchy. Mistakes can be forgiven or fixed with money. They can indulge in a kind of visceral animality that others cannot because they would receive no second chances. Could anyone but a wealthy white man behave like Donald Trump and keep the US presidency? If Trump's Supreme Court justice appointee Brett Kavanaugh had been anyone else but a white heterosexual man from a wealthy family, could he have gotten into all those drunken fights, possibly sexually assaulted women all through high school and college, and still not had his civility seriously doubted? Indeed, what makes people like Trump more appealing is the brazen expression of animality. Trump's persistent lying in his self-interest and absence of sophisticated analytical skill about most pressing issues were read as "authentic" for his single-term presidency. Privileges of masculinity, able-bodiedness, class, heterosexuality, and whiteness allow some people to "get on like animals" without consequences that could be terminal for marginalized subjects. The most striking recent illustration of this phenomenon is the stark difference between the US Capitol police's treatment of mostly peaceful Black Lives Matter protesters in 2020 and the force's lackadaisical and in some cases complicit response to the violent insurgency by Trump supporters on January 6, 2021. Had those insurrectionists been Black, no doubt the death toll and arrest rate would have been far higher and the condemnation more universal.

At both my Canadian high school and my university, white students, especially boys, openly transgressed lines that I knew would mark me, a nonwhite student from a working-class family, as less than human. In those prelegalization days, a pot-smoking white boy was just being a kid; a nonwhite one was a criminal. I am an easy drunk now (half a glass of wine is all it takes) precisely because I never built up a tolerance for alcohol. If in Trinidad becoming a "good boy" seemed like a negotiated choice, in Canada, I was very clearly told that any deviation from idealized social norms would be strictly punished. No room would be made for adolescent exploration. I quickly understood that no second chances were available to dark-skinned bodies for any of the indulgences that were viewed as a normal part of white adolescence.

The persistence of this instruction was underlined in *Our Oshawas*, a video that played alongside *Caution* at *All the Flowers*. The video resulted from three sets of conversations and tours of Oshawa with Sue Seto, an Asian Canadian woman about my age who grew up in the city. Her family established the city's first Chinese restaurant in the 1920s. In the audio for *Our Oshawas*, listeners hear us detour from a playful conversation about dating and teenage experiences to arrive at the realization that our dominant feeling of growing up as young persons of color in Canada was of persistent terror. The video shows me retracing part of Sue's walk home from school, which, it turned out, was exactly as long as mine—twenty-three minutes—and over which time, we discovered, we were often afraid: of racial slurs that might be hurled, of encountering police who might be bullying, of threats of physical violence that might appear. Both of us had experienced intimidating, aggressive encounters with local police around the age of sixteen. Officers visited her for allegedly skipping a class (she hadn't) and me for failing to notice that I might have nicked a car bumper in the mall parking lot (I likely did). In both cases, the officers warned us that we could face serious consequences, even jail, for such misdemeanors.

One of the things we discovered from our conversation was that despite our creative spirits, we played it very straight in school, as "good students" who never indulged in the necessary rituals of adolescence we witnessed around us. This feeling of terror meant there would be no drunken nights, no skipping out on school for a waffle run, and certainly no sex. We lived in fear of punishment for any deviance, however slight, however natural—and not from our parents but from the social institutions around us. We were thus robbed of the small window of time available for the kind of adolescent exploration that permits indulgence of one's wild desires. As suggested by another work in the exhibition, *Now and Then*, a pair of banners that announce in part, "70,000 species of flowers that go extinct before they are found," the very formative experiences of adolescent exploration have a fixed expiration date, and the loss of them has punishing consequences.

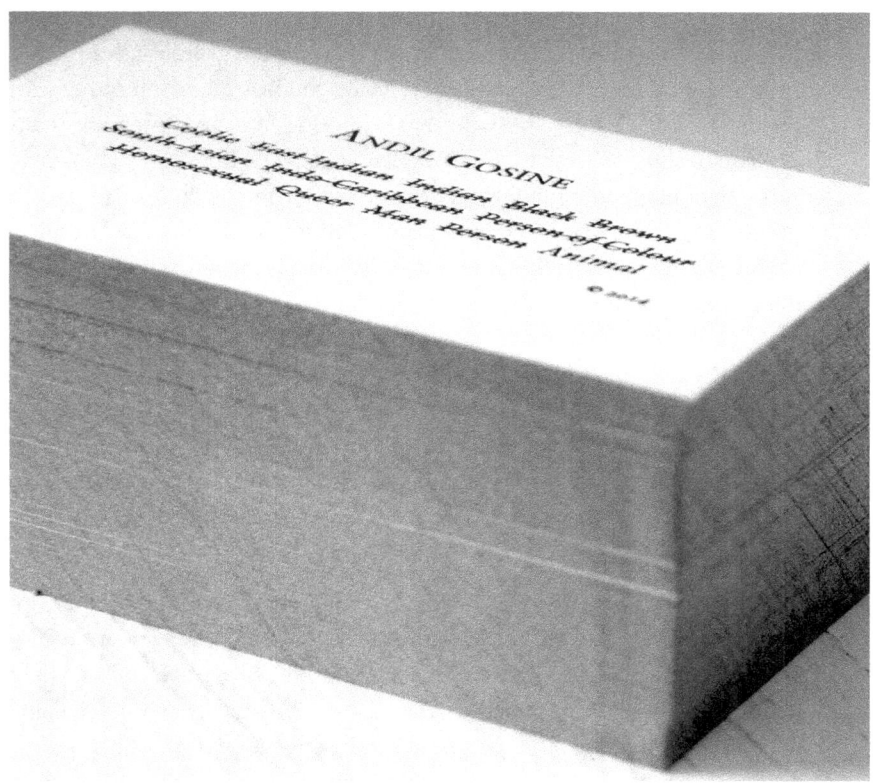

FIGURE 5.1 Andil Gosine, *Calling Card*, 2014.

This new awareness of lost adolescent experimentation in part led me to the question "Am I an animal?" *Calling Card* (figure 5.1) documents my determined reach for an answer. After decades of navigating mostly unchosen and always uncomfortable racial, ethnic, and gendered identities, *Calling Card* feels like a return to the first identity that properly fit me. It is not that the others don't count, of course. They lurk eternally, products of history that are impossible to leave entirely, if at all.

The claim of "animal" as an identity at this time is also an aspirational acknowledgment in two ways. First, it is a reach toward redemption from practices of excessive *discipline* and *production*. Second, it is a declaration of willful but not always achievable solidarity with all animals in a moment of global ecological crisis, when more than one million species are threatened with extinction—more than at any other moment in history (United Nations 2019). This gesture is not benevolent. I survive because animals give me life, both in the grander sense of planetary connectedness on which human life depends and in the most intimate sense: my dog Lulu has lifted me many times from feelings of despair.[7] In *Dangerous Crossings*, her study of racialization in relationship to animal rights, Claire Jean Kim concludes, "The effort to gain full humanity by distancing from nonhuman animals, like the effort to achieve moral considerability for animals through racially fraught, racism-denying analogies, is a misbegotten project: it has not succeeded and cannot succeed because race cannot be unsutured from species and dismantled while species categories motor on in force" (2015, 286). In her view, we must both contend with racial/imperial histories and the history of human domination over animals and oppose them. That is perhaps the challenge faced by human subjects whose marginalization is tied to their animalization. In 1873 *The Tennessean* published a speech by Frederick Douglass that underlined the importance of this proposition.

> There is no denying that slavery had a direct and positive tendency to produce coarseness and brutality in the treatment and management of domestic animals, especially those most useful to the agricultural industry. Not only the slave, but the horse, the ox, and the mule shared the general feeling of indifference to the right naturally engendered by a state of slavery. . . . It should be the study of every farmer to make his horse his companion and friend, and to do this, there is but one rule, and that is, uniform sympathy and kindness. . . . All loud and boisterous commands, a brutal flogging should be banished from the field, and only words of cheer and encouragement should be tolerated. A horse is in many respects like a man. He has the five senses, and has memory, affection, and reason *to a limited degree.* (quoted in Jackson 2016, 104)

As Jackson observes, here Douglass suggests that slavery *introduces* brutality into the lives of humans and animals. "While stopping short of foreclosing difference," she argues, Douglass's "understanding of (human) being, presumably including his being, does not arise in binaristic opposition to, or in negation of, 'the animal,'" as a "horse is in many respects like a man" (2016, 104). Douglass ends this section of his speech by declaring, "When young, untrained and untamed, he (a horse) has unbounded faith in his strength and fleetness. He runs, jumps, and plays in the pride of his perfections. But convince him that he is a creature of law as well as of freedom, by a judicious and kindly application of your superior power, and he will conform his conduct

Chapter Five

to that law, far better than your most law-abiding citizen" (quoted in Jackson 2016, 105). Jackson reads Douglass's statements as critically wrestling with slavery's hierarchies of being and feeling: "The 'humane' is an ideal that suggests humanity is gained by performing acts of kindness and attuning oneself to the suffering of those of inferior status and lesser capacity; as such, it does not posit humanity simply as an inherent or a priori aspect of being human" (2016, 105).

Scholar and former Black Panther Angela Davis takes up the mantle of animal justice more than a century later. Answering the critical question of "how we [can] not only discover more compassionate relations with human beings but [also] develop compassionate relations with the other creatures with whom we share this planet" (2012), Davis advocated reform of the whole capitalist industrial form of food production: "It would mean being aware— driving up the interstates or driving down the 5, driving down to LA, seeing all the cows on the ranches. Most people don't think about the fact they're eating animals. When they're eating a steak or eating chicken, most people don't think about the tremendous suffering that those animals endure simply to become food products to be consumed by human beings." For Davis, this blindness is connected to the commodity form. "I think the lack of critical engagement with the food that we eat demonstrates the extent to which the commodity form has become the primary way in which we perceive the world," she explained. "We don't go further than what Marx called the exchange value of the actual object—we don't think about the relations that that object embodies—and were important to the production of that object, whether it's our food or our clothes or our iPads or all the materials we use to acquire an education. . . . That would really be revolutionary to develop a habit of imagining the human relations and non-human relations behind all of the objects that constitute our environment." José Esteban Muñoz adds that while thinking outside the regime of human is simultaneously exhilarating and exhausting, "it is a ceaseless endeavor, a continuous straining to make sense of something else that is never fully knowable. . . . To think this thing we call inhuman is never fully knowable, because of our own stuckness within humanity, makes it a kind of knowing that is incommensurability" (2015, 209–10).

Made to feel immoral by the tenets of Victorianism, British colonial officers recuperated their humanness by producing the Others they encountered as animals. Postcolonial elites charged with leading nations like Trinidad and Tobago were similarly hamstrung by the demand to show themselves human. They found animals in fellow nationals, and complied with the continuation of punitive colonial legislation against vagrants, poor people, homosexuals, gender nonconforming people. Yet it has often been people living the conditions of the most marginalizing intersections who have offered the strongest rebukes against claims of inferiority. The police, acting under the direction of the postcolonial state, would want us all to believe that Kennty Dave Mitchell, a working-class man, a homosexual man, a man lacking formal education, ought to have to show how human he is, but Mitchell responds without doubt of his right to human dignity. He doesn't have to prove anything at all. When other Trinidadians I work with, academics and artists alike, ask where I'm from in Trinidad, the answer is almost always followed by confusion, sometimes arising from the fact of the place and often from simply not knowing of the space at all. Often, I add, "I'm from the bush." The confusion gets interrupted by a chuckle. Relief follows.

NATURES' WILD

The title of this chapter and book reference *Natures: A Guerrilla Girl Story* (plate 11), a video that I conceived as an adaptation of *The Clearing*, Lorraine O'Grady's photographic diptych (plate 1). *Natures'* subtitle references O'Grady's membership in the feminist activist group, where she used the pseudonym Alma Thomas. In my 2015 video, O'Grady's responses to my taped interview with her from five years earlier are laid over another diptych featuring interracial sexual desire, this time between two men, one of whom is me. *Natures'* opening scene provides context for what is about to unfold. As the video on the left appears, O'Grady asks, "What is love?" After audibly signaling hesitation, she continues, "It all depends if you're talking about sex or love, right? For me, I think love is everything." We are now twenty-five seconds in, and the two male figures begin to kiss passionately, right until the end of the seven-minute piece. O'Grady continues, "The problem with love is that it's every emotion, love and hate and distrust . . . giving over everything, at the extreme." A minute later, the screen is filled as the video on the right shows the rehearsal of the kiss on the left. At that point, O'Grady comments, "The sexual relationship is always already . . . imbricated in the social. The amazing thing is that when we're actually involved in the sexual act, we're not thinking socially, or we're not feeling socially. We are feeling totally individually. But then we're called to account. Once the orgasm is finished, then we're called to account." A moment later, she says, "I don't think most people want to think about the compromising, difficult parts of sexuality even among 'normally married couples,' you know. But they certainly don't want to hear about that difficulty in interracial relationships, or certainly they don't want to have the historical nature of this relationship exposed *en plein air*."

Both O'Grady's attempts to exhibit *The Clearing* and mine to share *Natures* exemplify the social hesitation to speak about the "difficult parts of sexuality." In 1993, Ellen Cantor asked O'Grady to participate in a show, *Coming to Power: 25 Years of Sexually X-plicit Art by Women* at the David Zwirner Gallery in New York. "The only piece that I had that was remotely sexually explicit was this piece," O'Grady recalls, "and so I gave her the diptych" (2010). But when O'Grady went to the show, she found that Cantor had decided to show only the left side of the diptych. "This show was about, you know, sexuality as an uncomplicated, positive blessing," O'Grady determined, "not sexuality as a complicated life issue or even sexuality as an issue far more complicated for women of color than for white women, you know, none of the modulations of sexuality were to be present in the show. And I said [laughs], 'What have you done? You've put my piece up and it's not my piece.' That was when I first began to realize that the two parts of *The Clearing* were a bit much for a certain audience." She would find similar resistance when she offered the piece to the Southeastern Center for Contemporary Art for its show on Black women. When the curator—"a very nice guy," O'Grady remembers—saw the piece, "it just threw him. And he said, 'That's not what sexuality is, or at least that's not what it's supposed to be.' 'But well,'" O'Grady replied, "' that's what it is'" (2010).

Twenty-five years after O'Grady's rebuke of Cantor's removal of half of her diptych, I was mounting *Natures* as part of my invited exhibition at the RMG in Oshawa. I was told by the curator that the gallery director had requested that the video projection be partially hidden. On the last day of installation, I was informed that a small sign that warned people "This exhibition contains mature content" would be added. I didn't protest, in part because I thought the addition of the blocking wall enhanced rather than diminished the presentation of the video and that the warning sign might actually make people more interested in seeing the work. The reason I was given for the light censorship was also flattering. I was told that even though there was no nudity or obscene language in the video, the passion of the kiss justified the censorship. Ignoring the likelihood that the explanation I was given was just a quintessentially Canadian way to couch homophobia, being told that just the way I kissed was too hot for the gallery did not upset me, first because the gallery was my return to the city where I spent four very sexless years of high school and where the notion that my body was an undesirable one was learned and most instilled, and second because I received the gallery staff's reaction as validation that my attempts to shake off discipline and production and embrace my animal desires were working.

Undoubtedly, however, what lies behind both the reluctance to show the second half of *The Clearing* and the attempt to hide *Natures* is anxiety about how sex threatens to expose us. As O'Grady says, sex reminds us of our animality and is "almost an affront to the ways in which culture has tried to circumscribe nature" (2010). In 1993, Cantor wanted to present interracial coupling as exemplary only of idealized "courtly love," making invisible the ways in which the violent history of the Americas has structured sexual relations, including those that O'Grady describes as foundational to its making: sex between white masters and enslaved Black women. In 2018, the staffers at the RMG enthusiastically overrepresented the queerness of *All the Flowers* in their descriptions of it, which were mostly couched in nationalist narratives of suffering and rescue, but were not comfortable with representations of actual homosexual desire.

Sexual desire is always threatening to the representation of ourselves as *human, not animal* precisely because no conscious effort can fully control our principal subconscious drive. Prior to colonization, antisodomy and antibestiality laws were logically conceived and coupled with civilization codes like sumptuary laws as a projection of anxieties by the powerful—that is, to mark themselves as *human, not animal* and the peasants, whom these laws would principally govern, as not quite human, closer to animal. Once colonization made available Black and Brown bodies for the projection of these anxieties, the laws traveled and were eventually less concerned with disciplining peasants, who were eventually reinvented as white. Following the retreat of European colonial states, postcolonial leaders such as Williams kept those laws in place, perhaps as a kind of reassurance that colonized subjects would continue to work toward civilization of themselves from *more animal* to *more human*. This imperative continues to inform many contemporary forms of sexual rights advocacy that argue that LGBTQI+ people aspire toward recognition of their belonging to the civilized/normalized.

Denial of our animal natures might be embedded in all formulations of the human as civilized beings, but not everyone's expression of animal desire, especially through sex, is treated equally. That *The Clearing* and *Natures* presented nonwhite bodies as desiring and desirous surely produced more anxiety than if all of the seen subjects were white. A few days before the end of my exhibition's run in Oshawa, the "mature content" warning sign was removed immediately after *one* gay white man complained that he was offended. *He* also immediately received an apology from the gallery, and a report on his experience received a prominent spot in Canada's most circulated newspaper, the *Toronto Star* (Szekely 2018) and was carried by other smaller papers. Underscoring the difference in how our erotic autonomies were viewed was that no journalist asked what I thought about any of it.

My kiss with a white lover in *Natures* is not a sign of any racialized sexual preference (I have none) but is more likely an expression of an ambivalent longing for the freer access that many white gay men seem to claim their animal desires. Contemporary gay culture is marked by a confident embrace of animal desire that contests old ideas of courtly love: open relationships, polyamory, a post-PrEP (pre-exposure prophylaxis) world that neuters anxieties about HIV/AIDS, and a plethora of digital tools like Grindr that afford quick, casual sexual connections. The failure of this menu of sexual liberation to align with my own desires, however, leaves me wondering how much that dissonance is a product of my own self-disciplining, perhaps in response to the civilizing imperatives that shaped my childhood. Perhaps my practices of stoicism inside a wild party is just a throwback to high school.

As signaled by the presentation of the scenes of raw and constructed desire in the *Natures* diptych as simultaneous, discerning how much the colonial mandate to civilize ourselves persists in contemporary culture is not an easy task. We often slip between recognition of our animal desires and trying to prove ourselves *human, not animal.* I went to see Nicki Minaj perform in concert in 2014. Her anthem "Anaconda" was ruling the airwaves, and her influence in the cultural zeitgeist was at its zenith. True to her persona, Minaj exuded powerful confidence on stage, leaving no doubt about who was in charge of *her* erotic autonomy.[8] The moments I most recognized her Trinidadianness were the frequent ones she took to encourage her fans to work hard and "stay in school." She even expressed admiration for some students she knew who were off to college. In the "Anaconda" video, Minaj signals her comfort with raw, animal desire, not only in how she telegraphs her sexual preferences in the lyrics and through her sexually charged choreography but also by placing herself in a forest. Is Minaj's persistent mention of education evidence of Williams's watchwords still hanging over her too, a possible subconsciously driven utterance to defend the potential characterization of her as animal? Or is Minaj simply skillfully reconciling contradictory thrusts of nature and culture?

Like Minaj's emboldened communication of her sexual desire, Kelly Sinnapah Mary's paintings of animalistic humans and drawings of hybrid human-chickens and my declaration of "animal" as an identity in *Calling Card* might suggest an embrace of wildness. But we are not so much championing animality as we are reporting what searches for truth have brought to the surface.

Sinnapah Mary's project is to make sense of her history and place in the Caribbean and of the region itself, and tensions about animality present themselves from this investigation. My declaration of "animal" as an identifier in *Calling Card* similarly refuses ethnonationalism, commits to the understanding of culture advanced by coolitude/*creolité*, and declares allyship with nonhuman animals; nonetheless, it is, like the title of this book, an observation.

What opens up for us, Caribbean people, when we are freed from proving ourselves *not animal*? Many of the Caribbean people mentioned in this book have already shown us what is possible. When sodomy was a crime in the country, Colin Robinson, Kenny Mitchell, and legions of same-sex-loving Trinbagonians *steupsed* in response to the imposition of heterosexuality as requirement to inhabit humanness. Risking violence and denigration, Isabella Persaud and the other litigants in the McEwan case challenged another archaic colonial law for over a decade, thereby underlining their humanness regardless of what clothing the law demanded for their bodies. The people who helped Shari Petti subvert the dress code at the government office, too, understood that her bare knees bore no relationship to her character or her civility. Ramsingh's disruption of Father Larry's orientation class on homosexuality and even the puhngah game in the Photography Club are also examples of how targeted peoples have exercised politics of resistance for just as long as strategies of dehumanization have been deployed. These resistances also operate in spaces that are often outside the radar of Caribbean intellectual inquiry, which continues to center and amplify the middle-class urban subject, and we need to pay more attention to them. Our understanding of the postcolonial experience requires that alongside Christopher Cozier's narrative of how deeply the colonial civilizing project constituted his educational experience in Port of Spain, we also consider its less evident influence in my George Village and ask about Kenny Mitchell's experience of that project. When social justice movements advance on the risks taken by activists removed from the center of power, shorthand explanations often emphasize the activists' extreme marginality and sense of desperation; however, we must also ask how their lesser indoctrination into the dominant discourses of power and its rituals provides a confidence to claim respect for their person. What other narratives of being might be operating further out from the center, stripped from their classist attachments to civilizing projects?[9]

What new strategies for social justice might emerge from taking our animal natures more seriously? Perhaps because they are formed around a concern for erotic autonomy, sexual rights efforts, particularly in relationship to

HIV/AIDS, have forced contention with difficult truths of sexual desires, but how might other approaches also develop from taking our animal desires more seriously? Many antiracist, feminist, and anti-ableist efforts are predicated on teleological narratives of civilization and an idealized human subject in the same moment that right-wing fascists, epitomized by Trump's "Make America Great Again" movement, gain traction from exuberant indulgence of animality. Does their "success" hold lessons for the Left?

For centuries, guardians of antisodomy laws have argued that these regulations were needed to protect against wild desires that threaten our humanness. But in no place has the decriminalization of sodomy produced this fantasy. Jason Jones's legal victory in Trinidad and Tobago has already prompted studies measuring the decision's impact, including one in which Jones is a collaborating investigator. Based on friends' accounts, media reports, and personal visits, I believe that what has changed since the decriminalization is that some people feel safer and that more people are educated about sexuality—and often kinder. It is also possible that Devindra Rampersad's ruling was playing catch-up with social and cultural shifts already in motion. What is at risk, then, if the dress codes go, too, along with the various punitive rituals performed across the Caribbean in the name of civilizing the youth—corporal punishment, high-stakes exams that crush childhood development, overpolicing, and all the other classist and racist injuries premised on assuming a humanness that is *not animal*? All that is at stake is the continued masochistic attachment to an epistemology that from its inception had no regard for our well-being, our pleasures, or our worth.

Chapter One. *Puhngah!*

1 Writing about his experience at another Roman Catholic high school in Trinidad during the same time period, Andre Bagoo suggests that "the choir" was a homoeroticized space. "I was in the choir of an all-male, Roman Catholic secondary school in the heart of Port of Spain. . . . It was only years later that I realised everyone in the choir was gay. (I say everyone but I really mean some of us . . .)" But, Bagoo continues, "I didn't get any action. Like a good Catholic, I remained a virgin" (2020, 46).

2 The goal here was to humiliate the boy by producing a squeal. An alumnus who described himself as "effeminate" during his time at Presentation in the 1970s revealed that he was so often a target of such bullying that he managed to control his reaction, learning not to audibly respond when it happened. At the same time, these incidents, he says, made him more curious to explore this new sensation. The rituals simultaneously villainize anal penetration and in-

troduce the possibility of pleasure from giving and receiving anal penetration even as it is conducted as a deliberate violation.

3 In 2019, students attending a boys' school, St. Michael's, in Toronto, Canada, were charged with sexually assaulting one of their peers with a broom handle in a manner that parallels poling. Witness testimony in the case characterized such events as frequent (Loriggio 2020). I am not aware of any charges in relationship to cases at Presentation College.

4 Saint Christopher and Nevis, Offences against the Person Act, rev. ed., 2002, Chapter 4.21.

5 Guyana, Criminal Law (Offences) Act 1998, Chapter 8:01.

6 Kamala Kempadoo's *Sexing the Caribbean* (2004) powerfully describes the persistent legacy of this eroticization of the region.

7 It was not really until the nineteenth century that these offenses were commonly prosecuted (Cook 2003, 15–49). From his review of cases over this period, Sean Brady concludes that the number of "indictments for sex between men was high in the 1870s and the 1890s, and that the increase in indictments between these years was relatively gradual" (2005, 100). For example, the career of painter Simeon Solomon collapsed when he was arrested and charged with attempting to commit sodomy. He was fined £100 in London in 1873 for his first offense and was imprisoned in Paris for three months for his second (Seymour 1997).

8 "Respectability" is a concept primarily used in anthropology and has been credited to Peter Wilson, who in 1969 paired it with "reputation" as a framework for linking domestic to broader social organization in the Caribbean. In this chapter, I rely principally on Stephen Kingsley Scott's (2002) approximation of Wilson's approach in his study of Trinidad.

9 Antigua and Barbuda Sexual Offences Act 1995, Section 12.

10 Jamaica Constitution, Section 13(12)(a), (b), and (c).

Chapter Two. Clothes Make the Man

1 This was no small achievement, since fashion is always being configured through gender. As Joanne Entwistle concludes from her studies, "the preoccupation with gender starts with babies and is played out through the life cycle, so that styles of dress at significant moments are very clearly gendered. . . . Such styles enable the repetitious production of gender" (2000, 329).

2 Sergeant Wallace, *Two Chamars*, ca. 1890, photograph, Royal Anthropological Institute, RA12722.

3 Civil Appeal No. 118, Trinidad, 2007.

4 Reflecting the fact that McEwan and other arrestees in this case do not fix their gender pronouns, I similarly vary the gender pronouns used in reference to each of them.

5 As indicated by a sign outside the courtroom (Sharples 2017, photo 3).

6 As indicated by a notice detailing what women can wear in public buildings (Chappell 2018, photo 3).

7 "Sumptuary Law," Wikipedia, accessed February 22, 2019. https://en.wikipedia
.org/wiki/Sumptuary_law.

8 For a fuller discussion of the deployment of sumptuary law in the colonial
Americas, see Earle 2019.

9 *The Attorney General of Guyana v. McEwan et al.*, 2018, Guyana, CCJ Appeal
No. GYCV2017/015.

10 Robinson's preferred acronym is GLBT. "I prefer to begin my listing with the
least specific and sometimes ungendered term, *gay*," he explained in this
interview.

Chapter Three. The Father, a Godfather,
and the Specter of Beasts Old and New

1 Even though Hindus comprised about a quarter of the island's population
throughout the twentieth century, not until 1986 was a Hindu cabinet minister
sworn into government.

2 "Tolerance" is a subdued characterization of the frankly impressive processes
of creolization that marked Trinbagonian society. Regardless of the persistence
of discourses of "race" and the structuring force of racism throughout the society, the innovation of new cultural forms from the mixing of once-distant
cultures is remarkable. "Tolerance" in practice meant that I grew up in a Hindu
home, went to a Hindu school, and regularly attended a Hindu temple, but at
all three sites, we celebrated new versions of Christian and Muslim festivals.
Christmas was certainly the biggest family celebration in my household. Unlike many contemporary iterations of state multiculturalism, this experience
was not of "tolerance" of cultures sealed off from each other but of ones mess-
ily remaking each other.

3 Included among Gandhi's eleven vows were *Brahmacharya* (self-discipline)
and *Sharirshrama* (bread labor). In a September 1, 1921, column for his newspaper *Young India*, he wrote, "Our children should not be so taught as to de-
spise labour. . . . It is a sad thing that our schoolboys look upon manual labour
with disfavour, if not contempt." In another column published on November
5, 1925, he explained that *bread labor* "means that everyone is expected to perform sufficient body labour in order to entitle him to [his living]. It is not,
therefore, necessary to earn one's living by bread labour, taking the word living
in its broader sense. But everyone must perform some useful body labour."

4 Zimbabwe's Robert Mugabe often referred to homosexuals as such (Moyo 2017).

5 Research projects have also been funded. "Sexualities in Conversation" was
made possible through my own access to a research grant from the Social Sci-
ences and Humanities Research Council of Canada, for example.

6 4Change gets its name from Section 4 (Recognition and Declaration of Rights
and Freedoms) of the Trinidad and Tobago Constitution. 4Change, formed
in 2007, was inspired by the successful lawsuit by maxi (taxi) driver Kenny
Mitchell after his humiliation by police officers for being gay. A main precursor

to CAISO, the Trinidad and Tobago Anti-Violence Project focused on various forms of homophobic violence.

7 We determined the invitation list together, but Tracy and I deferred to Carr about the final say on which activists from the region should be included. A few months before I would meet Colin Robinson, I had heard of his work and proposed to Carr that an invitation should be sent to him to join us in Barbados. Carr's response was quick, pointed, and firm. "Colin is bad news," he replied, "a careerist who wrecked his life in NYC and has decided that GLBT in the Caribbean is fertile ground for his ego" (email correspondence, 2008). We went back and forth about the decision, but Carr was adamant that Robinson be struck from the list. He was excluded from the meeting.

Personality conflicts are hardly unusual in social movements, particularly in high-stress situations where a small number of people are taking big risks and working in precarious conditions. Concerns around the approaching meeting in Barbados were not limited to Carr's hesitations about Robinson's inclusion. We decided it would not be an open or public event. Our main goal was to meet each other, share our work, and strategize ways of working together. Robinson and Carr would eventually also go on to work together as members of the Steering Committee of C-FLAG until Carr's untimely passing in 2011.

8 *Liming* is Trinidadian vernacular for socializing. Robinson shared his original notes to the authors in a July 6, 2011, email to me.

9 Trinidad and Tobago's 2005 national development plan to achieve developed-nation status in fifteen years was named Vision 2020, a play on the optometric concept of 20/20 vision. One of the country's popular aged rum brands is called 1919. At its founding, CAISO teased the government that it had a 1919 vision of sexual diversity.

10 Robinson has often criticized how the "pink press" constructs the Caribbean (e.g., C. Robinson 2018a).

11 On March 22, 1961, Williams delivered the speech "Massa Day Done" at Woodford Square in Port of Spain.

12 *TV6 Morning Edition*, June 29, 2018.

Chapter Four. *Désir Cannibale*

1 In her interview with me, Sinnapah Mary explained that the image is a reference to Hindu rituals that involve animal sacrifice.

2 That is not to say that some of this work is not also informed by the individual experiences of their creators. For example, my own *Cane Portraiture* project, in which I photograph subjects against the backdrop of sugarcane fields, has been broadly read as a social-historical project about indentureship. I have usually deferred to this explanation because it is, indeed, about the tensions of exile that indentured workers and their descendants are always negotiating. But at its heart, the project is specifically about not having enjoyed a consistent experience of home since the childhood one in which I lived, surrounded by cane fields.

Chapter Five. *Natures' Wild*

1 "I Am Isabella," YouTube, August 9, 2018, https://www.youtube.com/watch ?v=z_UbTZotroA.

2 Persaud, like most of the litigants in the case, switches gender pronouns.

3 In his essay about Freud's conception of human nature in *Civilization and Its Discontents*, Nicholas Ray weighs the psychoanalyst's contradictory statements about the animality of humans. "When Freud invokes the putative 'animality' of the human," Ray points out, "he does so in a tendentious way, exclusively to signify those aspects of man which are anterior, antithetical or antagonistic to civilization" (2014, 12). And yet Freud, Ray observes, also simultaneously points to nonhuman animals as exemplars of civilization: "Why do our relatives, the animals, not exhibit any such cultural struggle? We do not know. Very probably some of them—the bees, the ants, the termites—strove for thousands of years before they arrived at the State institutions, the distribution of functions and the restrictions on the individual, for which we admire them today. It is a mark of our present condition that we know from our own feelings that we should not think ourselves happy in any of these animal States or in any of the roles assigned in them to the individual" (Freud 1962, 123). This pervasive contradictory tension recurs in reference to other nonhuman animals (dogs, earthworms, insects, grass snakes, and so forth) throughout *Civilization*, thus producing, Ray says, "an instability that leaves [Freud] caught between suggesting that there is too much and suggesting that there is too little of the 'animal' about us humans ever to be contentedly civilized" (2014, 16).

4 Shraya now identifies as a trans woman.

5 Elsewhere (Gosine 2016a), I explain how I read that album, *Baby*, as a textual documentation of my mother's negotiations of various demands of gender and patriarchy in 1980s Trinidad. In the album, she often appears as doting mother, as would be expected for a baby album, and many photos mirror dominant narratives of femininity at the time. But others break from it. In the first few pages of the album, she is in pants and a tight-fitting short blouse that would be out of place in metropolitan North American cities at the time, but these were notable for 1970s rural Trinidad. About one-third of the images feature her, foregrounded most of the time. Much more than her self-representation in *Baby*, the images of me that she constructed and compiled demonstrate her consistent wrecking of normative representations of gender.

6 Green is more commonly associated with Indo-Caribbean Muslim culture.

7 As Donna Haraway argues in *The Companion Species Manifesto*, the historical relationship between humans and dogs is an example of the entwinement of human and nonhuman animal co-constitution. Using the concept of *nature-cultures* to challenge this dualism, Haraway points to the coevolution of dogs and humans (2003, 29), with humans and dogs continuously shaped by each other through the "successful evolutionary strategy" (30) of domestication. In conversation with Nicholas Gane, Haraway contends that "humans are products of situated relationalities with organisms, tools, much else," and are never

humans exclusive of our attachments and dependency on other species (2006, 146).

8 Perhaps in part due to the historical racialized sexualization of Black women, hip hop has a strong tradition of Black artists like Minaj claiming their erotic autonomy. In 2020, Megan Thee Stallion's "Savage" and her duet with Cardi B, "WAP," went even further than Minaj did in centering their sexual desires. Both were not merely ubiquitous as songs but ubiquitous throughout popular culture.

9 Gloria Wekker's study of the mati work culture of women loving women in *Politics of Passion* (2006) is one telling illustration of an alternative sexual culture.

WORKS CITED

Agamben, Giorgio. 2004. *The Open: Man and Animal*. Translated by Kevin Attell. Stanford: Stanford University Press.

Alexander, M. Jacqui. 1994. "Not Just (Any) Body Can Be a Citizen: The Politics of Law, Sexuality and Postcoloniality in Trinidad and Tobago and the Bahamas." *Feminist Review* 48 (Autumn): 5–23.

Alexander, M. Jacqui. 2005. *Pedagogies of Crossing: Meditations on Feminism, Sexual Politics, Memory, and the Sacred*. Durham, NC: Duke University Press.

Ali, Shereen. 2015. "Aria Lounge Policies under Fire." *Trinidad and Tobago Guardian*, December 14. https://www.guardian.co.tt/article-6.2.372681.dd771fedb8.

Alliance for Justice and Diversity (AJD). 2017. "Take Care of Each Other's Safety." March 23. https://justicediversitytt.wordpress.com/keep-safe/.

Arens, William. 1979. *The Man-Eating Myth: Anthropology and Anthropophagy*. New York: Oxford University Press.

Association internationale des critiques d'art—Caraïbe du Sud (AICACS). 2017. "*Hotmilk* de Kelly Sinnapah Mary." January 2. https://aica-sc.net/2017/01/02 /hotmilk-de-kelly-sinnapah-mary/.

Attai, Nikoli. 2017. "Let's Liberate the Bullers! Toronto Human Rights Activism and Implications for Caribbean Strategies." *Journal of Eastern Caribbean Studies* 42, no. 3: 97–121.

Bagoo, Andre. 2020. *The Undiscovered Country*. Leeds, UK: Peepal Tree Press.

Bahadur, Gaiutra. 2013. *Coolie Woman: The Odyssey of Indenture*. Chicago: University of Chicago Press.

Banning-Lover, Rachel. 2017. "Where Are the Most Difficult Places in the World to Be Gay or Transgender?" *The Guardian*, March 1.

Barcan, Ruth. 2004. *Nudity: A Cultural Anatomy*. Dress, Body, Culture. New York: Berg.

Barrow, Christine. 2001. "Contesting the Rhetoric of 'Black Family Breakdown' from Barbados." *Journal of Comparative Family Studies* 32:419–41.

Batchelor, Tom. 2017. "One of the World's Most Homophobic Countries Is about to Have a Transgender Model Appear at Fashion Week." *The Independent*, January 9.

BBC News. 2016. "Michelle Obama 'Ape in Heels' Facebook Post: Woman 'to Return to Work.'" December 13. https://www.bbc.com/news/world-us-canada-38301808.

Bedford, Kate. 2009. *Developing Partnerships: Gender, Sexuality, and the Reformed World Bank*. Minneapolis: University of Minnesota Press.

Bever, Lindsey. 2018. "H&M Apologizes for Showing Black Child Wearing a 'Monkey in the Jungle' Sweatshirt." *Washington Post*, January 8.

Bobb-Smith, Yvonne. 2020. Interview by Andil Gosine. August 14.

Boorstin, Daniel J. 1983. *The Discoverers*. New York: Knopf Doubleday.

Brady, Sean. 2005. *Masculinity and Male Homosexuality in Britain, 1861–1913*. Houndmills, UK: Palgrave Macmillan.

Brebion, Dominique. 2018. "Désir Cannibale." Association Internationale des Critiques d'Art—Caraïbe du Sud (AICACS). July 30. https://aica-sc.net/2018/07/30/desir -cannibale/.

Brereton, Bridget. 1979. *Race Relations in Colonial Trinidad*. Cambridge: Cambridge University Press.

Brock, Peggy. 2007. "Nakedness and Clothing in Early Encounters between Aboriginal People of Central Australia, Missionaries and Anthropologists." *Journal of Colonialism and Colonial History* 8, no. 1.

Brown, Dalvin. 2018. "'You Can't Just Treat People Like Animals': U.S. Prison Strike Prompts Solidarity Rallies." *USA Today*, August 22.

Bulkan, Arif, and Tracy Robinson. 2018. "Modern Vagrancy, LGBTQI Lives, Discrimination, and Strategic Litigation in the Caribbean." Presentation, University of Toronto, December 3.

Carter, Marina, and Khal Torabully. 2002. *Coolitude: An Anthology of the Indian Labour Diaspora*. London: Anthem.

Césaire, Aimé. 1971. *Cahier d'un retour au pays natal*. Paris: Présence africaine.

Chapman, Steve. 2018. "Roseanne Barr and the Persistence of Prejudice." *Chicago Tribune*, May 30.

Chappell, Kate. 2018. "Jamaica to Roll Up Sleeves and Review Sexist Clothing Rules: 'We Must Evolve.'" *The Guardian*, July 25.

Chong, Shao Yuan. 2020. "To Shame or to Hide? Print Media Reporting of Sexualised Hazing in Taiwanese and Singaporean Conscript Institutions, 1990s to 2010s." Undergraduate thesis, University of British Columbia.

Coalition Advocating Inclusion of Sexual Orientation (CAISO). 2010. *Against Equality: Queer Critiques of Gay Marriage*. Edited by Ryan Conrad. Lewiston, ME: Against Equality Publishing Collective.

Coalition Advocating Inclusion of Sexual Orientation (CAISO). 2018. "Joy, Vulnerability, Re-Focus on Parliament Follow Court Ruling Ending Criminalization of Consensual Sex." April 14. https://www.facebook.com/notes/982571302220073.

Cohn, Bernard S. 1996. *Colonialism and Its Forms of Knowledge: The British in India*. Princeton, NJ: Princeton University Press.

Cook, Matt. 2003. *London and the Culture of Homosexuality, 1885–1914*. Cambridge: Cambridge University Press.

Cooper, Carolyn. 2004. *Sound Clash: Jamaican Dancehall Culture at Large*. New York: Palgrave Macmillan.

Crichlow, Wesley. 2004. *Buller Men and Batty Bwoys: Hidden Men in Toronto and Halifax Black Communities*. Toronto: University of Toronto Press.

Cuvier, Georges, and Étienne Geoffroy Saint-Hilaire. 1824. "[Espéce Humaine] Femme de race Bochismann [de face]." General Research Division, New York Public Library. https://digitalcollections.nypl.org/items/510d47d9-6bf0-a3d9-e040-e00a18064a99.

Davis, Angela. 2012. "A Holistic Approach: Justice, Access and Healing." March 2. https://www.radioproject.org/2012/02/grace-lee-boggs-berkeley/.

De Andrade, Oswald. 2011. "Manifesto Antropófago—Edição crítica e comentada." *Periferia* 3, no. 1. https://doi.org/10.12957/periferia.2011.3407.

De Andrade, Oswald, and Leslie Bary. 1991. "Cannibalist Manifesto." *Latin American Literary Review* 19, no. 38: 38–47.

"Désir Cannibale." 2018. Press release. http://www.fondation-clement.org/Decouvrir-les-expositions/Desir-Cannibale-Exposition-collective.

Douglas, Sean. 2018. "CAISO: Don't Panic over Gay Court Case." *Trinidad and Tobago Newsday*, March 17. https://newsday.co.tt/2018/03/17/caiso-dont-panic-over-gay-court-case/.

Douglass, Frederick. 1845. *Narrative of the Life of Frederick Douglass, an American Slave*. Boston: Anti-Slavery Office. http://www.gutenberg.org/files/23/23-h/23-h.htm.

Du Bois, W. E. B. 1920. "Negro Writers." *The Crisis* 19 (April): 298–99.

Dyer, Richard. 1985. "Male Gay Porn: Coming to Terms." *Jump Cut: A Review of Contemporary Media* 30 (March): 27–29.

Earle, Rebecca. 2001. "'Two Pairs of Pink Satin Shoes!!': Race, Clothing and Identity in the Americas (17th–19th Centuries)." *History Workshop Journal*, no. 52 (Autumn): 175–95.

Earle, Rebecca. 2012. *The Body of the Conquistador: Food, Race and the Colonial Experience in Spanish America, 1492–1700*. Cambridge: Cambridge University Press.

Earle, Rebecca. 2019. "Race, Clothing and Identity: Sumptuary Laws in Colonial Spanish America." In *The Right to Dress: Sumptuary Laws in a Global Perspective, c. 1200–1800*, edited by Giorgio Riello and Ulinka Rublack, 325–45. Cambridge: Cambridge University Press.

Ehrenstein, David. 1980. "Added Attraction: Within the Pleasure Principle or Irresponsible Homosexual Propaganda." *Wide Angle* 4, no. 1: 62–65.

Ellis, Daveny. 2019. "Activist Finds Untruths in Rainbow Road Story about Bajan Lesbians." *Loop News*, December 19. http://www.loopcayman.com/content/activist-finds-untruths-rainbow-road-story-about-bajan-lesbians-0.

Entwistle, Joanne. 2000. "Fashion and the Fleshy Body: Dress as Embodied Practice." *Fashion Theory* 4, no. 3: 323–47.

Esplen, Emily. 2017. *Women and Girls Living with HIV/AIDS: Overview and Annotated Bibliography*. Brighton, UK: Institute of Development Studies, University of Sussex.

Everts, Sarah. 2013. "Europe's Hypocritical History of Cannibalism." *Smithsonian Magazine*, April 24. https://www.smithsonianmag.com/history/europes-hypocritical-history-of-cannibalism-42642371/.

Fanon, Frantz. 1967. *Black Skin, White Masks*. New York: Grove.

Fawcett, Leesa. 2016. "Rats! Being Social Requires Empathy." In *Animal Subjects 2.0*, edited by Jodey Castricano and Lauren Corman, 457–72. Waterloo, ON: Wilfrid Laurier University Press.

Ford-Smith, Honor. 2007. "Keynote: Cannibals, Colonial Scholars and Performance as Postcolonial Caribbean Knowledge Production." *Caribbean Quarterly* 53, nos. 1–2: 8–22.

Foucault, Michel. 1978. *The History of Sexuality*. New York: Pantheon.

French, Patrick. 2008. *The World Is What It Is: The Authorized Biography of V. S. Naipaul*. London: Picador.

Freud, Sigmund. 1962. *Civilization and Its Discontents*. New York: Norton.

Fuson, Robert H. 1987. *The Log of Christopher Columbus*. Camden, ME: International Marine.

Gandhi, M. K. 1921. "National Education." *Young India*, September 1. Reprinted in *The Complete Works of Mahatma Gandhi*, vol. 24. https://gandhiserve.org/cwmg/VOL024.PDF.

Gandhi, M. K. 1925. "A Hotch-Pot of Questions." *Young India*, November 5. Reprinted in *The Complete Works of Mahatma Gandhi*, vol. 33. https://gandhiserve.org/cwmg/VOL033.PDF.

Gane, Nicholas, and Donna Haraway. 2006. "When We Have Never Been Human, What Is to Be Done? Interview with Donna Haraway." *Theory, Culture and Society* 23, nos. 7–8: 135–58.

Gaskins, Joseph, Jr. 2013. "'Buggery' and the Commonwealth Caribbean: A Comparative Examination of the Bahamas, Jamaica, and Trinidad and Tobago." In *Human Rights, Sexual Orientation and Gender Identity in the Commonwealth: Struggles for Decriminalisation and Change*, edited by Corinne Lennox and Matthew Waites, 429–54. London: School of Advanced Study, University of London.

Georgetown Law Human Rights Institute Fact-Finding Project. 2018. *Trapped: Cycles of Violence and Discrimination against Lesbian, Gay, Bisexual, and Transgender Persons in Guyana*. Washington, DC: Georgetown Law Human Rights Institute.

Ghisyawan, Krystal. 2016. "Queering Cartographies of Caribbean Sexuality and Citizenship: Mapping Female Same-Sex Desire, Identities and Belonging in Trinidad." PhD diss., University of the West Indies.

Gill, Lyndon K. 2018. *Erotic Islands: Art and Activism in the Queer Caribbean*. Durham, NC: Duke University Press.

Githire, Njeri. 2014. *Cannibal Writes: Eating Others in Caribbean and Indian Ocean Women's Writing*. Urbana: University of Illinois Press.

Glad Day Bookshop. 2018. "Defending LGBTQ Rights in Barbados." Facebook, July 12. https://www.facebook.com/events/235721367229615.

Goldberg, Jonathan. 1992. *Sodometries: Renaissance Texts, Modern Sexualities*. Stanford: Stanford University Press.

Gosine, Andil. 2004. *Sex for Pleasure, Rights to Participation, and Alternatives to AIDS: Placing Sexual Minorities and/or Dissidents in Development*. Brighton, UK: Institute of Development Studies, University of Sussex.

Gosine, Andil. 2006. "'Race,' Culture, Power, Sex, Desire, Love: Writing in 'Men Who Have Sex with Men.'" *IDS Bulletin* 37, no. 5: 27–33.

Gosine, Andil. 2009a. "Monster, Womb, MSM: The Work of Sex in International Development." *Development* 52:25–33.

Gosine, Andil. 2009b. "Speaking Sexuality: The Heteronationalism of MSM." In *Sexuality, Social Exclusion and Human Rights: Vulnerability in the Caribbean Context of HIV*, edited by Christine Barrow, Marjan de Bruin, and Robert Carr, 95–115. Kingston, Jamaica: Randle.

Gosine, Andil. 2010. "Non-White Reproduction and Same-Sex Eroticism: Queer Acts against Nature." In *Queer Ecologies: Sex, Nature, Politics, Desire,* edited by Catriona Mortimer-Sandilands and Bruce Erickson, 149–72. Bloomington: Indiana University Press.

Gosine, Andil. 2012. "Caribbean: Crossroads of the World." *Art in America*, June 13. https://www.artinamericamagazine.com/reviews/caribbean-crossroads-of-the-world/.

Gosine, Andil. 2015. *Rescue, and Real Love: Same-Sex Desire in International Development*. Brighton, UK: Institute of Development Studies, University of Sussex.

Gosine, Andil. 2016a. "My Mother's *Baby*: Wrecking Work after Indentureship." In *Indo-Caribbean Feminist Thought*, edited by Gabrielle Hosein and Lisa Outar, 49–60. London: Palgrave Macmillan.

Gosine, Andil. 2016b. "*Puhngah*/Men in Skirts: A Plea for History." In *The Palgrave Handbook of Gender and Development: Critical Engagements in Feminist Theory and Practice*, edited by Wendy Harcourt, 551–60. London: Palgrave Macmillan.

Works Cited

Gosine, Andil. 2018. "Rescue, and Real Love: Same-Sex Desire in International Development." In *Routledge Handbook of Queer Development Studies*, 193–208. Abingdon, UK: Routledge.

Hall, Stuart, with Bill Schwarz. 2017. *Familiar Stranger: A Life between Two Islands*. Durham, NC: Duke University Press.

Handy, Gemma. 2018. "Archaeologists Say Early Caribbeans Were Not 'Savage Cannibals,' as Colonists Wrote." *The Guardian*, April 24.

Haraway, Donna. 2003. *The Companion Species Manifesto: Dogs, People, and Significant Otherness*. Chicago: Prickly Paradigm.

Hartman, Saidiya. 1997. *Scenes of Subjection: Terror, Slavery, and Self-Making in Nineteenth-Century America*. New York: Oxford University Press.

Haworth, Abigail. 2013. "Why Have Young People in Japan Stopped Having Sex?" *The Guardian*, October 24.

Hollibaugh, Amber, and Margot Weiss. 2015. "Queer Precarity and the Myth of Gay Affluence." *New Labor Forum* 24, no. 3: 18–27.

Hulme, Peter. 1998. "Introduction: The Cannibale Scene." In *Cannibalism and the Colonial World*, edited by Francis Barker, Peter Hulme, and Margaret Iversen, 1–38. Cambridge: Cambridge University Press.

Human Rights Watch. 2008. *This Alien Legacy*. New York: Human Rights Watch.

Hyam, Ronald. 1991. *Empire and Sexuality: The British Experience*. New York: Manchester University Press.

Jackson, Zakiyyah Iman. 2016. "Losing Manhood: Animality and Plasticity in the (Neo)Slave Narrative." *Qui Parle* 25, nos. 1–2 (Fall/Winter): 95–136.

Jane, Cecil, trans. 1960. *The Journal of Christopher Columbus*. New York: Bramhall House.

Joffe, Hélène. 1999. *Risk and "the Other."* Cambridge: Cambridge University Press.

Jones, Jason. 2018a. "We Won in Trinidad. Now It's Time to End All Homophobic Laws in the Commonwealth." *The Guardian*, April 14.

Jones, Jason. 2018b. "What an amazing year for me and my small team of lawyers . . ." Facebook, December 21. https://www.facebook.com/jasonjonesesquire.

Joseph, Ralina L. 2011. "Imagining Obama: Reading Overtly and Inferentially Racist Images of Our 44th President, 2007–2008." *Communication Studies* 62, no. 4: 389–405.

Kamugisha, Aaron. 2007. "The Coloniality of Citizenship in the Contemporary Anglophone Caribbean." *Race and Class* 49, no. 2: 20–40.

Karras, Ruth Mazo. 2005. *Sexuality in Medieval Europe: Doing unto Others*. New York: Routledge.

Kempadoo, Kamala. 2004. *Sexing the Caribbean*. New York: Routledge.

Kim, Claire Jean. 2015. *Dangerous Crossings: Race, Species, and Nature in a Multicultural Age*. Cambridge: Cambridge University Press, 2015.

King, Rosamond S. 2014. *Island Bodies: Transgressive Sexualities in the Caribbean Imagination*. Gainesville: University Press of Florida.

Kitzinger, Jenny. 1995. "The Face of AIDS." In *Representations of Health, Illness and Handicap*, edited by Ivana Markova and Robert Farr, 49–66. London: Harwood Academic.

Koblin, John. 2018. "After Racist Tweet, Roseanne Barr's Show Is Canceled by ABC." *New York Times*, May 29.

Kumar, Preity Rajanie. 2018. "Women Lovin' Women: An Exploration of Identities, Belonging, and Communities in Urban and Rural Guyana." PhD diss., York University.

Lambert, Steve. 2019. "Viral Video of Manitoba Newborn Being Apprehended by CFS Prompts Family to Speak Out." *Global News,* January 11.

Larcher, Akim Ade, and Colin Robinson. 2009. "Fighting Murder Music: Activist Reflections." *Caribbean Review of Gender Studies,* no. 3: 1–12.

Leap, William, ed. 1999. *Public Sex/Gay Space.* New York: Columbia University Press.

Lee, Phillip. n.d. "About." *His Way Out Ministries.* Accessed November 14, 2011. http://hiswayout.com.

Levine, Philippa. 2008. "States of Undress: Nakedness and the Colonial Imagination." *Victorian Studies* 50, no. 2 (Winter 2008): 189–219.

Levine, Philippa. 2013. "Naked Truths: Bodies, Knowledge, and the Erotics of Colonial Power." *Journal of British Studies* 52, no. 1 (January): 5–25.

Linnaeus, Carl. 1758. *Systema Naturae.* Ed. 10, vol. 1. http://linnean-online.org/119965/.

Loriggio, Paola. 2020. "Teen Wanted to Change Schools after Sexual Assault at Toronto Private School: Witness." CBC, December 9. https://www.cbc.ca/news/canada/toronto/st-michaels-trials-1.5834577.

Lunenfeld, Marvin. 1991. *1492—Discovery, Invasion, Encounter: Sources and Interpretations.* Lexington, MA: Heath.

MacLean, Geoffrey. 2010. "Remembering Our History (Know Your Country)." CAISO, February 17. http://gspottt.wordpress.com/2010/02/17/remembering-history/.

Massad, Joseph A. 2007. *Desiring Arabs.* Chicago: University of Chicago Press.

McCaskell, Tim. 2016. *Queer Progress: From Homophobia to Homonationalism.* Toronto: Between the Lines.

McClintock, Anne. 1995. *Imperial Leather: Race, Gender, and Sexuality in the Colonial Contest.* New York: Routledge.

McNeal, Keith E., and Rachel Afi Quinn. 2016. "Transgressive Bodies, Caribbean Sexualities, and Queer Feminisms." *Social and Economies Studies* 65, no. 4: 131–41.

Mercer, Kobena. 1990. "Black Art and the Burden of Representation." *Third Text* 4, no. 10: 61–78.

Minshall, Peter. 2013. "Mas Man Unmasked." *Trinidad and Tobago Guardian,* February 3. https://www.guardian.co.tt/article-6.2.394690.6d35a57b84.

Mohabir, Nalini. 2018. "Hidden Stories in the Family Photo Album: The 'Brown Sugar Diaspora.'" The Conversation, December 10. https://theconversation.com/hidden-stories-in-the-family-photo-album-the-brown-sugar-diaspora-107261.

Mohabir, Rajiv. 2021. *Antiman: A Hybrid Memoir.* Brooklyn: Restless Books.

Mohammed, Patricia. 1999. "From Myth to Symbolism: The Definitions of Indian Femininity and Masculinity in Post-Indentureship Trinidad." In *Matikor: The Politics of Identity for Indo-Caribbean Women,* edited by Rosanne Kanhai, 62–99. St. Augustine, Trinidad and Tobago: University of West Indies.

Mohammed, Patricia, dir. 2009. *Coolie Pink and Green.* Film. Trinidad and Tobago.

Moran, Leslie. 1996. *The Homosexual(ity) of Law.* London: Routledge.

Moran, Padraig. 2018. "Indigenous Women Kept from Seeing Their Newborn Babies

Until Agreeing to Sterilization, Says Lawyer." CBC, November 13. https://www.cbc
.ca/radio/thecurrent/the-current-for-november-13-2018-1.4902679/indigenous
-women-kept-from-seeing-their-newborn-babies-until-agreeing-to-sterilization
-says-lawyer-1.4902693.

Morrison, Ryan. 2020. "Columbus' CANNIBAL Claims May Have Been True after All."
Daily Mail, January 10. https://www.dailymail.co.uk/sciencetech/article-7872651
/Columbus-Caribbean-CANNIBAL-claims-true-all.html.

Mowlabocus, Sharif, Justin Harbottle, and Charlie Witzel. 2013. "Porn Laid Bare: Gay
Men, Pornography and Bareback Sex." *Sexualities* 16, nos. 5–6: 523–47.

Moyo, Jeffrey. 2017. "Worse than Dogs and Pigs: Life as a Gay Man in Zimbabwe." Reu-
ters, September 3. https://www.reuters.com/article/us-zimbabwe-rights-lgbt
/worse-than-dogs-and-pigs-life-as-a-gay-man-in-zimbabwe-idUSKCN1BF03Z.

Muñoz, José Esteban. 2015. "Theorizing Queer Inhumanisms: The Sense of Brown-
ness." *GLQ: A Journal of Lesbian and Gay Studies* 21, no. 2: 209–10.

Murray, David A. B. 2009. "Bajan Queens, Nebulous Scenes: Sexual Diversity in
Barbados." *Caribbean Review of Gender Studies* 3. https://www.researchgate.net
/publication/238682208_Bajan_Queens_Nebulous_Scenes_Sexual_Diversity_in
_Barbados.

Nicol, Nancy, Nick Mulé, and Erika Gates-Gasse. 2014. "Envisioning Global LGBT
Human Rights: Strategic Alliances to Advance Knowledge and Social Change."
Scholarly and Research Communication 5, no. 3: 1–16.

Noble, Louise. 2011. *Medicinal Cannibalism in Early Modern English Literature and Culture*. New York: Palgrave Macmillan.

Noble, Louise. 2013. "'And Make Two Pasties of Your Shameful Heads': Medicinal
Cannibalism and Healing the Body Politic in Titus Andronicus." *ELH* 70, no. 3:
677–708.

O'Grady, Lorraine. 1998. "Olympia's Maid: Reclaiming Black Female Subjectivity." In
Art, Activism, and Oppositionality, edited by Grant H. Kester, 268–87. Durham,
NC: Duke University Press.

O'Grady, Lorraine. 2010. Interview by Andil Gosine. June 21.

Outar, Lisa. 2016. "Art, Violence, and Non-return: An Interview with Guadeloupean
Artist Kelly Sinnapah Mary." In *Indo-Caribbean Feminist Thought*, edited by Gabrielle Hosein and Lisa Outar, 93–112. New York: Palgrave Macmillan.

OutRight Action International. 2017. "Excerpt: What Has Been the Conservative Response in Trinidad to Your Court Case?" YouTube, March 2. https://www
.youtube.com/watch?v=FEXDJYOvRZs&feature=youtu.be.

Paul, Annie. 2003. "Christopher Cozier." *Bomb*, January 1.

Puar, Jasbir. 1999. "Transnational Sexualities and Trinidad: Modern Bodies, National
Queers." PhD diss., University of California, Berkeley.

Puar, Jasbir. 2007. *Terrorist Assemblages: Homonationalism in Queer Times*. Durham,
NC: Duke University Press.

Puri, Shalini. 2004. *The Caribbean Postcolonial: Social Equality, Post/Nationalism, and
Cultural Hybridity*. New York: Palgrave Macmillan.

Ramjag, Rawle. 2016. "Dress Codes in Carnival Country." National Workers Union,

September 20. http://www.workersunion.org.tt/where-we-stand/nwu-news
/dresscodesincarnivalcountrybyrawleramjag.

Ray, Nicholas. 2014. "Interrogating the Human/Animal Relation in Freud's *Civilization and Its Discontents*." *Humanimalia: A Journal of Human/Animal Interface Studies* 6, no. 1: 10–40.

Reddock, Rhoda. 1986. "Freedom Denied: Indian Women and Indentureship in Trinidad and Tobago, 1845–1917." *Caribbean Quarterly* 32, no. 3: 27–49.

Reddock, Rhoda, Sandra Reid, and Jane Parpart. 2011. *Breaking the Silence: A Multi-Sectoral Approach to Preventing and Addressing Child Sexual Abuse in Trinidad and Tobago*. Port of Spain: University of West Indies.

Robinson, Colin. n.d. "The Work of Three-Year-Old CAISO." Accessed September 6, 2016. https://www.caribbeanhomophobias.org/node/20.

Robinson, Colin. 2010. "Sexual Rights: Protection of Sexuality as Something Good, Natural, Precious, Essential—at the Core of Human Expression . . . Human Freedom . . . Human Community." CAISO, March 23. http://gspottt.wordpress.com /category/trans/.

Robinson, Colin. 2011–18. Interviews by Andil Gosine.

Robinson, Colin. 2018a. "Making Up the Caribbean." *Trinidad and Tobago Newsday*, September 16. https://newsday.co.tt/2018/09/16/making-up-the-caribbean/.

Robinson, Colin. 2018b. "The Small-Man Court." *Trinidad and Tobago Newsday*, November 17. https://newsday.co.tt/2018/11/17/the-small-man-court/.

Robinson, Colin. 2019. "My Memories of Marlene." *Trinidad and Tobago Newsday*, August 18. https://newsday.co.tt/2019/08/18/my-memories-of-marlene/.

Robinson, Tracy. 2007. "A Loving Freedom: A Caribbean Feminist Ethic." *Small Axe* 11, no. 3: 118–29.

Robinson, Tracy. 2017. "New-Old Law in the Postcolony: Regulating Sex in the Anglophone Caribbean." Paper presented at the Penn Program on Democracy, Citizenship, and Constitutionalism (DCC), Tenth Annual Conference, "Citizenship on the Edge: Sex/Gender/Race," University of Pennsylvania, Philadelphia, May 5.

Robinson, Tracy, and Arif Bulkan. 2017. "Enduring Sexed and Gendered Criminal Laws in the Anglophone Caribbean." *Caribbean Review of Gender Studies*, no. 11: 219–40.

Rodriguez, Mathew. 2019. "Trump's Plan to Decriminalize Homosexuality Is an Old Racist Tactic." *Out*, February 19. https://www.out.com/news-opinion/2019/2/19 /trumps-plan-decriminalize-homosexuality-old-racist-tactic.

Romero, Ivette, trans. 2018. Excerpts from Dominique Brebion, "Désir Cannibale." RepeatingIslands.com, August 1. https://repeatingislands.com/2018/08/01/art -exhibition-desir-cannibale/.

Rowe, Acey. 2019. "'I'm Free': How Canada's Rainbow Railroad Helped a Barbados Couple Fleeing Persecution Find Peace." CBC, December 17. https://www.cbc.ca /radio/docproject/i-m-free-how-canada-s-rainbow-railroad-helped-a-barbados -couple-fleeing-persecution-find-peace-1.5393927.

Rubenstein, Jay. 2008. "Cannibals and Crusaders." *French Historical Studies* 31, no. 4: 525–52.

Sanatan, Amílcar. 2019. "'Writing Is an Arsenal': An Interview with Colin Robinson." *Small Axe* 32 (October). http://smallaxe.net/sxsalon/discussions/writing-arsenal -interview-colin-robinson.

Sauer, Carl. 1966. *The Early Spanish Main.* Berkeley: University of California Press.

Scott, David. 2000. "The Re-Enchantment of Humanism: An Interview with Sylvia Wynter." *Small Axe* 8 (September): 119–207.

Scott, Stephen Kingsley. 2002. "Through the Diameter of Respectability: The Politics of Historical Representation in Postemancipation Colonial Trinidad." *NWIG: New West Indian Guide/Nieuwe West-Indische Gids* 76, nos. 3–4: 271–304.

Seymour, Gayle M. 1997. "Simeon Solomon and the Biblical Construction of Marginal Identity in Victorian England." *Journal of Homosexuality* 33, nos. 3–4: 97–119.

Shakespeare, William. 1992. *The Merchant of Venice.* New York: Washington Square Press.

Sharples, Carinya. 2017. "Guyana's Transgender Activists Fight Archaic Law." *BBC News,* March 26. https://www.bbc.com/news/world-latin-america-39292599.

Sheller, Mimi. 2003. *Consuming the Caribbean: From Arawaks to Zombies.* London: Routledge.

Sheller, Mimi. 2012. *Citizenship from Below: Erotic Agency and Caribbean Freedom.* Durham, NC: Duke University Press.

Silvera, Makeda. 1992. "Man Royals and Sodomites: Some Thoughts on the Invisibility of Afro-Caribbean Lesbians." *Feminist Studies* 18, no. 3: 521–32.

Simpson, Joel. 2018. Interview by Andil Gosine. January 2.

Sinnapah Mary, Kelly. 2018. Interviews and email correspondence with Andil Gosine.

Sital, Krystal A. 2018. *Secrets We Kept: Three Women of Trinidad.* New York: Norton.

Smith, Faith. 2017. "Queer Livity in the Caribbean: Rosamond S. King's Island Bodies." *Small Axe* 21, no. 1: 223–40.

Smith, Matthew Ryan 2020. "Andil Gosine's 'Cane Portraiture' and the Aesthetics of Indenture." *BlackFlash,* March 4. https://blackflash.ca/2020/03/04/andil-gosine -cane-portraiture-and-the-aesthetics-of-indenture/.

Smith, Raymond T. 1967. "Social Stratification, Cultural Pluralism and Integration in West Indian Societies." In *Caribbean Integration: Papers on Social, Political and Economic Integration,* edited by Sybil Farrell Lewis and Thomas G. Matthews, 237. Rio Piedras: Institute of Caribbean Studies, University of Puerto Rico.

Stabroek News. 2009. "He Wore Blue Velvet . . . ? Seven Fined for Cross-Dressing." February 10. https://www.stabroeknews.com/2009/02/10/news/guyana/he-wore -blue-velvetseven-fined-for-cross-dressing/.

Stewart, J. O. 1973. "Coolie and Creole: Differential Adaptations in a Neo-Plantation Village—Trinidad, West Indies." PhD diss., University of California, Los Angeles.

Stoler, Ann Laura. 1992. "Sexual Affronts and Racial Frontiers: European Identities and the Cultural Politics of Exclusion in Colonial Southeast Asia." *Comparative Studies in Society and History* 34, no. 3 (July): 514–51.

Stoler, Ann Laura. 1995. *Race and the Education of Desire: Foucault's History of Sexuality and the Colonial Order of Things.* Durham, NC: Duke University Press.

Sullivan, Jacob, and Michael Hegenauer. 2017. "LBGTQ Travel Index: Which Countries

Are the Most Gay Friendly?" Kayak, April 4. https://www.kayak.co.uk
/magazine/gay-travel-index-2017/.

Strasser, Max. 2014. "Top Twelve Most Homophobic Nations." *Newsweek*, February 27.

Szekely, Reka. 2018. "Oshawa Gallery Apologizes for Putting Mature-Content Warning on Exhibit with Gay Themes." *Toronto Star*, March 21. https://www.thestar.com /news/gta/2018/03/21/oshawa-gallery-apologizes-for-putting-mature-content -warning-on-exhibit-with-gay-themes.html.

Thompson, Akola. 2019. "Trans History and Remembrance: Beyond the Stereotypes." *Stabroek News*, November 22. https://www.stabroeknews.com/2019/11/22 /features/the-minority-report/trans-history-and-remembrance-beyond-the -stereotypes/.

Torabully, Khal. 1992. *Cale d'étoiles: Coolitude*. La Reunion: Azalées Edition.

Tsuji, Teruyuki. 2008. "Villaging the Nation: The Politics of Making Ourselves in Postcolonial Trinidad." *Callaloo* 31, no. 4: 1148–74.

Turner, Darwin T. 1974. "W. E. B. Du Bois and the Theory of a Black Aesthetic." *Studies in Literary Imagination* 7, no. 2: 1–21.

UNICEF. 2010. *Child Sexual Abuse in the Eastern Caribbean*. Bridgetown, Barbados. https://www.unicef.org/Child_Sexual_Abuse_Publication.pdf.

United Nations. 2019. "UN Report: Nature's Dangerous Decline 'Unprecedented'; Species Extinction Rates 'Accelerating.'" May 6. https://www.un.org /sustainabledevelopment/blog/2019/05/nature-decline-unprecedented-report/.

Upchurch, Charles. 2009. *Before Wilde: Sex between Men in Britain's Age of Reform*. Berkeley: University of California Press.

Wahab, Amar. 2012. "Homophobia as the State of Reason: The Case of Postcolonial Trinidad and Tobago." *GLQ: A Journal of Lesbian and Gay Studies* 18, no. 4: 481–505.

Waites, Matthew. 2013. "United Kingdom: Confronting Criminal Histories and Theorising Decriminalisation as Citizenship and Governmentality." In *Human Rights, Sexual Orientation and Gender Identity in the Commonwealth: Struggles for Decriminalisation and Change*, edited by Corinne Lennox and Matthew Waites, 145–81. London: School of Advanced Study, University of London.

Ward, Jane. 2015. *Not Gay: Sex between Straight White Men*. New York: New York University Press.

Wehner, Peter. 2019. "Pete Buttigieg's Very Public Faith Is Challenging Assumptions." *The Atlantic*, April 10.

Wekker, Gloria. 2006. *The Politics of Passion: Women's Sexual Culture in the Afro-Surinamese Diaspora*. New York: Columbia University Press.

Whitehead, Neil. 1984. "Carib Cannibalism: The Historical Evidence." *Journal de la société des américanistes*, no. 70: 69–87.

Williams, Eric. 1942. *The Negro in the Caribbean*. Gloucester, MA: Haskell House.

Williams, Eric. 1962. "Message to the Youth of the Nation." August 30. https://ufdc.ufl .edu/AA00012809/00001.

Wilson, Sascha. 2007. "Victim of Public Ridicule Speaks Out." *Trinidad and Tobago Guardian*, July 21.

Wynter, Sylvia. 2003. "Unsettling the Coloniality of Being/Power/Truth/Freedom: Towards the Human, after Man, Its Overrepresentation—An Argument." CR: The New Centennial Review 3, no. 3: 257–337.

Young, Robert J. C. 2005. Colonial Desire: Hybridity in Theory, Culture and Race. London: Routledge.

Page numbers in italics refer to figures.

abominable crime of buggery 23–24, 26, 30, 76, 91–92

Africa 16, 39, 40

Africans 17, 21, 25, 27–28, 31, 102, 106, 109

Afro-Trinidadians 29, 102

Agamben, Giorgio 3

Alexander, M. Jacqui 4, 9, 29, 30

Alice & Goliath 115

Alice's Adventures in Wonderland (Carroll) 115

Alliance for Justice and Diversity (AJD) 93

All the Flowers 139–142

America 16, 20, 39, 40, 54

Amerindians 21, 105, 107

Anderson, Winston 57

Andrade, Oswald de Souza 108

animal/animality 3, 16, 19, 102; accusations of 109; anxieties 4, 6; arbiter of 38; behavior 50; in *Calling Card* 150; Caribbean peoples 7, 8, 38, 109; carnivorous 111; civilize colonized peoples 24; claim of 143; colonial accusations of 8; colonial and postcolonial-era cultures 4; colonized peoples 17;

animal/animality (*continued*)
demarcation of human 8; desire
148–49; history of 40, 46; human/
humanity 3–6, 8, 10–12, 16–17, 23, 39,
41, 46–47, 58–59, 73, 116–25; hybridity
118, 125, 128; Indigenous peoples 19,
72; Kalinago/Caribs as 5; lack of civilization 40; laws about 26–27; men
who had sex with 24; non-Europeans
as 25; nonhuman 11, 116, 126; nonwhite homophobe as 7; nonwhite
people 39; rights 144; sexual desire 4;
sexuality 107; slaughtering of 18; social 111
Animal Farm (Orwell) 56
animalistic act/desire 24, 27, 73, 117, 125,
136
animality 19, 25, 38, 44, 68, 102, 109, 126
Antigua 30
anxieties 20, 23–24, 37, 72
Arab 74
Arens, William 107
Arif, Bulkan 46
Asia 16, 39, 40
Attack of the Sandwich Men (Cozier)
28, 29
Attai, Nikoli 75
Australia 41

Baartman, Sara 40
Bagoo, Andre 64
Bahadur, Gaiutra 33
Balboa in Quarequa 37
Banana Bottom (McKay) 50
Banjo (McKay) 50
Barbados 56, 76
Barbados Sexual Offences Act 76
Barbuda 30
Barcan, Ruth 39
Barrow, Denys 57
beast 16–31
Bedford, Kate 29
Belize 74
Beloved (Morrison) 10
Berkeley, Cherisse 64
Bernardino of Siena 37

bestiality 6, 24, 72; homosexuality and
24; masturbation and 24
Black Gay Men 63
Black Hearts Collective 63
Black women 3
Bobb-Smith, Yvonne 54–55
Bomb (magazine) 28
Botswana 74
breathing air 56–61; *see also* natural as
breathing air
Brereton, Bridget 27
Brief History of Seven Killings (James) 71
British colonies 23, 25
British Empire 24
British Home Office 24
British slavery-replacement system 32
British West Indies 25
"Buy Crix" 86–99

Cale d'etoiles (Torabully) 32
Calling Card 143, 143–46
Canada 36, 75, 103
Canadian Broadcasting Corporation 76
Canadian HIV Legal Network 75–76, 81
cannibalism 104–8, 110; hypocritical his-
tory of cannibalism 107
cannibals 104–5
Cannibal Writes (Githire) 106
Caribbean Court of Justice 56
Caribbean homophobia 74
Caribbean Indigenous peoples 20
Caribbean International Resources Net-
work 130
Caribbean Postcolonial (Puri) 111
Caribbean Queer Visualities (Belfast)
136–39
Caribbean Vulnerable Communities
(CVC) 80
Carroll, Lewis 115
Catholicism 27
Cempaloa 19
Charter of Fundamental Rights and
Freedoms 30
childhood socialization 37
China 52
choir practice 13

Christian: missionaries 41; model 23; theology 39

citizenship 9, 10, 11, 70

Citizenship from Below (Sheller) 9

civilization/civilized 30, 40; behavior 23, 27, 140; common sense 67; humans 41, 136

Clearing, The (O'Grady) 3, 19

clothes/clothing 32–61; absence of 39; arbitration over 39; civility right and 39; feature of being human 39; female 45; men 45; morality and 39; moral reasons for 44; role of 39; symbolic use of 39; variously and simultaneously 39; vis-à-vis items of 44

Coalition Advocating Inclusion of Sexual Orientation (CAISO) 78–86

colonial antisodomy laws 30

colonial-era anxieties 38

colonial missionaries 20

colonial stigmatization 84

colonization 4, 72, 88; advance 6, 19; afterlives of 7; Black and Brown bodies 148; British 21, 23; Caribbean 43; of civilized peoples 17; dominant logic of 37; European 4, 17, 39, 41; France 118; of Global South 67; heritage of 133; heteropatriarchal 29; rejection of 64; Spanish 21; use of sex 72; violence of 52

Columbus, Christopher 104

Coolie Colors (Glasgow) 136–39

Coolie Coolie Viens 133–36

Cortés, Hernán 3, 19, 72

Cozier, Christopher 28–29

criminal codes 23

Criminal Law (Offences) Act 26

Crix 86

Cuba 104

culture 3; American right-wing 117; British 27; contemporary popular 117; destruction of 32; Euro-American 134–35; gay 101, 149; gender affairs 78; Indian 112; Indian heritage and 112; Indo-Trinbagonian 99; national 84; normative 4; possession of 27;

re-creation of 113; rural forms of 101; Trini 83; Western 107

Cuvier, Frédéric 40

Daily Mail 106

d'Anghiera, Peter Martyr 18

Daniel Boone's First View of Kentucky (Ranney) 21, 22

Darwin, Charles 41

Dass, Rishi 91

de Balboa, Vasco Núñez 17

de Bry, Theodore 17, 18, 19, 105

decriminalization of sodomy 63, 70, 92, 95, 151

de Horta, Blas 40

dehumanization 5, 11, 20, 43, 47, 58, 72, 98, 131, 150

del Castillo, Bernal Díaz 19

del Fuego, Tierra 41

De Orbo Novo (d'Anghiera) 18

de Oviedo, Gonzalo Fernández 20

Désir Cannibale 8, 103–129

desire 20, 25; animal 148–49; cannibal 108, 112; to embody traditional femininity 37; free animal 21; romantic 135; sexual 2–4, 12, 31, 68, 125, 136, 146, 148–49

discipline: production 67–68, 139–41, 143, 148; through sexuality 29–30, 138

Douglass, Frederick 16

Drabble, Richard 91

dress code: gendered 52; for humans 48–56; as mark of civility 52; persistent investment in 52; signage in Port of Spain 53; *see also* clothes/clothing

dressing 47; *see also* clothes/clothing

Dutch Caribbean islands 54

Earle, Rebecca 54

Edwards, Jeremy Steffan 64

"Elephant's Walk" 14–15

Elliott, Richard 81, 82

Emanuel, Antonio 91

England 24, 54

English emissaries 25
Entwistle, Joanne 39
Envisioning Homophobia 74
erotic autonomy 4, 30, 149
Euro-American culture 4, 134, 135
Euro-American narratives 101–2
European colonization 4, 17, 39, 41
Evangelicals 93–95
Everts, Sarah 107

Facey, Laura 131
familial attachments 17
Fanon, Frantz 10, 11, 37, 84, 101
fashion 33, 35–36
Fashion Institute of Technology (FIT)
    132
Fleta 23
Florida Museum of Natural History 106
Foucault, Michel 21, 23
French, Patrick 119
Fung, Richard 12, 137

Gandhi, Mohandas 68
Gaskins, Joseph 26
gay: in Barbados 77; Black 98; Carib-
    bean men 33; in Caribbean territory
    77; conversion therapy 86; culture 101,
    149; global community 86; identity 83;
    international activists 7; internation-
    alism 90; international narratives 85;
    law 75; male bodies 36; masculinity
    36; media 95; men 97, 120, 149; move-
    ments 87; rights to marriage 79; sex
    tourists 74; sexual identities 73, 102;
    visible activist 63; white men 21
Gay International 73
gender 24, 101; ambiguity 37; coded
    dress 37; confines of 35; confusion
    137; criminalization of 131; criminal
    laws 23; demonstrated leadership on
    89; determinant rules 49; dress codes
    52; expressions of 31, 47; gigantic 50;
    humanity and 43; identities 45, 72,
    79, 143; Indo-Surinamese dancer 97;
    lighthearted stereotype of 62; male

137; nonconforming characters 37;
    nonconforming identities 48; norma-
    tive behaviour 57; norms 20, 33, 37;
    personal identity and 57; policing ges-
    ture 35; policy-for-some green paper
    78; as restrictive disciplining tool 33;
    rights 9; socialization 139; visual art
    with 39
Georgetown Botanical Gardens 130
Georgetown Law Human Rights Insti-
    tute 38, 46–47
Ghisyawan, Krystal 101
Githire, Njeri 106
Goldberg, Jonathan 72
Gonzalez-Torres, Félix 12
Gospel 13, 16, 36, 74
Grady, Leor 12
Grenada Revolution 63
gross indecency 26
Guardian, The 64, 80, 85, 92, 105
Guyana 26, 74; colonial antisodomy 30;
    domestic violence 33; LGBTQI people
    in 38; marginalized groups in 86;
    National Cultural Centre in George-
    town 45; SASOD in 86; *Sunday Chron-
    icle* 38

Hall, Stuart 27–28
Hanamji, Rudy 64
Hemings, Sally 3
heteronormativity 24
heterosexual family 30, 138
Hill, James 50
Hindu/Hinduism 112, 113, 155n1; cabi-
    net minister 155n1; Catholicism and
    112; deity 138; flags 137; forms of mar-
    riage 23; gods and goddesses 112, 113,
    118; heritage 118; Indian conch 112;
    Indo-Caribbean community 67; Ma-
    habharata 55; pundit (priest) 112, 113;
    reincarnation 113, 118; rituals of 113,
    127, 156n1; school 118, 155n1; temple
    155n1
History of Jamaica, The (Long) 17
Home in Harlem (McKay) 50

homoerotic: sexual socialization 13; socialization 13, 14; homoerotic homosexual agenda 86; *see also* Buy Crix
homosexuality 5, 37, 78, 150; anxieties about 11, 21, 94; bestiality and 24; condemnation of 14; fears about 24; historical visibility of 83; immorality of 6; masturbation and 23; normalization of 71; regulation of 4
homosexual sex 20, 134, 138
homoshaming/homoeroticizing ritual 14
homosocial behavior 13
Hosein, Gabrielle 64
Hotmilk 125–26
human/humanity 3, 16; animals/animality and 3–6, 8, 10–12, 16–17, 23, 39, 41, 46–47, 58–59, 73, 116–25; demarcation of 8; dress code for 48–56; gender and 43; as more animal 16; sexuality 23
Huxley, Thomas 40

identity 39; animal as 143, 149; authentic 113; ethnic 113; gay/lesbian 83; gender 72, 79; LGBTQI 73; personal 57; power and 4; reconstruction of 128; self-constitution of 4; self-determined constitution of 46; sexual 9, 39, 43, 101–2
India 52, 74
Indian indentures 23, 106, 109, 111, 114
Indigenous Jamaicans 17
Indigenous peoples 5, 19–20, 31, 41, 72, 104, 106–7, 111, 131
Indigenous victims 19
Indo-Caribbean peoples 127, 129; cultural forms 102; domestic violence 33; morality 60; visual arts 127–29
Indo-Guadeloupean community 112
Indo-Guyanese 101
Indo-Trinidadians 32, 102
Institute of Development Studies at Sussex University 134
interracial sex 4, 146–48
Inward Hunger (Williams) 100
Island Bodies (King) 37

Jackson, Zakiyyah Iman 10, 17
Jacob-Gomes, Shannon 52
Jamaica 26, 30, 56, 74
James, King 54
James, Marlon 71
Jefferson, Thomas 3
jokes 16, 20

Kalinago (Carib) 19
Kamugisha, Aaron 9
Kenya 74
King, Rosamond 9, 37
Kumar, Priety 101

Laveaux, Mélissa 103
lesbian 46, 73, 74, 76, 83, 86, 89; *see also* gay
Levine, Philippa 39–41
LGBTQI movement 80
LGBTQI people 38, 71, 74
Linnaeus, Carl 39–40
Long, Edward 17
Long Way from Home (McKay) 50

MacLean, Geoffrey 64
Made in Love 133–36
male sexualities 71
Malinche, La 3, 19
"man" beyond metropole 99–102
mancebos 107
Man-Eating Myth (Arens) 107
Manifesto antropófago (Andrade) 108
Maraj, Kennedy Everett 64
Mary, Kelly Sinnapah 8, 108–16, 124–25
masculinities 71; femininity and 37; gay, in pornography 36; performance of 32; privileges of 141; signaling 137; transgressions of 137
masturbation: bestiality 24; homosexuality and 23; mutual 14
McDonald, Marlene 78
McKay, Claude 49
Medicinal Cannibalism in Early Modern English Literature and Culture (Noble) 108

62 Men and 63 Women (Facey) 131
men who have sex with men (MSM) 134
Mercer, Conrad 68
Mercer, Kobena 126
Merchant of Venice, The (Shakespeare) 44
Mexico 41
Minshall, Peter 56
missionaries 16, 20, 41; *see also* Christian, colonial missionaries
Mitchell, Kennty Dave 78
Monkman, Kent 21, 31
Morrison, Toni 10
Mottley, Sharon 64
Muslim 74
Muslimeen 94
My Green Hills of Jamaica (McKay) 50

Nahua woman 19
naked/nakedness 6, 36, 39, 43–44; kind of dress 41; native 40; quite 41; stylized 41
Nanan, Wendy 12
National Geographic 41
National Policy on Gender 78
natural as breathing air 56–61
Natures 146–51
Nevis 24
new beasts 70–78
Newsweek 73
New York City 63
Nicol, Nancy 74
Nixon, Angelique 64
Noble, Louise 108
North Carolina State University 106
Notebook of No Return (Mary) 8, 109–16
nudity 39; ashamed and shamed 41; condemnation of 40, 41; *see also* naked/nakedness

O'Grady, Lorraine 3–5, 7, 12, 19, 21, 125, 132–33
Olympia's Maid (O'Grady) 3
oral sex 13
Ortiz, Tomás 19
Orwell, George 56

Pandora's box 23
patriarchal power 24
Paul, Annie 28
People's National Movement (PNM) government 50, 79
People's Partnership (PP) 79
Person Act 24, 25
Petti, Shari 50, 59–61
Photography Club 15
political independence 28, 30, 33, 56
politics of respectability 7, 27, 29, 45, 92, 129
pornography 36
Port of Spain 50, 54, 101
postemancipation Caribbean 25
Presentation College 13–15, 35–36, 58, 62, 71, 138
production 67–68, 139–41, 143, 148
Puar, Jasbir 101
puberty 13
Puhngah 13–31; "game" 15; joke 20; man and beast 16–31; sodomy 17
Puri, Shalini 111

Quarequa (now Panama) 17–18
queer 19, 43, 68
queer internationalism 72, 77
Queer Corner Caribbean 64

race 10, 19; discursive articulation of 24; in relationship 27
racism 70, 72, 111, 117–18, 136, 140
Rajnauth-Lee, Maureen 57
Ramjag, Rawle 55
Ramlochan, Shivanee 64
Rampersad, Devindra 91
Ranney, William Tyee 21
recolonization 29; *see also* colonization
redemption 21, 143
ritual(s) 14; of adolescence 142; hazing 14; of Hinduism 113, 127, 156n1; homosexuality in 14; homoshaming/homoeroticizing 14; not-infrequent 13; punitive 151; ridiculous 28; sexual assault 15
Robertson-Ogle, Melissa 58
Robert Village Hindu School 34, 68

Robinson, Colin 59, 62–63, 77
Robinson, Tracy 23, 30–31, 46
Rodney (Sur), Sur 12
Rowe, Acey 76
Roy, Terry-Ann 64

sadomasochism 14
Saint-Hilaire, Étienne Geoffroy 40
Saint Kitts 24
same-sex kissing 14
Same Village, under Christianity, The
    (Sterndale) 42
San Fernando 35
Saunders, Adrian 57
savings clauses 56
Scott, David 99
sculptures 39, 114
secularism 58
sex: act 3, 6; with animals 24; anxieties
    23; attitudes toward 26; civil param-
    eters of 4; homosexual 20; as effec-
    tive method 6; interracial 4; oral 13;
    between white masters and enslaved
    Black people 3
sexual assault 14–15
sexual attachments 17
sexual citizenship 9, 10–11
sexual desire 2–4, 12, 20, 31, 68, 125, 135,
    140, 148–49
sexual experimentation 15, 119–20
sexual freedoms 74
sexual heterodisciplining 15
sexuality(ies) 17; license 26; rights 78;
    tinged 19
Sexuality, Health and Empowerment
    (SHE) 76
Sexual Offences Act 30
sexual violence 19
shadowed hillock 19
shame 20, 45, 119
Sheller, Mimi 9, 107
Silvera, Makeda 60
Silver Lining Foundation 64, 93
Simpson, Joel 58
Sinette, Luke 64
single 16

Sital, Krystal 33
slavery 23, 25, 89, 109, 144
Smithsonian Magazine (Everts) 107
socialization 14; childhood 37; evidence
    of 19; experiences of 140; formative 35;
    gender 139; homoerotic 13, 14; toward
    sadomasochism 14
Society against Sexual Orientation Dis-
    crimination (SASOD) 58
sodomy 15; British legislation 23; brutally
    punished 20; decriminalization of 63;
    evidence of 17; fear 20; imagined act
    of 21; indictments for 26; normative
    Western moral significance 17; partici-
    pation in 17–18; puhngah joke 20; sex-
    ual vice of 19; shame 20; stigma 20
Soomarie, David K. 64
Spanish Inquisition 20
Stabroek News 48, 55
St. Lucia 74, 80, 97
Summary Jurisdiction (Offences) Act
    26, 46

Thompson, Akola 37
Tobago 28, 30, 55, 56, 58, 59, 64
tolerance 67, 155n2
Tomlinson, Maurice 82
Torabully, Khal 32, 57
transgender 30, 47, 57, 73–74
Trans United Guyana 130
Trinidad 21, 28, 30, 52, 54, 55, 56, 58, 59,
    60, 63, 64, 101
Trinidad and Tobago Newsday 64, 80
Two Chamars (Wallace) 41, 43

Uganda 74
undressing 41, 47; *see also* clothes/clothing

vagrancy laws 88
Victorian era 6, 23
Village in Pukapuka, A (Sterndale) 41, 42
violence 20; act of 21; agents of 19; of
    colonization 52; institutional accom-
    modation 14; against Marxist gov-
    ernments 63; sexual 19; against sexual
    minorities 46

visual art 39; after indentureship 126–29, 133

Wallace, Sergeant 41
wanton sexualities 25
Ward, Jane 14–15
Williams, Eric 7, 64, 67, 68, 70–71, 77, 81, 83–84, 89, 92, 98–100, 138–40, 148, 149

Wit, Jacob 57
World Is What It Is (French) 119
wrecking work 32–33, 57
Wynter, Sylvia 7, 10–11, 67, 70, 72, 99–101, 106, 131

youth of the nation 16, 64